the
Millennial
Narrative

jaco j. hamman

the Millennial Narrative

sharing a good life with the next generation

Abingdon Press

Nashville

THE MILLENNIAL NARRATIVE:
Sharing a Good Life with the Next Generation

Copyright© 2019 by Abingdon Press

This book is printed on acid-free paper.

Library of Congress Cataloging-in-Publication Data has been requested.

ISBN 978-1-5018-3913-9

19 20 21 22 23 24 25 26 27 28—10 9 8 7 6 5 4 3 2 1
MANUFACTURED IN THE UNITED STATES OF AMERICA

*To the student and friend residents in the
Friendship Houses of Our Place Nashville.
You are witnessing the good life to us.*

Contents

Acknowledgments

This book was drafted in and for many communities. I am grateful for: the God of compassion who restores; the prophet Joel, for recognizing the locusts in our world and for showing us the essence of the good life; the co-writers who collaborated with me on a specific chapter: Kyle and Natalie, Julian Galette, Kelsey Davis, A. Keller Hawkins, Lindsey Krinks, and Rj Robles; and Melanie Bockman, a fellow in the Program in Theology and Practice and doctoral student in homiletics and liturgics, for being my research assistant.

The following "millennials" read early drafts of each chapter, engaged me in conversation, provided wonderful feedback, and helped shape the project: Katie Baker, Aly Benitez, Jessica Bratt, Joy Bronson, Kelly Brouwer, Rachel Brownson, Kelsey Davis, Nicholas Donkoh, Anne Elzinga, Ariel Franklyn, A. Keller Hawkins, Attie Jansen Van Vuuren, Caleb Larmey, Leah Lomotey-Nakon, Jordan Luther, Colleen Maki, Katie Morris, Aaron Palmer, Josh Rodriguez, Anna Skates, J. P. Sundararajan, Brett Vanderberg, David Veldt, Jennaba Waggy, and Tim Woods. I'm also grateful to seasoned pastors and leaders for their wisdom: Joanne Lindstrom, John Luth, Viki Matson, Kenny Nollan, Kim Nollan, Scott Smith, Bill Stroo, and Quinton Walker.

I also wish to thank gifted musicians, coordinated by a dear friend and gifted artist, Christopher Williams (Joel and *The Millennial Narrative* can be listened to as a music album); and Vanderbilt University for supporting my research and writing.

I am especially indebted to Chris Benda in the Vanderbilt University Divinity Library; the many faith communities that allowed me to explore the meaning of the book of Joel in their presence; and the leadership at Abingdon Press and editor Paul Franklyn. Thank you for believing in this project.

Jami and Michaela Hamman: thank you for showing me the power in doing faith differently.

Michelle Hamman: you flow unfailing love, support, and affirmation over me, even as you endured early-morning alarms, preoccupied moments, and evening weariness. You create the belonging where I and many others can receive restoration.

Introduction

What is the witness or testimony to human life that we find in the narrative many millennials are living? I suggest that they are telling us that loss and trauma cannot be lightly brushed away or ignored, that loneliness is too painful to tolerate and the freedom to define one's own communal experience where vulnerability can be risked is essential, that nurturing one's spiritual life is important, that we need to hold each other accountable and work toward social justice, and that millennials are and hope to be a difference in the world. Of course, there is much more to this generation, which has been described as the next great generation.[1] The traits mentioned here link the millennial generation to a significant, but mostly unknown biblical narrative.

Cultural commentators, psychologists, and the church remain critically uncertain about this generation, often referring to them as "Post-Christian," or "Generation Me," or even narcissistic "Trophy Kids." They note how millennials are "colliding" with other generations, how they find themselves "lost in translation," and how millennials in the US seem to be "coming up short" compared to their international peers and prior generations.[2] Here we actively resist the cultural labels attached to the millennial generation, not because we turn a blind eye toward their particularities, but because negative comments can be made about any generation, especially boomers (with their self-centeredness, impatience, and iconoclasm) and Gen Xers (with their free agency, social splintering, and cultural exhaustion), who birthed and parented millennials. It is no surprise that millennials turn toward gathering, community, patience, trust, and a new focus on action.

The Millennial Narrative seeks to invite a generation to discover a narrative worth living into and empowering church leadership to meet young adults where they are already active in the world. The book seeks to empower pastoral leaders seeking to partner with those who do religion differently, those who are often described as "the nones." It is not a book *about* young adults, per se, but *for* and *with* young adults and those seeking to partner and lead with them. Many in mainstream ministries are discovering that meeting this generation is a challenge, for the Pew Research Center suggests that "the recent decrease in religious beliefs and behaviors is largely attributable to the 'nones'... particularly in the millennial generation, who say they do not belong to any organized faith."[3] "The stereotypical 'none' is younger, urban, white, a bit more likely to be male than female, slightly more likely than most Americans to have completed college or graduate school."[4] It is good to remember that before 2012, the category of "nones" hardly existed. Polls from Pew, Gallup, Nielsen, and other research firms constructed this label. And not all young adults are white, with 43 percent of this generation being persons of color. *But who would prefer to be called a "none"?* "None" after all, denotes exclusion, being of no group or people and lacking the essential qualities of recognition and belonging.[5]

Following contemporary scholars who warn that the descriptor "millennial" was drafted to focus advertising for a specific generation, this book also refers to "young adults," yet we cannot so easily remove ourselves from the "millennial" label. This generation gathers and creates community, but prefers to do so outside the church or without specific membership, as 70 percent (56 million) of young adults do; they believe, but do so otherwise as doctrines and statements of faith are not appealing or persuasive.[6] The church is experiencing much uncertainty and anxiety vis-à-vis young adults. Despite mainly being raised in the church as children, young adults are choosing different ways of seeking membership and believing. An estimated 70 percent of "nones" grew up in households that were affiliated with a specific religious tradition and then they left the fold and seem slow to return.[7] Referring to the millennial generation as "nones," even though a popular term among scholars, researchers, pundits, and those seeking to fill empty pews, may reflect anxious concern, but it also exposes a spirit of moral judgment, of being threatened and of seeking control. Certainly, the label itself exposes much about the person or group assigning the label. Simply put, the identification "none" does not reflect all we know about today's young adults, especially the gifts, skills, and interests they bring.

In *Choosing Our Religion: The Spiritual Lives of America's Nones*, religious studies professor Elizabeth Drescher reminds us that besides the "nones," there are also the "somes"—those young adults who are religiously affiliated, and also the "nones-in-some's-clothing," persons who pretend to believe to protect themselves from judgment.[8] The lives of the "nones" are deeply intertwined with the lives of the "somes" and the "nones-in-some's-clothing" as they all share the very themes this book explores. The unaffiliated, Drescher reminds us, are not limited to the millennial generation, but persons of all ages who choose nontraditional ways of believing, belonging, and behaving. Also, they are embedded in spiritual *practices* that sustain their spirituality and faith, much like traditional religious practices do for mainline Christians. Drescher also finds "'none' is a 'negative definition.' It describes people who *do not* identify as belonging to a specific group, who *are not* affiliated with one institutional religion or another."[9] Her research indicates that those labeled as "nones" by religious leaders, demographers, researchers, and educators do not appreciate the label.

What is a minister or a faith community to do? Faulting young adults for adopting "moral therapeutic deism"—a label attached to millennial faith (see chapter 3)—does not help. We are told they believe in a creator God watching over human life who is not particularly involved, except in a time of crisis; a God wanting persons to be good and happy; and that good people go to heaven.[10] Labeling someone's faith "moralistic therapeutic deism" is unlikely to persuade them to join a church, even if that congregation prides itself in being welcoming or affirming. An older generation labeling millennials in critical terms is not an approach that communicates "You are welcome here!"

Sorry, that's not for me

Sarah is one person I held in mind while writing *The Millennial Narrative*. I met Sarah as we were both working toward affordable housing for urban populations. She is a twenty-four-year-old who grew up in a moderate Christian home, but she left the Protestant faith in her early teens when the judgmental attitudes of the church toward her lesbian, gay, and transgender friends reached a breaking point. Once she left the church, Sarah discovered she did not miss it much. She did not reject Christianity as much as grew out of (or away from) it. Sarah still sees Jesus as a model to follow—Gandhi and Nelson Mandela being models too—identifying especially with Jesus's affiliation with the marginalized. She believes there is much wisdom in the world to draw upon as she nurtures her spirituality. Yoga, as the embodiment of space, and the practice of meditative silence are important to Sarah; so too is social activism. Coffee shops and listening to podcasts nurture and educate. A number of experiences in her young life influenced her decision to let go of traditional faith: the church not practicing the love it is preaching; a friend who committed suicide; a date rape; her parents' divorce; study abroad programs that took her to India, South Africa, and Brazil; and living with underemployment and significant student debt. She carries these moments on her body, tattooed in a rainbow of colors on her arms, lower legs, and back. The tattoos remind her of her resilience and honor friendships, relationships, and places that brought pain, pleasure, and promise. Other than a deep desire to do good and not doing harm to herself, others, or the earth, Sarah has no concrete vision that governs her life and has worked for a number of nonprofits since graduation. Knowing that I am an ordained pastor in the Presbyterian Church (USA), she was not surprised when I asked her whether she could imagine finding any meaning in the Protestant tradition that shaped her early life. Sarah responded without hesitation: "Sorry, that's not for me." I believe her, especially if the tradition famed for always reforming itself resists doing so.

How does a pastoral leader, embedded in traditional structures and beliefs—even if it is only in the perception of others—befriend and partner with a person like Sarah?

A trialogue for a world come of age

Whereas a traditional approach to Christian ministry would argue that young adults should know about personal sin and the need for salvation and for meeting Jesus, *The Millennial Narrative* contends that all people—young and old—need a narrative to live into. Narratives do not exclude a relationship with Jesus, but they are bigger than a personal relationship. The traditional entrance into a life of faith in the Christian tradition is questioned by many young adults: *Virgin birth? Resurrection? Jesus as the only way to salvation?* The answers to these questions, which the church defensively provides with doctrine rich in history, rarely convince. For many today, statements of faith are not the entry point into a life of faith and rarely inform their personal belief. Rather, they find themselves immersed in a religionless world that has come of age, as theologian Dietrich Bonhoeffer envisioned in a prison cell in 1944. Bonhoeffer prophetically stated:

> ...we are moving towards a completely religionless time; people as they are now simply cannot be religious any more. Our whole nineteen-hundred-year-old Christian preaching and theology rests on the religious *a priori* of mankind. But if one day it becomes clear that this *a priori* does not exist at all, but was a historically conditioned and transient form of human self-expression and if therefore man becomes radically religionless—and I think that that is already the case (else how is it, for example, that this war, in contrast to all previous ones, is not calling forth any religious reaction?) what does that mean for Christianity? It means that the foundation is taken away from the whole of what has up to now been our "Christianity."[11]

In a world come of age, Bonhoeffer warned, apologetics are "pointless." He knew that not everybody would be positive about a world come of age and stated that "anxious souls will ask what room there is left for God now; and as they know of no answer to the question, they condemn the whole development that has brought them to such straits."[12] Still, Bonhoeffer was positive about a world come of age, seeing it as an invitation for the Christian faith to redefine itself. Rarely can one argue another person into faith or force someone to accept Jesus, for faith and a relationship with Jesus are discovered. A focus on the suffering of Jesus, Bonhoeffer believed, will lead to new discoveries for a religionless society. *The Millennial Narrative* does not follow Bonhoeffer to the suffering of Jesus, though we agree with Bonhoeffer. Rather, we argue that an entrance into a life of faith is a focus on *personal* suffering and that the good life resides in finding oneself in a bigger narrative.

Furthermore, we do not follow the Christian tradition to read scripture through a christological lens—that one can find Jesus in all of scripture or that scripture is completed by Jesus. This would not only mute Joel for all who do not embrace this way of reading scripture, but would suggest that Joel, as a narrative that predates Jesus by a few hundred years, had no meaning for the very people who received the narrative. Rather, we believe that the book of Joel has autonomy enough to not be dependent upon Jesus as a lens. Of course, many who will read this book do have a personal relationship with Jesus and can see how Joel reflects the life and ministry of Jesus. The history of reading and interpreting the Bible—see below—shows that reading scripture is always personal, contextual, and historical. We want to offer the narrative of Joel to persons who do not have a relationship with Jesus as their Lord and Savior. One need not despair, not for the lack of Jesus in *The Millennial Narrative* nor the lack of offering New Testament wisdom to young adults. If we believe that scripture is inspired, that God's Spirit reveals itself to people and that God tends the church, then any one, through Joel, can discover Jesus and the church anew. Claiming that one has to work through Jesus to find God and meaning in life does not reckon with the mystery of God and that the image of God is alive in every person.

Since meeting and partnering with young adults demand a fresh approach to life and faith, a unique trialogue informs this project: The lives of *young adults* (also referred to as *millennials*) are placed in conversation with the story found in the book of Joel, as *narrative* becomes the bridge not only between a person and his, her, or their life but also between a person and community and a person and God. The narrative that defines *The Millennial Narrative* can be given as an answer to a question:

Q: How do you desire to live your life?

A: I seek to find myself in a bigger story as I mourn my losses, seek healing for my wounds and traumas, and build life-giving communities. I nurture my spirituality by being in relationship with a compassionate God who promises restoration and pours out the Spirit over me. I hold myself and others accountable for decisions made and actions taken. I commit to participate with others in God's restorative work as we build a just society and foster sustainable living.

This answer—similar to a credo—captures the themes of the narrative discovered in the book of Joel and as the opening sentences here indicate, the narrative corresponds with the experience the majority of young adults share. Some may find the fact that the good life begins with loss and mourning ironic, possibly even off-putting. It is the counterintuitive wisdom of Joel that not only catches us by surprise but also opens the possibility for a new approach to life and faith. The question "How do you desire to live your life?"—modeled after the question-and-answer format used by Martin Luther in the early 1500s and seen in the Heidelberg Catechism of 1563—also receives answers from culture.

Popular wisdom provides many narratives to live into: you can be whatever you want to be; get a good education; if you work hard, you can go from rags to riches; the poor are poor because they are lazy; wealth (or consumption) brings happiness; be a winner; diets work; medicine can heal you; technology will save us; guns do not kill, people do; time heals; and more. Epic American narratives also include how the West was won and lost, America as protector of the free world, the American Dream, Silicon Valley and two boys starting something big in a garage (or the entrepreneurial spirit). Gender, race, class, and sexuality come wrapped in these cultural narratives, which orient a person's life. With no exception, cultural narratives fail, despite the promises they hold or the wisdom they proclaim.

With chapters exploring the individual elements of the narrative, we find in Joel seven core foci and assumptions that drive our inquiry. They include concern about the future of the Christian church, the life millennials are seeking, the role of narratives in our lives, embracing the transformative power of scripture, empowering a new religious leadership, awakening hope, and honoring shared similarity and personal individuality. Specifically, the seven foci and assumptions are the following:

First, the future of Christianity and especially how it manifests in the church depend greatly upon today's young adults. If the church as we know it today in its denominational colors cannot find a way to join and partner with today's young adults, the institutionalized church will continue to experience diminished relevancy. Sustaining systems and buildings will increasingly burden the church due to the lack of financial and relational capital. Some might say that it is time for denominations to fade away, but that would be a sad day as denominations sustain many other structures on which society and the world depend. That view also does not reckon with the fact that it is God's church and the body of Christ, which will be sustained as it has been for millennia. For the church, the questions of relevancy and presence, which came into prominence in the 1960s, are escalating. Extending hospitality to millennials and partnering with them can revitalize the church.

Second, millennials are interested in the good life. Historically, Christianity has proclaimed *the good news*, which is often limited to introducing a loving "Father," encouraging a personal relationship with Jesus, offering salvation from personal sin, and extending an invitation to join the church as the body of Christ. Young adults, generally speaking, have no personal connection with these particular foci. Rather, they are interested in *the good life*, a present and future that seem elusive amid student debt, underemployment, financial uncertainties, and an earth straining under climate change. The good life speaks to the very narrative that guides this inquiry: finding ways to flourish when loss and trauma are intimate enemies; building community; nurturing one's spirituality; living an accountable life with boundaries; and making a positive difference in the lives of others and the world. We envision what is most fundamental to human belonging and flourishing—to what it means to be human per se—the care *of* self and others, care *about* persons and moments and situations, and care *with* like-minded folk.

Third, humans live by and love stories. Psychologists, anthropologists, sociologists, and neuroscientists all agree that narratives are central to how we find meaning and how our brains organize sensory input. From the moment we are born, parents and caregivers read stories to us. As children, we find much pleasure in hearing our birth narrative. These stories paint portraits of the world in which we can live with moral values, purpose, and meaning. Stories, with a beginning and an end in endless repetition, place boundaries around us and thus contain us. The power of a story is that once heard, it is *appropriated* in a very personal way. No two persons hear a story the same way.

Fourth, scripture has the power to disclose important truths or insights, also new realities. The narratives in the Bible—such as the story found in the book of Joel—tell us something fundamental about what it means to be human, reveal essential elements of lived experience, and introduce us to a compassionate God longing to be in relationship with us. This power invites, witnesses, restores, convicts, and empowers. It is thus important that persons receive biblical stories, whether it is through verbal, written, or even musical means. As one commentator writes: "The Bible shapes readers by showing them what lies beyond the self."[13]

Fifth, religious leadership needs a new vision for the twenty-first century. Ministry, as it has evolved over two thousand years with its foci of counseling, preaching, teaching, as well as reconciling, liberating, and administrating, is less effective in a world come of age. The traditional practices of leadership may hinder more than help in meeting and partnering with young adults, or at least they should be informed by different values and content. This implies that the pastoral identities of pastoral leaders need transformation.

Sixth, hope is the only antidote to the feelings of despair, anxiety, worthlessness, and apathy. Society has come of age and this comes at a great cost: existential despair. To hope, however, is inherently risky as one anticipates a benign yet unknown future. God, who consistently seeks us out and restores our brokenness, is the source of our hope. When one person tells another to have hope, it is poor care and can border on abuse, especially if the hopeless person is marginalized, in a situation of despair, or is experiencing social injustices (see chapter 1). Hoping is often confused with wishing, which knows exactly what it wants as it sets its sights on a specific outcome. Our individualistic consumer culture thrives on wishing. We are bombarded by advertisements for products that promise to change our world. Powerful algorithms know what we want before we do. Attempting to partner with young adults without meeting them with hope is a futile effort.

A seventh core assumption that permeates these pages is that narratives are personally appropriated. As such, we are all alike in some ways, even if we are very different in other ways. Addressing the relationship between culture and personality, Harvard anthropologist Clyde Kluckhohn and his colleague, psychologist Henry Murray, warn:

EVERY MAN is in certain respects
a. like all other men,
b. like some other men,
c. like no other man.[14]

Each person's journey, like all, like some, like no other....Although it is difficult to imagine that the narrative explored in these pages will not deeply resonate with every person (especially with young adults), the way the narrative will be appropriated will be unique to each person. For some years I have been reflecting on Joel's narrative with persons between the ages of twelve to ninety on four continents (North America, Africa, Asia, and Australia). I'm yet to meet a person who does not associate with loss and trauma, who does not long for belonging and community or yearns for a vibrant spirituality, who does not thirst for a compassionate God, and who does not want to make a difference in the world. My research and partnering with young adults—together we create intentional communities where persons with intellectual and/or developmental disabilities live with graduate students—convinced me, however, that Joel's narrative is the affirmation our young people need to receive.

The tripartite foci—the experience of young adults, the story found in the book of Joel, and the importance of narratives in our lives—hold much promise, for they draw on what is essential to both human nature and the witness of scripture.

A studied generation, but misunderstood

Given a year or two on either side, the young adults envisioned in these pages are those born between 1980 and 2000, called millennials, though strict generational lines are usually not helpful.[15] Someone born as a "cusper," whose birth coincides with the ending and the beginning of two generational eras, for example, may associate with both. We do love our labels, from baby boomers to Xers to millennials. Australian sociologist Dan Woodman refers to himself and his peers as "Xennials," a microgeneration within the millennial group, referring to those born between 1977–83, persons who grew up with the rotary phone but who live close to their smartphones.[16] *The Millennial Narrative* generally focuses on "young adults," a broad category of more than 75 million persons and the largest generation in the United States. With 43 percent of young adults non-white and 6.4 percent identifying as lesbian, gay, transgender, or queer, they are also the most diverse generation to date.[17] With only 14 percent living in rural areas, young adults are mostly found in suburban (54 percent) and urban (32 percent) areas. With a median household pre-tax income of $35,300, almost one in five young adults lives in poverty. Important for this project is the fact that today's young adults are less connected with traditional institutions than earlier generations.[18] Those who came to the United States as children show higher levels of cultural affiliation, with significant connection to family, heritage, community, and language compared to young adults born in the US.[19]

Much has been written on the millennial generation, including their relationship with the Christian tradition and how they approach faith.[20] Whereas the generation received initial affirmation, recent works show a more critical stance, even overtones of judgment.[21] Research does paint an ambivalent picture about this generation. Professors of education Arthur Levine and Diane Dean studied five thousand freshmen across 270 diverse colleges and universities matriculating between 2005 and 2014. In their *Generation on a Tightrope: A Portrait of Today's College Student*, they find young adults tension-filled:

> [Young adults entering college] are struggling to maintain their balance as they attempt to cross the gulf between their dreams and the world in which they live. They seek security but live in an age of profound and unceasing change. They desperately want the economic opportunity their parents enjoyed but are coming of age during a deep recession with reduced career prospects. They want to believe in the America [*sic*] Dream and are optimistic about their personal futures but they are pessimistic about the future of the country. They want to be autonomous grown-ups but seem more dependent on their parents and the people around them than any modern generation. They want intimacy—a partner and a family—but they are isolated, weak in face-to-face communication skills and live in a hook-up culture. They want to play by the rules but they don't know the rules and the rules are in flux because of the dramatic changes in our economy, the rise of new technologies, the condition of our public and private institutions and a world growing flatter. They want to live in an internet world.[22]

Today's young adults received a world unlike the one that welcomed their parents. A global economy, technological advances, and threats by political extremists color their world, and each come with profound personal, emotional, relational, and professional costs. Their experience is amplified by the reality of constant change, weaker familial ties, increased racial tension, limited employment opportunities, debt burdens, and a widening class gap. The shift from an analog to a digital world and an information economy has not been easy.

Counseling centers at universities and colleges see a significant rise in mental health concerns in their students. *The Chronicle of Higher Education*, reporting on the American academic landscape, identifies an "Epidemic of Anguish" as anxiety, depression, and suicidal ideation have reached an all-time high on college and university campuses.[23] Young adults today can only benefit from hope, that invisible force that positively informs one's here-and-now as one anticipates a benign, inviting future. The church, of course, is the historical *agent* of hope, but this is changing for today's young adults. We may best return to the *source* of our hope: God. The book of Joel, placing God at the center of its narrative, is a book of hope, written for a people in crisis. It is *the* story today's young adults need to hear.

Without a doubt, those named the millennial generation are being misunderstood. That so much is being written on young people indicates culture's desire to make sense of a generation that is already beginning to be dominant socially and politically, if not yet economically. *The Millennial Narrative* will not remove this misunderstanding, but by emphasizing core traits—even if some are painful—within a larger narrative, pastoral leaders will receive an approach to ministry that will not only empower them in partnering with young adults but will also remove the sharp focus culture places on the negative traits many assign to younger adults.

Joel: A person, a book, and a narrative

Imagine a life-giving narrative few know about. This is Joel—a person and a short story—with a powerful plot: There was a people whose lives and landscapes were devoured by different kinds of locusts. They were in crisis and mourning, lamenting their losses and coming together as a sacred assembly. The people cried out to God, who met them as a compassionate Being who does not anger easily but rather abounds in love. God responded: "I will repay you for the years that the cutting locust, the swarming locust, the hopping locust, and the devouring locust have eaten" (Joel 2:25a). The restoration includes God pouring out God's spirit on all people, young and old, men and women, slave and free. Empowered by the God now dwelling over and in persons, the people are held accountable especially where injustices are found. As some expect judgment for their actions, others experience water flowing from God's throne, nurturing the earth wherever it flows, a sign of blessing. It is a powerful narrative that has been resonating with people for more than twenty-five hundred years!

Joel the person is quite a mystery, much like young adults are to older generations. Little is known about him. We know his name means "Yahweh is Elohim/God" and that he was the son of Pethuel, though we do not know who Pethuel was. In ancient Near East culture, Joel was a nobody. There are also significant questions regarding when he lived and where he roamed, making Joel truly a "mysterious prophet."[24] He probably lived in or around Jerusalem, given the frequent references to the temple.[25] Some scholars date Joel as early as the ninth century (the early preexilic time in Israel's history), whereas others date Joel after the exile (515–350 BCE). Most seem to think that Joel was written somewhere between 586–555 BCE, thus the late preexilic period or the immediate aftermath of exile.[26] "[Since] Joel's superscription has no date, this implies that his message is not related to a specific situation within the history of Israel, but to something more far-reaching and thus to a more important phenomenon."[27]

The content of Joel also brings more questions than answers. Commentators are not in agreement as to the central issue or theme in the book. Does the book address a locust plague, warn about the Day of the Lord, or lament a drought brought on by dry sirocco winds?[28] Furthermore, the nature of the book is highly disputed: is it prophecy, a theodicy, lament, or apocalyptic? As one of the twelve Minor Prophets—with Hosea, Amos, Obadiah, Jonah, Micah, Nahum, Habakkuk, Zephaniah, Haggai, Zechariah, and Malachi—Joel is wedged like a "problem child" between Hosea and Amos.[29] He roamed the southern kingdom of Judah as an unconventional prophet. Judah was a tiny agrarian province that included Jerusalem and its surrounding area. We learn about farmers, wine makers, and priests, for those are the vocations demanded by the narrative. Joel does not describe much joy in the life of the Judeans, but envisions better days ahead where nature is transformed, the Davidic dynasty is restored, and an era of peace has settled.[30]

The inscription, "The LORD's word that came to Joel, Pethuel's son" (Joel 1:1) is not meant to introduce the author as much as introduce a genre. In the Hebrew Bible, the opening line identifies a prophetic book with some apocalyptic elements and tells of what could be expected: "oracles accusing Israel of wrongdoing and calling for repentance, assurances of well-being and declamations against foreign nations."[31] Joel, however, diverts from this tradition in telling ways: Judah's sin is not identified and God is introduced as the compassionate God, slow in anger, but ready to restore. Resembling a prophetic book, Joel is a book of instruction as it seeks to initiate in us the wisdom we need to thrive in life as we face the locusts of life. Commentator John Barton reflects, "Joel belongs to the period when the prophetic task was no longer condemnation and denunciation but encouragement."[32]

With the book of Lamentations, Joel gives us a glimpse of life for those who remained in Judah after the exile of 587 BCE. Joel reminds us that the longing for God does not end when people do not assemble in and bring offerings to the temple. "In the absence of the Temple, [the people] thought that there was no way to return to God.... [Joel] argued that the covenant with God could continue in the ruined precinct of the house of YHWH, in contrast to the people, who thought that the destruction of the Temple signified a severing of the bond of God."[33] Joel is not an apocalyptic book—it lacks supernatural revelation—even though, as with the apocalyptic genre, the book wants to instill hope.[34] When lives and institutions are experiencing ruin, Joel is the messenger of hope.

A short book, merely 73 verses and 957 words, Joel has been contained in three chapters since the early thirteenth century, departing from Hebrew texts that have the same number of verses placed in four chapters.[35] There are two clear sections, with the first two chapters dealing with the destruction of locusts and the second with holding people accountable, or in more traditional language, the Day of the Lord. The two parts of Joel raise questions regarding whether the book was written by two authors, or by a single author at different times.[36] Structural and linguistic considerations as well as the use of similar terminology support the view that Joel's two sections form a unit and were probably written by a single author. Joel's compelling message calls on his listeners to hear, weep, awake, sound an alarm, return, rejoice, fast, lament, assemble, and more. It is a "demanding" book with forty-three commands and "a relatively high overall rate of use of imperatives, approximately three commands in every five verses."[37]

Promising personal and also political salvation, Joel is best read as one narrative.[38] Identifying the book of Joel as a narrative worth living into is not new. Historian and church father Jerome (347–420 CE) saw the book of Joel as a *narratio*—a narrative—that not only "[teaches about] the mysteries (*sacramenta*)," but also "[narrates] a simple story (*historium*)" about events past.[39] As a story, the book of Joel has "information gaps."[40] Information we need to understand the text is not given. We do not know, for example, why God calls on Judah to return to YHWH. No sin is mentioned and God is not portrayed as an angry God. Whereas Hosea is clear that natural disasters come from God, Joel does not follow Hosea's tradition. Unknowns abound as we do not know why God would become "jealous of the land" (2:18). Furthermore, we do not know if the people returned to the Lord as called upon. We do know, however, that in Joel, God's compassion turns against God's heart of anger and triumphs.

Joel reuses texts that were already authoritative in his time and weaves them into a story that brings hope to the hopeless and gives direction for those wanting to build a future. Like any story, the words are important, but not more so than the overarching themes within it. Joel wants to bring his listeners over to his view of the world. His rhetorical genius compels his listeners to look at things differently—to take the story to heart—as they move from scenes of devastation to promises of restoration. The fact that the book lacks sufficient data to identify a historical event does not diminish its transformative and instructive potential for a modern people. Like the first listeners of Joel, we too cannot remain neutral to Joel's "fantastical story" where the good life with a compassionate God begins in profound loss.[41] Either one recognizes the weight of loss/trauma, community, spirituality, restoration, accountability, and making a difference or one does not.

Living according to an opera, not by hit singles

Psychologists, sociologists, and linguists remind us that narratives are found in every culture.[42] "A narrative in its most basic sense refers to a recounting of a sequence of events that is told from a particular point of view."[43] Per definition, narratives tell of something past or future, of events other than the here and now. Always holding a specific point of view, that view can be changed, altering the meaning of a narrative. When a narrative is told and retold, as with Joel's, the narrative begins to inform culture. University of Utah linguist Bradford Hall reminds us that narratives "are essentially *actions* taken by *characters* in relation to a *problem* and the perceived *outcome* of those actions."[44] Through characters, problems, actions, and outcomes and by storing and presenting information, narratives inform and give meaning.

Hall argues that narratives (1) teach us the ways the world works, giving general principles and also particular contexts; (2) describe our place in the world as it shapes personal and communal identities, who we are and what we are like; (3) advise us how to act in the world, both effectively and appropriately; and (4) provide a framework on how to evaluate or judge what goes on in the world, what is good or bad and what might be safe or dangerous.[45] These are just some of the functions narratives play. Due to narratives being interpreted or appropriated, they have diverse personal meanings. The truths we resonate with in a narrative compel us to make the story our own, even if there might be elements within the story we find troublesome or even irrelevant. Earlier I identified this aspect as the power of scripture to disclose compelling insight.

The narrative in the book of Joel contains the four elements Hall identifies. Joel has the courage to lament what we know, yet so often dare not name—that locusts still stalk our lives. Joel's courage thus empowers and invites us to name the locust we witness or may even have become. Yes, Joel affirms we can live as a blessing to others. He reminds us that lamenting and gathering are appropriate responses when touched by locusts and that a relationship with a compassionate God promises restoration. Now, living with blessing and not as a people devoured by locusts, we begin to live and act differently, holding ourselves and others accountable as we become a blessing to others.

With regard to biblical studies, our narrative existence is best embraced by a way of reading scripture where the reader greatly determines the truth discovered in the text. This postmodern approach, called reader-response criticism, believes that individuals and communities bring their own concerns to receiving and interpreting a text. All interpretation is personal and historical. Commentator John Barton, reflecting on this hermeneutical approach, writes that we cannot "stand outside our own interests when we approach a text; always we bring ourselves to the text and this is not a drawback to be avoided if possible, but the only way we have, as humans, of knowing anything."[46] We hear narratives through our own ears and read them through our own eyes. Some theorists (Stanley Fish is one proponent) argue that a narrative has no meaning until it is appropriated, while others (like Wolfgang Iser) argue that narratives and texts do have meaning, but that meaning takes active form only in the lives of persons. It is this very act of personal appropriation that creates the space for the book of Joel to inform our lives. Reader-response theory inevitably leads to reception theory—with Hans Robert Jauss its biggest proponent—which asks how a community received (or reads) a text, as well as a history of consequences, which is concerned with how a text influenced other faith traditions, the arts, and popular culture and how it was used by readers and communities (Leong Seow is the pioneer in this regard).[47]

Reader-response and reception theories invite us to find new meaning in the book of Joel, each of us from our own unique setting in life.[48] I rediscovered Joel in a way that shifted my boundaries when I read feminist theologian Denise Ackerman's *After the Locusts: Letters from a Landscape of Faith*, in which she sees apartheid South Africa as a locust devouring lives and landscapes.[49] I read Joel as a White South African and an immigrant to the United States, as an ordained pastor and professor, and also as a husband and the father of two teenagers who are unlikely to worship and do church the way I do. When I read Joel, these factors, more than others, create the horizon (or boundary) that determines my appropriation of the narrative. My horizon, no doubt, will shift in the next years as not only I change, but as my contexts and relationships change, too. Jauss believed encountering the "other," especially the marginalized, inevitably shifts one's horizon. For us, Joel is the "other." Before a narrative's meaning can be found, however—before it can be perceived and appropriated—the story, as an opera with many acts, needs to unfold and be heard.

A significant problem we face in this virtual age, though, is that we might be losing the presence of narratives in our lives. That is the argument of media theorist Douglas Rushkoff in his *Present Shock: When Everything Happens Now*. Rushkoff reminds us:

> Experiencing the world as a series of stories helps create a sense of context. It is comforting and orienting. It helps smooth out obstacles and impediments by recasting them as bumps along the way to some better place—or at least the end of the journey. As long as there is enough momentum, enough pull forward and enough dramatic tension, we can suspend our disbelief enough to stay in the story.[50]

As we live notification to notification, driven by a multiverse and one newsflash or text replaces another, we lose the deeper connections to stories. The moment, captured in a selfie or a few lines, becomes all-important. Rushkoff provides a lovely image, saying we need to live by operas with many acts, when most persons choose to listen to hit singles.[51]

Joel is *the* narrative (or opera) for a world come of age. When framed as a short story, the narrative of Joel reads as follows:

> There was a person who knew the locusts of life. The locusts caused devastation, loss and trauma. He/she/they mourned the losses and sought healing for the traumas by building life-giving communities and nurturing his/her/their spirituality. He/she/they discovered the compassionate God who promises restoration and pours the Spirit over all. The person(s) embraced accountability, knowing that decisions made and actions taken have consequences. He/she/they participated in God's restorative work toward a just society and a sustainable earth. The person(s) lived the good life.

The millennial narrative: What to expect

Each chapter of *The Millennial Narrative* builds on a specific narrative marker in the book of Joel. The first chapter, "RECOGNIZE: The Locusts of Life and the Promise of Lament," embraces the ironic fact and paradoxical twist that the good life begins with loss.[52] We identify and describe six types of loss, crisis, trauma, and anxiety caused by the locusts of life. Nearly twenty-five hundred years ago, Joel bluntly stated: "Joy fades away from the people" (1:12). Nothing has changed. Still, young adults continue to find creative ways to grieve and lament the losses that touch their lives. We can learn from them even as creative pastoral leaders can facilitate the work of mourning for young adults.

Chapter 2, "GATHER: The Isolation of Loss and the Promise of Community," follows Joel as he calls on persons touched by locusts to gather. "Request a special assembly," Joel demands (1:14). Young adults, we discover, are really good at gathering, most often outside church walls. Effective pastoral leaders join the communities young adults are building and empower them to create new places of belonging.

Chapter 3, "DISCOVER: The Compassionate God and the Promise of Personal Restoration," introduces a God "merciful and compassionate, very patient, full of faithful love" (2:13), a God who "will repay you for the years [the locusts] have eaten" (2:25). Every person longs to discover this responsive, caring God, who is much different from the God who is perceived as distant and not really interested in our predicaments, or the God who is fast to judge and punish.

Chapter 4, "RECEIVE: God's Spirit and the Promise of Spiritual Practices," embraces Joel's God as the divine's spirit is poured out upon everyone and as young adults begin to prophesy, dream dreams, and see visions (2:28). When mainline Christianity argues that millennials are "spiritual but not religious," the judgment is harsh, for the statement almost always means "You are not religious in the ways we have been for generations." Receiving God's Spirit speaks of vitality and new creation. The theologies on which congregations and denominations are built are inherently static, identified in themes such as *predestination* (all things are preordained by God), *election* (God already chose who the faithful would be), *reprobation* (God condemns nonbelievers), an *unchangeable* God, *sanctification* (the process of becoming holy, whether through works or faith) and *justification* (saved by Christ), and also *historical confessions*. Effective ministers and pastoral leaders are vision catchers, not vision casters. They recognize that we are shifting from spiritualities of dwelling (place) and seeking a spirituality of practice. Today's young adults provide a vision of hopeful living and are showing us the importance of spiritual practices.

Chapter 5, "BE ACCOUNTABLE: A Just God and the Promise of Political Restoration," follows Joel into what is often referred to as "the day of the Lord," a day where humanity will be held accountable for the choices we made. "The day of the LORD is near in the valley of judgment," Joel warns (3:14). We need not fear this day, for the God who is slow to anger and who repays us for the damage caused by the locusts is the One who holds us accountable. The church, which has neglected ecological and social justice concerns for so long, can learn from young adults and their keen sense of social justice and inclusion. When a leader can join her millennials in the social causes they champion, a congregation may discover wonderful partners doing God's work on earth.

Chapter 6, "RESTORE: The God Who Nurtures and the Promise of Renewal," concludes the narrative of Joel as Joel envisions blessing that flows from God's throne into neighborhoods, where the water nurtures and restores (Joel 3:18). We are called into God's restorative work. Young adults already flow with God's love, grace, and justice to persons, communities, and the earth. Effective leaders will join them in the blessings they embody. When one meets young adults where they are, one will discover the narrative of Joel already present.

I invited six young adults, named in the acknowledgments, to coauthor a portion of each chapter with me. They are persons who enriched my life and introduced me to what a faithful and even prophetic life looks like in today's world. They would be the first to say there is nothing special about them, but that would not hide the gifts they bring or the difference they are making in especially my hometown. A group of twenty, mostly millennials but also some from older generations, read each chapter and provided feedback. Their voices too permeate these pages. I am deeply grateful for all the contributions many young adults made to inform this project. They were not research subjects; they are partners in life and ministry.

The Millennial Narrative embraces the challenge to introduce teenagers and young adults to a narrative worth living into. That narrative is constructed around embracing one's losses and seeking restoration for one's traumas; gathering and building community; discovering a compassionate God; nurturing one's spirituality; and being accountable, ultimately being a difference-maker in this world. Be prepared—you are about to hear a life-changing story.

Chapter One

RECOGNIZE

The Locusts of Life and the Promise of Lament

A good life knows loss. Teenagers and millennials are intimately aware of this fact. In a meeting room at a downtown market, a youth group of thirteen- to nineteen-year-old teens and their leaders are having lunch. All have gotten their favorite fare and we are ready to do some work. Earlier, the teens heard me preach from the book of Joel. Setting the stage is brief: "The losses that touch our lives are many and greatly affect the joy we experience in life. Loss, like the locusts we read about this morning, easily becomes an unbearable burden that ruins our lives and relationships. I wonder, what losses have you experienced and how do they affect your life?"

As a leader wheels a whiteboard to the front of the room, there is silence and the teens stare at their food. The silence does not last long. One after the other speaks. Some mention a grandparent who died—an expected death. Others mention moving, a friendship that ended, a pet that died—other expected deaths. Soon they turn to losses that feel heavy with gravitas. One teen tells of significant struggles with depression and loneliness after his parents' divorce as he moved with his mother into a small apartment. A young woman about to leave for college tells of being in an emotionally destructive relationship for a number of years, unable to extract herself from her partner's abusive grip. With courage, she describes paralyzing anxiety and waning self-confidence. She is working hard at regaining confidence and looks forward to her college years. A fifteen-year-old tells the group about being bullied at school, how his grades began to drop, and how he found relief in computer games, which alienated him from family and friends. A number of the teens tell of a friend at school or a relative who committed suicide. I try to recall how old I was when someone close like that committed suicide—sometime in my late twenties. We fill the board in no time, wondering together how we can lament these locusts of life. As we do so, we validate research that found many teenagers and millennials have experienced economic concerns, chronic illness, the death of a family member, divorce, substance abuse, violence and bullying, painful sexual experiences, and learning and developmental disabilities.[1]

Every theme of Joel explored here can be an entry point into the life of a young adult (or another person). Creating community, introducing a compassionate God, nurturing a rich spirituality, appreciating accountability, or even being a blessing are wonderful gateways to relationships and a life of faith. The narrative of Joel, however, opens with loss. The experience of loss—alongside being nourished, being loved, experiencing shame, and feeling the need to believe—makes *each person like all other persons*. From the experience of birth, loss permeates our lives as no person escapes the power of loss. Even friendship, the philosopher Jacques Derrida reminds us, is colored by loss, for one friend knows he or she will die first.[2] From the moment we enter into a relationship, Derrida finds, we begin to mourn, for we know the relationship will end. Relationships are inherently prodigal. Loss, however, comes in a variety of experiences, even if relationship loss or death might be the first things we think of when we are asked to reflect on loss and mourning.

Sadly, our families poorly prepare us for identifying, naming, and working through our losses. Rather, our families reflect Kathleen O'Connor's. O'Connor, a Hebrew Bible scholar who writes on lament, paints a vivid picture of her family:

> My expressive, loving family practiced denial. It forbade anger, ignored sorrow, and created a culture of silence about hard things. From generation to generation, we practiced denial: we looked on the bright side, walked on the sunny side, and remembered that tomorrow is another day. Like many assimilating immigrant groups, deaths went ungrieved, anger lurked but could not speak, and broken dreams were barely noticed. Some of us lost great chunks of ourselves along the way.[3]

Effective leadership is greatly defined by the ability to facilitate the work of mourning for persons and in communities. Change, the result of effective leadership, inevitably awakens loss, as with change something has to end. Should a leader remain stuck in O'Connor's family, not having grown out of and away from destructive emotional processes, then it is nearly impossible for the leader to facilitate the work of mourning in others.

Emily Kaiser, like O'Connor, knows loss. Emily, who identifies herself as "28 and single," is a digital producer, a journalist, and a writer. She left Washington, DC, where her first job took her, to be closer to her mother after her mother was diagnosed with cancer. Two years after her mother's death, Emily wrote "How Millennials Mourn" for the *Washingtonian*.[4] Her experience identifies a young adult feeling unsupported by older generations. Emily tells of extreme loneliness—feeling that those around her were far removed from their parents' mortality. Seeing her mother succumb to the illness was extremely painful for Emily. Despite her mother's assurances that she would beat the cancer, Emily knew better. Age-wise grown-up, but missing the grown-up credentials her mother achieved at Emily's age, such as being married, Emily was terrified. "She and I never talked about [the cancer]," Emily writes. Neither did they talk about family. "We didn't go near any conversations about the big things she'd miss out on, like the moment I'd find the man I wanted to marry or sharing the excitement of my wedding day. We just focused on the trivial little things that had always connected us." The trivial things included sending funny cat videos to each other and even adopting two cats, Ramona and Harriet, who became the connection to her mom.

The first six months after her mother's death, a deep gloom came over Emily and she could barely function. "It was as if I'd become estranged from everyone in my life," she writes. Even her colleagues with elderly parents, parents who had also died, were unable to communicate the empathy Emily needed and the disconnect grew larger. "The brutal specifics of it felt so different from those of my colleagues who had buried 80-year-old parents," she writes. "Didn't they realize?" A conversation with Human Resources widened an already immense gap. "Plenty of people get uncomfortable about death and say tone-deaf things to the bereaved. But there seemed to be a common thread here: My loss, I think, required a different kind of vocabulary, one that my colleagues—and most other people—didn't have," Emily concludes. Her alienation from friends and coworkers deepened.

What Emily wanted, she came to see, was "not quite the juvenile-bereavement tragedy, but not quite the adult way-of-the-world one, either." Alone in her anger and grief, things began to change for Emily when she joined a grief group with a number of other young adults. They vented in anger—especially at empty platitudes—and contemplated what getting married and having a child without their loved one would be like. As the group's relationships deepened, they started meeting socially too, despite differing vocations, worldviews, and other divergences. Through her group, Emily began to feel the emerging adult she is. Emily's work of mourning—essentially finding a new identity after a loss—continues. She reminds us that for millennials, grieving is fused with the search for a new identity. Finding a new identity can be a slow and difficult process.

Joel resonates with Emily's need for a "different kind of vocabulary." Such is the impact of loss that even Joel asks whether such a thing has ever happened. He recommends lament, which was an established tradition in the ancient Near East, but one forgotten in our day. I wonder how Emily would have experienced her mother's death if she was empowered to lament arguably the most significant loss of her life as of yet. But then again, maybe she lamented in a modern idiom. Lament is the language of being confused and hopefully anticipating a changed world. This language is best spoken in community, as chapter 2 argues. Just as Emily sought community, Joel calls people together. Restoration colors both narratives. Emily's need for a "different kind of vocabulary," however, exposes an older generation's inability to connect with their younger coworker. This disconnect, I believe, is far more prevalent than one would believe. An effective leader is willing to learn new ways of connecting and seeks ways to bring age-old wisdom to a new generation.

In this chapter, we take a closer look at the opening act of the book of Joel. For Joel, the metaphor of loss is that of being devoured by locusts—four different kinds, to be precise. Singular in their destruction, they devour lives and landscapes with devastating consequences. Joel recommends lament as one response to loss. Joel's narrative is then brought into sharper focus by looking at the varied nature of loss. We identify six types of loss that touch all, for they are inherent to life, but we place them in the context of the experiences of young adults. Identifying different kinds of loss is important, for the church has rituals to deal with some losses, such as death, but not others, such as divorce or early pregnancy loss. Moreover, one cannot grieve or approach every loss in the same way. We also look at common reactions to loss, such as feeling disoriented and searching for someone powerful who might undo the loss that occurred. The chapter concludes with practical guidelines on how best to facilitate the work of mourning with millennials.

Has something like this ever happened before?

Joel knows how to make an entrance. Upon addressing "everyone in the land" (1:2), we read,

> Has anything like this ever happened in your days,
>   or in the days of your ancestors?
> Tell it to your children,
>   and have your children tell their children,
>   and their children tell their children.
> What the cutting locust left,
>   the swarming locust has eaten.
> What the swarming locust left,
>   the hopping locust has eaten.
> And what the hopping locust left,
>   the devouring locust has eaten....
> It has destroyed my vines,
>   splintered my fig trees,
>   stripped off their bark and thrown it down;
>   their branches have turned white.
> Lament like a woman dressed in funeral clothing,
>   one who has lost the husband of her youth.
> The grain offering and the drink offering are gone from the LORD's
> temple.

The priests and the LORD's ministers mourn.
. . . The crops of the field are destroyed.
The grapevine is dried up;
    the fig tree withers.
Pomegranate, palm, and apple—
    all the trees of the field are dried up.
Joy fades away from the people. (Joel 1:2-4, 7-10, 12)

What an opening act! Joel invites us into the good life by recognizing the locusts of life, acknowledging the devastation they cause, and offering concrete ways to respond. It's a summons for us all to attend to the very thing that is happening in our midst.[5] With "hear," "tell," and "lament," as well as "wake up," "scream," "be shocked," "dress [for a funeral]," "demand (a fast)," and "gather," Joel begins with a list of powerful imperatives.

Joel drew on older sources, for his opening words echo a hymn dedicated to the goddess Nanaya, a prayer on behalf of Sargon II, king of Assyria (721–705 BCE).[6] Nanaya's hymn, which was probably used in the dedication of a temple, has two types of locusts bringing destruction to crops and fields. Other parallels include prayers of blessing and the cutting off of grain from the temple. Whether Joel relied on Nanaya, or both narratives relied on an even older source, remains uncertain.

We are told of complete agricultural failure, which for a people of the land is devastating: "locusts, or a series of increasingly severe locust plagues, have ravaged the crops; in addition to the locusts, an unrelenting drought has consumed the land and destroyed the harvests; and on top of the drought, a fire has swept across the countryside, destroying the trees and drying up any remaining sources of water."[7] It's been almost one hundred years since the United States knew a locust plague. Pesticides and the tilling of soil prevent such catastrophes. The rest of the world, from Australia to Africa and even Egypt and Israel, knows the dangers of locust plagues. Their devastation cannot be underestimated. Augustine of Hippo, in his *City of God* (written in 410 CE) tells of a "prodigious" North African locust plague, which killed eight hundred thousand people when the swarm died en masse after consuming all the food and the locusts' rotting bodies brought on typhoid to an already devastated land and people. Of a garrison of thirty thousand soldiers, Augustine writes, only ten survived.[8]

Some commentators believe that the locusts metaphorically refer to a human army that attacked (possibly the Assyrians, Babylonians, the Medes, or even Romans). Others see an eschatological and apocalyptic attack against Judah, while yet others state that the text refers to a real locust plague or even a debilitating drought. Contemporary commentators also interpret the locusts as reality or through a political lens.[9] All, however, see spiritual and intellectual truth in the locusts.[10] The different interpretations are not mutually exclusive, and commentator Elie Assis suggests that "the locusts have a double meaning, a literal one and a metaphorical one."[11] The double meaning causes "deliberate ambiguity," which invites a range of responses.[12] The ambiguity is also an invitation to return to God (see chapter 3). God contributes to the confusion, as God refers to the devastation that lasted "years" (2:25) and no plague lasts that long. In four different oracles (1:2-12; 1:13-20; 2:1-14; 2:15-17), the reality of the locusts is announced and Israel is called to lament, fast, gather, and return to God.[13]

Embracing the metaphorical nature of Joel, we can say that the locusts' appearance is *like* that of an army, the locust head being seen as similar to the head of a horse; the sound of them devouring the land is *like* approaching chariots; they move *like* mighty men. In Joel 2, we note, no distinction is made between the destruction of the locusts and the devastation of drought. Structurally, the locusts in the first chapter drive all the references to invasion and destruction in Joel and tie Joel to ancient Hebrew traditions. As early as 1879, commentators found a parallel between the plagues that prepared Israel's exodus (Exod 10:14) and the locusts of Joel that initiate God's intervention on earth.[14] Joel's narrative transports us to the exodus and thus becomes "double-voiced."[15] For us, solving the dilemma of whether the locusts are real or not does not preclude embracing the narrative's truth. The imagery of a force on the move that causes devastation might be enough, for emotionally and relationally we know such forces intimately. As commentator Pablo Andiñach writes, Joel, with apocalyptic overtones, "summons [his readers] to mourning and lamentation before the tremendous tragedy of the plague."[16]

He calls on a liturgical response—to lament, to fast, to gather, and to return to God—a divine response to a human tragedy.

Joel 1:4 is a pivotal verse in this opening act: "What the cutting locust left, the swarming locust has eaten. What the swarming locust left, the hopping locust has eaten. And what the hopping locust left, the devouring locust has eaten." In a four-stage procession, the totality of disaster is shown. The cumulative destruction not only increases the tension in the story, but it leaves no one untouched. Whereas some translations just refer to "locusts," the Common English Bible refers to the *cutting* locust, the *swarming* locust, the *hopping* locust, and the *devouring* locust. The Hebrew text, in turn, identifies four different plagues. There is the *gazam* (the cutter; that which cuts off); the *gasil* (the chewers, devouring palmerworms, cankerworms), *slow moving*, but devastating; the *yelek* (the eaters or consumers); and the *arbeh* (a swarm of locusts), *fast moving*, but just as deadly.[17] The Hebrew scriptures know these plagues, but only in Joel are they given in one sentence. The precise meaning of these words, however, is unclear, and the interpretation of the locusts has remained a hermeneutical problem.[18] Some argue that these insects describe different life stages and behaviors of locusts, whereas others see the four different references as pointing to total devastation. Some disagree that Israel had a rich vocabulary for locusts.[19] Whether a crawling worm or the locust that can ride the winds on its wings, Joel describes a fierce enemy. The locusts have teeth (and can pounce) like a lion (1:6), make sounds like chariots coming to launch an attack (2:5), enter a house through a window like a thief (2:9), or constitute a mighty army (2:11). Joel seeks out rich imagery to describe the vulnerability we experience in the presence of the locusts of life and their threat of devastation.[20] As a metaphor, however, the locusts describe crises, even small ones, that slowly unfold in our lives and other crises that surprise us, often with a phone call. Collectively, they are intricately tied to personal, social, political, and ecological salvation.[21] The *tetrad yeter* ("what [the cutting locust] left") makes one point: "Nothing can remain after a four-fold assault."[22]

Locusts inevitably awaken existential and spiritual crises. They initiate a reaction no one can avoid. The "drunkards" and "wine-drinkers" are the first to receive Joel's calls to weep. Reading Joel, one inevitably remembers Jesus being called a glutton and a drunkard (Matt 11:19). "In no biblical source does the word 'drunkard' refer to someone who drinks wine but does not become intoxicated," Assis reminds us.[23] Joel does not reproach the drunkards, a term he uses to metaphorically represent the whole nation. Rather, their behavior reveals the abundance of wine in a time of blessing. The spiritual crisis reaches a climax when the priests pray for mercy in 2:17: "Between the porch and the altar let the priests, the LORD's ministers, weep. Let them say, 'Have mercy, LORD, on your people, and don't make your inheritance a disgrace, an example of failure among the nations. Why should they say among the peoples, 'Where is their God?'" Asking *Why, God?* or *Where is God?* is a natural response to tragedy. Holding the paradox between a life in ruin and a loving God is not easy. This dilemma, also called theodicy, is best answered by practices such as friendship or lament or confession, rather than trying to rationally solve the tension.[24] God is not indifferent and hears the prayer of the priests, as chapter 3 will indicate.

Joel describes four responses to devouring locusts: lament, build community (see chapter 2), return to God (or repent; see chapter 3), and fast. These practices prevent denial and nostalgia as acts of resistance. The call to a prayer of lament is not a traditional prophetic response to calamity, for the tradition is most likely to say that what happened was deserved: retribution for sinful ways. *Joel is a different prophet.* There is no reason given for the presence of the locusts. Rather than being punitive, he is empathic and calls on Israel to pray, another novel step. In Joel's time, established prayer—as seen in the book of Lamentations—was neither custom nor institutionalized. Rather, "prayer is seen as a spontaneous outburst of a person in need."[25] Feeling remote from God and with no temple to pray in, Israel also abstained from prayer. Joel faults Israel for not praying and beckons them to return to God, also in prayer. He argues that the place where the temple stood will suffice to call out to God. The call to pray at the temple site is not a generic call for prayer, for it has a specific history and location, albeit unknown to us. Lament, we will shortly argue, is a powerful prayer and act of resistance in the face of tragedy.

Using the locusts of Joel as a metaphor for the millennials' experience opens three possibilities: First, we can *substitute* the two experiences and argue that as locusts devour landscapes and lives, anxiety, despair, isolation, insecurity, and underemployment devour too. Here the emphasis is on the outcome or result of a plague or power. By substituting one experience for another, new meaning is found. Second, we can *compare* locusts with something else—the pressure that leads to teen suicide or the economic realities of millennials, for example—and turn the metaphor into a condensed simile: A is like B. The emphasis is not on the outcome or result, but rather on the destructive power inherent to locusts and isolation, for example. We can embrace the *interactional* nature of metaphor. A metaphor contains at least two meanings, one literal and the other not and as these two (or more meanings) interact with one another, new understanding or meaning is created.[26] We entertain both the damage a locust plague can bring *and* the despair and lack of opportunity student debt induce, for example. As Joel describes locusts that may also be a human enemy and an apocalyptic warning, so too can we add analogies to the experience of young adults. We need not choose between these different meanings, for metaphorical and literal meanings are invited by the text, even as ambiguity and contradiction enter our discernment because of the interactional nature of metaphors.

Our opening salvo ends with "Joy fades away from the people." The locusts of life not only induce loss, they get into one's mind, changing one's outlook on life.[27] Emily witnessed this fact. What happened externally is now an internal reality. Depression, anxiety, and despair thrive in the wake of locusts devouring landscapes and lives. Recognizing this impact of the locusts on the people, Joel calls on them to build community and to return to God, an exhortation we explore in the next chapters. One cannot sustain oneself by positive thinking or sheer willpower in the face of tragedy. Finding meaning without engaging larger systems of thought or authorities is impossible, as we are embedded in relationships, even ones we wish to deny.

Recognize the losses initiated by crises, Joel advises. Every person knows those crises that surprise and those slowly moving toward us over distant horizons. Both kinds of crisis are inescapable. Whether personal or relational, social or financial, locusts abound. They come in various forms of abuse and violence, touching especially the lives of children, women, and the elderly; they come as failing and failed relationships; they come as illness and pandemics or as social structures that continue to support unjust systems. The locusts of life destroy hope and humanity, lives and land and relationships and reason. The first response of resistance is to recognize loss and hold it in vision, for that makes lament possible.

The diverse face of loss

The losses induced by the locusts of life are multilayered, even for a single catastrophe. Pastoral theologians Kenneth Mitchell and Herbert Anderson warn that "for many persons, the loss occasioned by death is the only loss worthy of significant attention; but the losses…to which we do not pay intentional heed may have a more profound impact on us in the long run."[28] They identify six types of loss that magnify the prevalence of loss in our lives. Each type of loss can visit with us at any point on our human journey, though some losses are more prevalent during certain life stages. As with every locust, a single event often contains many types of loss. The first type of loss they describe is *material loss*. "Material loss is the loss of a physical object or of familiar surroundings to which one has an important attachment."[29] Losing or breaking one's cell phone immediately catapults one into material loss. The teen who had to move into a small apartment after his parents' divorce experienced this loss. So too the teen whose pet died, as well as Emily leaving the city to be with her mother. Millennials know material loss in many other ways: moving from one affordable rental space to another; not having secure, well-paying employment; through the burdens of study debt; and not building equity as fast as previous generations did. If economists' warnings prevail that young adults are not planning for retirement and that systems that currently provide for the elderly are likely to fail, then material loss will follow this generation into mature adulthood.[30] Joel is clear that the locusts of life, without exception, cause material loss. This is a difficult loss to grieve as most religions—especially Christianity—typically discourage adherents from attachment to earthly possessions. If you are not allowed to attach to material possessions, money for example, but do, how are you to grieve the loss?

A second loss Mitchell and Anderson define is *relationship loss*: the loss induced through "the ending of opportunities to relate oneself to, talk with, share experiences with, make love to, touch, settle issues with, fight with, and otherwise be in the emotional and/or physical presence of a particular human being."[31] Whether one is the person leaving or the one being left behind, relationship loss touches every person since no relationship lasts, as Derrida reminds us. We imagine deaths, breakups, or persons drifting in separate ways. Relationship loss can be traumatic, as with date rape or a divorce filled with conflict. Sometimes relationship loss has an early start, as one anticipates the ending of a relationship or the coming of a death in anticipatory grief. Relationship loss can be like a slow-moving caterpillar or surprise you with the speed of the flying locust.

"Intrapsychic loss is the experience of losing an emotionally important image of oneself, losing the possibilities of 'what might have been,' abandonment of plans for a particular future, the dying of a dream."[32] It reckons with the fact that external events often have inner costs. The very personal nature of *intrapsychic loss* makes it both difficult to communicate and a challenge to grieve. How can Emily tell those around her that she is grieving the fact that she will not be able to introduce her future husband to her mother? Furthermore, in a culture where we are told, "You can be whatever you want to be"—a lie rarely challenged—possibilities often do not match reality. Intrapsychic loss is also experienced when a person is not recognized in ways longed for or when a sudden change in perception sets in. Waning confidence and self-esteem, as the brave teen told the youth group of her struggle, speaks to this place of emptiness. Bullying, whether online or in person, devours in a similar way. So too when a college graduate or a recently divorced person has to move back into a parental home after dreams and expectations of independence. Joel's woman—a virgin—as she imagined herself a wife, a mother, and a grandmother, reflects deep inner turmoil as possibility faded away. Here, we imagine a husband dying after the bridal price was paid but before the consummation of the marriage, or a woman whose husband left her and a relationship ended. She cries out to God in helplessness—God who is yet to be mentioned. Her future is uncertain.

A fourth loss Mitchell and Anderson name is *functional loss*, "when we lose some of the muscular or neurological functions of the body."[33] This loss indicates our embodied nature, and as such, the aging process brings functional loss to every person. When one loses a limb, the grief can be intense. But so too is discovering that conceiving a child is a difficult challenge after parenthood took a back seat to one's career or that a longed-for unborn child is genetically malformed. Early pregnancy loss would indicate relationship loss, intrapsychic loss, as well as functional loss. In our body-conscious culture, one's relationship with one's body can be filled with ambivalence and loss. Functional loss resists easy solutions until one accepts one's own mortality.

Role loss is "the loss of a specific social role or of one's accustomed place in the social network."[34] Parenting and retirement initiate significant role losses of adulthood. Millennials, however, may experience role loss in the many transitions they experience as professional persons. It is estimated that the typical millennial will have at least ten *career* changes (not *job* changes) in his or her professional life.[35] In Western culture, who you are and what you do often come fused as roles and identities converge, increasing the intensity of role loss. Emily describes role loss as her role shifted from daughter to being a caregiver, a role "forced" upon her even as she readily accepted the role.

The final loss Mitchell and Anderson name is *systemic loss*. It is the loss that sets in when "[belonging] to some interactional system in which patterns of behavior develop over time" ceases.[36] This loss also accepts that we are dependent on services delivered by systems. When those services end, loss can be experienced. Young adults, Mitchell and Anderson write, are especially vulnerable to this loss as they leave communities to pursue education or employment. Since systems resist change, millennials may receive emotional pressure that discourages them from leaving the system, even as the system makes it difficult for them to feel welcome and stay. When systemic loss is fused with relationship loss and intrapsychic loss, the feeling of loss can be intense. Young adults, who generally reject climbing corporate ladders, are vulnerable to this loss as they frequently exit and enter systems.

The work of mourning

Our losses, whether avoidable or unavoidable, temporary or permanent, actual or imagined, and even anticipated or unanticipated, catapult us into grief. William Worden, a grief theorist, reminds us that the face of grief is varied. It ranges from sadness, anger, guilt or self-reproach, anxiety, loneliness, fatigue, and helplessness, to shock, yearning, emancipation, relief, and numbness.[37] We respond physically, with a hollowness in stomach, a tightness in chest and throats. We can be sensitive to noise and have a sense of "I am not really me" (also called depersonalization). We can be short of breath, our muscles can go weak, our mouths can go dry, we may lack energy.[38] Our thoughts can be filled with disbelief, confusion, preoccupation, a sense of presence (person still here), and even hallucinations (seeing a person who died, hearing their voice).[39] With our whole being impacted, we can behave oddly, with sleep and appetite disturbances. If we can sleep, we may dream of the deceased or the loss. We can be absentminded, socially withdrawn, avoid reminders of the deceased, or call out to the person; we can be restless and cry, seeking to visit places or objects that remind us of a time prior to the loss.[40]

Worden reminds us that thinking of stages of mourning is not helpful. Rather, he identifies four *tasks of mourning*:

1. *Accepting the reality of the loss* by resisting denying that the loss occurred;

2. *Working through the pain of grief* by feeling the pain and resisting finding "reasons" for why the loss happened (such as, "She is now in a better place");

3. *Adjusting to a changed environment,* as loss always changes one's identity and one cannot be the same person nor inhabit the same space after a loss has occurred;

4. *Emotionally relocating the deceased or loss and moving on with life.*

Worden's language of "tasks" provides us with a sense of direction; one can become unstuck and feel one is moving forward. "Mourning has a quite precise psychical task to perform: its function is to detach the survivors' memories and hopes from the dead," Worden writes.[41]

It can take up to two years to complete the tasks of mourning, but three to four years is not uncommon for a significant loss. Completing the tasks of mourning is greatly determined by certain mediators, indicating the nature of the loss.[42] These mediators include: *Who was the person who died?* A close friend or relative, a distant acquaintance, or a stranger? *What was the nature of the attachment?* Was the relationship secure or ambivalent? At peace or conflictual? Were there emotional, economic, or other dependencies in the relationship? *What was the mode or cause of death and/or loss?* Was it natural, accidental, suicidal, homicidal? Was violence and trauma involved? Was it an ambiguous death, such as in the case of a missing person where the body is never found? Maybe the death or loss is filled with stigma, as is often the case with suicide and HIV/AIDS. *What are historical antecedents?* How were previous losses grieved? Is there a history of depression? *Is the person resilient, optimistic, and can call on coping skills? Does the person have a strong social network? Are there concurrent stressors?*

The locusts of life unleash turmoil in our lives, always. In addition to the face of grief and the tasks and mediators of mourning we receive from Worden, psychiatrist Silvano Arieti proposes another key aspect of recognizing loss in our lives: "the psychodynamics of sadness."[43] When a loss occurs, a gap (or discrepancy) sets in between "the way it is" (a loss occurred) and "the way it should be" (I should be untouched by loss). A large gap turns loss and grief into depression. Because the difference between "the way it is" and "the way it should be" indicates an emotional burden, Arieti identifies the yearning for a "dominant other" who will miraculously turn the way it is into the way it should be. God, of course, is the optimal "dominant other" in this regard. However, when we seek all ways possible to eradicate the discrepancy that sets in, our sadness and/or depression deepens. Rather, we need a "significant other," someone who can help us explore "the way it is" as we work through the tasks of mourning. By looking at "the way it is," we discover a new identity and the gap toward "the way it should be" narrows. Effective leaders are thus persons who can assist young adults who are grieving in exploring "the way it is."

This exploration is a challenge since loss also induces shame, that feeling of being naked, vulnerable, with a deep sense that something is fundamentally wrong with one's self when one does not measure up to internalized standards. Joel, following the Wisdom tradition (Prov 10:5), recognizes shame in farmers and winegrowers who cannot fulfill their promises and potential due to the damage the locusts caused. Here shame is different from guilt, which would be not meeting external standards.[44] In shame, the self evaluates itself; in guilt, the self is being evaluated by an outside authority. As such, shame is a deeper wound than guilt. Still, there is a close correlation between loss, grief, and shame as mourning and shame awaken deep emotion. Putting on sackcloth, as Joel urges, also carries the connotation of having shame.[45] Both loss and shame are *embodied* experiences leading one to seek cover! Similar to the locust of loss, shame devours lives. As it destroys one's relationship with one's self, it destroys one's relationships with others, for one can only offer one's self to partners, friends, and colleagues. God, as we'll discover in chapter 3, recognizes the close relationship between loss and shame and affirms the restoration of lives: "You will eat abundantly and be satisfied, and you will praise the name of the LORD your God, who has done wonders for you; and my people will never again be put to shame" (2:26). God, proclaiming Lordship, repeats: "Never again will my people be put to shame" (2:27).

Lament as resistance and as mourning
(Cowritten with Kyle Cummins)[46]

Joel, who has an intuitive sense of how to respond to the locusts of life, recommends that the people lament, fast, build community (see chapter 2), and return to God (see chapter 3). "Lament like a woman dressed in funeral clothing, one who has lost the husband of her youth," Joel advises (1:8). In scripture, psalms of lament are not uncommon, as we can see in the book of Lamentations, one-third of the Psalms, and the book of Joel. The transformative power of a lament is not that it gives answers, but rather that we experience suffering again while we have a hearing. We speak and God listens. In doing so, our sorrow, pain, and fear are transformed. A psalm of lament invites personal and communal identification with the emotional, relational, and spiritual worlds of not only the psalmist but also with all who cried out to God: "Why?" or even "What the hell!" For about twenty-five hundred years, psalms such as Psalm 22, 23, 32, 37, and 71 comfort the frustrated, disillusioned, embittered, conscience-stricken, or fearful.

In the Hebrew tradition, lament has a certain form:[47]

1. *Address to God*: The address to God is usually a brief cry for help, but is occasionally expanded to include a statement of praise or a recollection of God's intervention in the past (Ps 71:1-3).

2. *Complaint*: God is informed about diverse problems or concerns that individuals (or a community) experience. In penitential psalms, the complaint can acknowledge one's sins (Ps 71:4).

3. *Confession of trust*: The psalmist remains confident in God despite the circumstances and begins to see personal problems differently (Ps 71:5-8).

4. *Petition*: Filled with confidence in God, the psalmist appeals to God for deliverance and intervention. Reasons why God should intervene might be expressed (Ps 71:9-13).

5. *Words of assurance*: The psalmist expresses certainty that the petition will be heard by God (Ps 71:14a).

6. *Vow of praise*: The lament concludes with the psalmist's promise to witness to God's intervention (Ps 71:14b-24).

Praying a psalm of lament takes one on an emotional roller coaster. It awakens the intense emotions, including the shock and anger we experience when touched by loss. Praying this way, however, places us in a bigger narrative, one where God seeks the best for us—yes, God is a seeker too.

Kyle is a youth minister. He and his partner, Natalie, serve the inner city of Los Angeles. The youth and young adults they love and serve come from families and other systems that failed them. Many are in foster care. Kyle and Natalie discerned to grow their family through adoption and became certified foster-to-adopt parents. One day they received a call regarding a thirteen-day-old baby girl in need of a home. They gave her the nickname Aria, for music is important to the couple and *arieh* in Hebrew means "lion," a strong association for a young girl to take into a world still dominated by men. Kyle and Natalie received assurances that their foster care would lead to adoption. For eight months, there was no word from the birth mother as they built their family. The courts, however, stonewalled completion of the adoption process. Accusations from Aria's extended family suddenly arose as identity politics entered the conversation. Sixteen months after taking Aria into their home, Kyle and Natalie received notice that Aria had to be returned to her birth mother. The life of Aria's birth mother, however, has been filled with trials of addiction and the responsibility of another pregnancy. Against the recommendations of social workers, child psychologists, and the foster care/adoption agency, Aria was returned to her birth family. The couple was broken—how could they not be? Hope flickered briefly as Aria's birth family reached out to Kyle and Natalie, expressing a desire to return Aria to them. Aria's birth mother wrote a note stating she could not provide care for her children and would prefer Aria be adopted by Kyle and Natalie, for she has seen their love for Aria. Her request too was denied. By 2018 a year passed since Kyle and Natalie received any information regarding Aria's well-being or the adoption process.

During a ministry leadership conference, Kyle was encouraged to write a psalm of lament on a deep sadness and/or trauma. He wrote his lament, which he called "Lament for our Lioness," about Aria:[48]

Creator God, Good Father & Perfect Son

Why did You take away our beloved Aria? Am I not meant to be a dad? Why did You give me such hope & peace that she would be ours? Was I not enough for You to want to keep our family together? I am scared to heal, to let go of anger, for it feels like that is forgetting her or accepting that she is not with us. I am so mad at You that I have even stopped praying for her. I struggle to trust You to meet her wants and needs. I am grieving as a father and it's disabling me as a husband. You did not create me strong enough to endure this. What is Your perfect plan, for it surely cannot be this? Are You the God of empty promises? Your silence is deafening!

You have revealed Yourself to me before, reveal Yourself again. You are the light in the darkness; shine here and now. Though I cannot see it now, I know You desire shalom.

Father God, You know the loss of a child, but Yours was returned. Return our daughter to us. Let us embrace her again. Jesus, as a Son You felt forsaken by Your Father; please guard her from feeling forsaken by me. Protect her memories of us. Remind her of our love for her. I am asking the great and powerful Lion of Judah to watch over our precious lioness! Even though we could not adopt her, we pray, we plead that You do! Restore joy to our marriage, our home.

Be my anchor because I cannot survive this storm, I am lost at sea. Bring beauty from these ashes!

You have created all things good, so we await this despair being replaced by hope. I will shout for joy when Your garden returns, when Your kingdom comes. I am Yours, we are Yours, she is Yours.

"Has anything like this ever happened in your days, or in the days of your ancestors?" Kyle and Natalie echo Joel's opening question. As a young couple, they are asked to endure much, even as they reflect the deep commitment of making a difference in this world, a strength many millennials bring. With much pain and sadness, they discovered the locusts that come in the form of systems, powers, and principalities. Kyle's relationship loss is palpable. His material loss is unmentioned, but present. His intrapsychic loss as hopes and dreams faded catapulted him into self-doubt. Kyle's role loss of being a father is obvious. The locusts of life induce significant and painful loss, even for a young couple seeking to make a difference in a vulnerable child's life. With his lament, Kyle is reaching out to the God who restores, the compassionate God who sees the damage the locusts caused and also our tears. God hears our complaints. Of course, when we lament, we rarely experience this God's presence. Lament is not God's coming close to us, it is our reaching out to God, who like a loving parent is present all along, even if we cannot locate God. With our lament, we say in the face of the locusts that they are not the ones determining the narrative of our lives. They may claim a moment of victory, even as the opening act, but as the narrative unfolds the locusts will be destroyed, we will be restored and a new resolution will set in.

As a leader, will you be able to become a significant presence to young adults such as Emily, Kyle, and Natalie?

RECOGNIZE: Five practices for significant leaders

Effective leaders are called to recognize the locusts in people's lives and to facilitate the work of mourning. Dominant forms of leadership—poor listening, claiming authority and control, superficial relationships, and being threatened—will lead a leader nowhere. Leaders *can* listen to the losses of people's lives without an anxious reactivity that wants to smooth things over or fix. In the language of Arieti, an effective leader is a significant other. A significant other recognizes the presence of locusts in the lives of millennials and the devastation they cause, facilitates the work of mourning, and witnesses God's gift of reparation in their lives. Being a dominant other, someone ready to step in and fix, inevitably fails. Fixing often comes naturally to pastoral leaders and resisting doing so is not easy. Rather, being a significant other, someone who can hold the tension inherent to exploring the way things are, is courageous. Five practices will assure that you remain an effective leader to young adults: mourn your personal losses, empathize with young adults, support the tasks of mourning, empower young adults to write psalms of lament, and witness the birth of a new identity.

First, *practice awareness* to the pervasiveness of loss. Every pastoral leader benefits from naming, grieving, and mourning his or her personal losses. Pastoral leaders know loss intimately, often from childhood as their families mirrored Kathleen O'Connor's. Often, their losses remain ungrieved. Since our emotional lives do not know time, the losses can be as raw as when we first experienced them. Then there are the losses one experiences as a pastoral leader, from relationship loss to intrapsychic loss to role loss. Financial loss often follows pastors. No leader escapes the fact that ministry is grief work.[49] Without engaging one's personal work of mourning—completing Worden's tasks of mourning—it will be impossible to facilitate the work of mourning for others. Rather, the fact that many young adults, like Emilie, Natalie and Kyle, walk toward their losses will be a threat, prompting one to fix others as fast as possible. Mourning personal losses implies, at least, being curious how your loss shaped you. Furthermore, it requires having written or prayed a psalm of lament before asking another to do so.

Second, *practice empathy*. Kara Powell, Jake Mulder, and Brad Griffin of the Fuller Youth Institute, the authors of *Growing Young: Six Essential Strategies to Help Young Adults Discover and Love Your Church*, identify empathizing as the key strategy.[50] Empathy—"feeling *with* young adults"—includes "the work you do to understand people. . . . It is your effort to understand the way they do things and why, their physical and emotional needs, how they think about the world, and what is meaningful to them."[51] Deeper than care or sympathy, empathy is a powerful dynamic that initiates change and instills a sense of belonging. We are reminded that millennials are different from previous generations: they have "a later finish line" (people marry later or stay longer with their parents, for example), while they also have "an earlier starting line" (as puberty sets in around age twelve to thirteen and children are mature for their age).[52] Between an earlier start and a later finish, young adults are longer in the race. The authors suggest that three questions asked by young adults are foundational to empathizing: "Who am I?...Where do I fit in?...What difference do I make?"[53] The questions speak to identity, belonging, and purpose. Joel's narrative speaks directly to these questions as it addresses the individual, affirms community, and empowers persons to be a blessing to others. In the context of locusts, the three questions might be, "What have the locusts destroyed? How can community buffer and protect against the locusts of life? How do you manage to be a difference in this world even with the presence of locusts in your life?"

Third, *practice mourning.* Earlier, Worden identified the tasks of mourning as (1) accepting the reality of the loss by resisting denial that the loss occurred; (2) working through the pain of grief by feeling the pain and resisting finding "reasons" for why the loss happened; (3) adjusting to a changed environment as loss always changes one's identity; and (4) emotionally relocating the deceased or loss and moving on with life. The first task asks a leader to invite a young person to tell what happened. If the loss was that of a loved one who died, how did the news break? Was the death expected or unexpected? How did she react upon receiving the news? What rituals did she and her family call upon? Many other questions can invite a person to share more deeply. As a leader, you can listen to the ways the person defends against the loss, but need not react to what you observe. Defenses are purposeful, and when they are no longer needed, usually cease. Since loss is painful, we often rationalize the loss ("Grandpa died at age eighty; he had a good life. I should not be so sad...") or we place our attention elsewhere (suddenly applying for a new job takes all the attention and energy). Sometimes we deny that the death has any meaning ("He was a mean person"). The second task of mourning invites the mourner to reflect on the physical, emotional, and spiritual pain the loss unleashed, as well as on the behavioral changes it initiated. It tasks a person to tell how difficult life is after the loss. The third task sees a young person slowly learning how to cope with a changed environment. As a leader, you can ask how the person is preparing to go home for Thanksgiving, the first without Grandpa. You may also ask about internal changes that are occurring. "How are you anchoring yourself in life now that Grandpa, the pillar of the family, died?" You can ask about shifts in identity and the presence or absence of meaning. "How did the death change you? What meaning have you discovered in Grandpa's death?" Moments of regression and childlike behavior are not uncommon during this task. Lastly, an effective leader can witness the changes observed in a person and share those observations. "I've noticed that you are more introspective after your grandpa's death..." or "How might your recent volunteer work be related to your grandpa's death?" Remembering anniversaries is central to being a significant other, so make a note on your calendar to check in with the young person who will experience a sense of loss anew as the loss's anniversary approaches.

Fourth, *practice empowerment.* A significant leader equips and inspires young adults to write laments about the presence of locusts in their lives. Of course, one does not begin a relationship with a request to write a lament, but after conversation, relationship building, and a deepening trust as a result, a lament can be the natural next step in one's work of mourning. In *Helping Youth Grieve: The Good News of Biblical Lament,* campus minister Bob Yoder explores the reparative power of lament in the face of eating disorders, depression, suicide, and other locusts in the lives of young adults.[54] "Since youth are abandoned by the adult institutions in their lives," Yoder writes, "they are forced to deal with pain and fear on their own."[55] Yoder faults the church for not introducing lament to young adults despite Jesus calling out Psalm 22 on the cross. There is a formfulness to lament—it takes one on an emotional, relational, and spiritual journey and as an act of protest gives voice to the sufferer. Yoder uses laments during retreats, some over a weekend and others a day long.[56] He creates space for millennials to tell about their struggles and the losses they've experienced, to meditate and pray their way through the outline of a psalm of lament. Yoder's work with lament taught him that, far from being depressing, community is built, and emotional, spiritual, and relational healing is experienced. Lament is not only countercultural, it restores. Furthermore, lament anticipates building community, the focus of chapter 2.

Fifth, *practice hope*. Defining hope is difficult despite being an enduring human trait. It speaks to the hoper desiring (or yearning for) a possible or certain outcome perceived as good. Judah, we'll discover, hoped for a locust plague to leave and crops to return. From a spiritual perspective, to hope is to imagine a benign future, created by God, slowly unfolding in one's midst. It is not being optimistic, being positive, or having grit and resilience—though hope informs all those traits. Philosopher Ariel Meirav writes that hope is *resignative*, by which he means that in hoping one realizes one has no ultimate control over the outcome. Also, resignation does not mean despair (even if the two dynamics are linked), reduced intensity, or the fact that one does have influence over one's own future.[57] Spiritual hope's resignation anticipates something will happen despite oneself.[58] As such, spiritual hoping as the kind we find in Joel is related to, but different from, psychological hoping. Rick Snyder, a pioneer in research on the psychology of hope, defines hope as "a cognitive set that is composed of a reciprocally derived sense of successful (1) agency (goal-directed determinism) and (2) pathways (planning on ways to meet goals)."[59] In Snyder's definition there is no resignation, but hope is "energetically pursuing one's goals and being able to generate multiple strategies to devote effort and make progress.... Hope = Agency Thoughts X Pathways Thoughts."[60] For Snyder, hope is a belief that one can do something, that there is possibility, and imagining the something to be done. Such agency complements being empowered, our fourth practice. The hope awakened and the outcome sought in the book of Joel are not internally driven. Judah cannot chase off the locusts, create rain, or return from exile on their own accord (see chapter 5). One can, of course, devise ways of coping with drought or adversity.

Drawing on power beyond ourselves, philosopher Jonathan Lear argues for "radical hope," the kind of hope one needs when one stares total devastation in the face, as Judah experienced with the locusts. Lear writes how the Crow nation, led by Chief Plenty Coups, exhibited much courage as they experienced the destruction of their culture by White Domination. Lear writes: "What makes this hope radical is that it is directed toward a future goodness that transcends the current ability to understand what it is. Radical hope anticipates a good for which those who have the hope as yet lack the appropriate concepts with which to understand it."[61]

Lear suggests that it was the dreams that Chief Plenty Coups had (see chapter 4 on dreaming and seeing visions) that led him to lead his people differently compared to other Nations who faced the same plight. The dreams told him and his people to listen, learn, and do the best to survive in a new reality. This courage helped the Crow Nation to survive the destruction of their culture, retain some land, and discover new ways of flourishing in a White world.

Whether spiritual or psychological, hoping is central to personal flourishing, distress management, success, and meaning. Whereas some persons will hope if no outcome is possible, others will despair even if an outcome is possible, and others yet will hope for a changed future with a backup plan in place that is less than their anticipated future. Theologian Miguel De La Torre warns us in his *Embracing Hopelessness* that one cannot offer hope to or expect hope from an oppressed people, turning hope into a utopian vision. Rather, "to engage in liberative ethical analysis, requires accompanying the distressed in their struggles; leaving the safety of ivory towers to occupy precarious spaces along the disenfranchised. In short, one must be ¡Presente!" (see chapter 6).[62] "To hope against inhumanity becomes counterproductive for those hoping to survive."[63] When the very people who are calling on hope are the ones fueling hopelessness as they participate in unjust practices, it requires a social justice stronger than utopian hope. We will see that the God of Joel will judge those who do so harshly (see chapter 5).

Hoping anticipates being open-minded. It includes recognizing the new identity that is emerging after the losses the locusts induced. In a world where selfies rule and connection is sought via social media, few people have someone trustworthy in their lives who can mirror the changes loss initiates. To do so, deeper levels of intimacy and conversation are needed than we often find online. Discovering a new identity is not easy. Both the wrestling to find a new identity and the joy of settling on one can be reflected as compassionate resistance to the presence of locusts in our lives. Since hoping brings people together, exploring the hope and dreams persons have (see chapter 4) can stimulate restoration and renewal. Hoping is a habit best practiced often, for hope is a way of being.[64] It defines one's current experience, not only one's future.

Toward mourning and lament

"Tell it to your children, and have your children tell their children, and their children tell their children" (1:3). The opening act of Joel's narrative demands memory. The elders—parents and grandparents and leaders—are the ones leading the work of mourning. There is instruction involved, as well as memory. It is the same memory that recalls leaving Egypt and the redemption God provided. This act of memory resists nostalgia (from the Greek, *nostos*—return, homecoming; and *algos*—suffering, pain, or distress). Nostalgia suggests an inability to lament and an incomplete mourning process. Hankering for the past can become a locust by the sheer weight of not being able to face the way it is. As Judah longed nostalgically in exile for a return, however, nostalgia sustained them, such is the ambivalent nature of this very human dynamic.[65] Joel will remind us soon that God is the one who remembers and our remembering is merely following God. As with the exodus, salvation and restoration, here too are grace received from God.

Those who know Jesus—the Man of Sorrows—have discovered that Jesus is intimately acquainted with loss and resists the way it is. The image, drawing on the prophet Isaiah (53:3), sees a despised and suffering servant, a text the Christian tradition interprets as reflecting Jesus, who cried when his friend Lazarus died (John 11:35), but also carried a cross (Luke 23), wore a crown of thorns (John 19:5), was crucified, cried out, and died (Matt 27:50). It was especially during the Middle Ages that this image of Jesus flourished. The wounds Jesus received at the hands of bystanders and soldiers were visible on his body, much like the devastation of the locusts were apparent to all. It is in the identification with Jesus as the Man or Sorrows that one can receive comfort and also recognition. The embrace and support of friends (see chapter 2) and meeting the God of Compassion (see chapter 3) are equal graces. The locusts of life leave no one untouched, not even Jesus.

An ancient Algerian story tells how Satan scoffed at God that he could make a better creation. God heard this and gave Satan power to bring to life whatever he might create. Wandering around, Satan saw the pride of a horse and carried the horse's head off to hell. He admired the long horns of the antelope and the gentle eye of an elephant. They joined the horse's head. Seeing a bull fighting with a lion, he took the bull's neck and the lion's breast. Thinking of what he might need to round out his animal, he took the strong thighs of a camel, the legs of an ostrich, the stomach of a scorpion, and the wings of an eagle. From these animals, Satan created a creature and showed God. As promised, God brought the creature to life. God, now scoffing at Satan's creation, said: "Is that then your handiwork? O Satan! As a sign of your weakness may this creature multiply the earth and teach humanity that there is no God but God."[66] Locusts still abound.

Joel's opening act provides a visual and acoustic description of loss and mourning. The damage the locusts caused can be seen in the faces and on the bodies of the people and the emaciated livestock mirror the devastated land. Thank God that Joel's narrative takes us far beyond this opening act. Soon we'll hear that the catastrophe stops rather abruptly as a compassionate God intervenes. It is grace to know that, should locusts invade one's life, it is but one act in a larger narrative. Devastation will not have the last word, as Joel reminds us (2:25-26):

> I will repay you for the years
>> that the cutting locust,
>> the swarming locust, the hopping locust, and the devouring locust have eaten—
>> my great army, which I sent against you.
> You will eat abundantly and be satisfied,
>> and you will praise the name of the LORD your God,
>> who has done wonders for you;
>> and my people will never again be put to shame.

Before we experience this grace, however, we need to gather, for that is Joel's demand.

Chapter Two
GATHER

The Isolation of Loss and the Promise of Community

Millennials find hope in belonging. All people do. While other generations might find belonging at church, millennials gather outside the church's vision. Church leadership needs to discover, embrace, support, and join this actuality before millennials might discover church anew. In *How We Gather*, Angie Thurston and Casper ter Kuile explore the varied ways millennials build community.[1] Written while they were graduate students at Harvard Divinity School, the authors show an interest in their own generation, especially nonreligious millennials. "Churches," they state, "are just one of many institutional casualties of the internet age in which young people are both more globally connected and more locally isolated than ever before. Against this bleak backdrop, a hopeful landscape is emerging. Millennials are flocking to a host of new organizations that deepen community in ways that are powerful, surprising, and perhaps even religious."[2] As Thurston and ter Kuile looked at a myriad of millennial communities, some of which have bridged to other generations, they found six common themes among organizations that attract millennials:[3]

1. *Community*: Valuing and fostering deep relationships that center on service to others.

2. *Personal transformation*: Making a conscious and dedicated effort to develop one's own body, mind, and spirit.

3. *Social transformation*: Pursuing justice and beauty in the world through the creation of networks for the good.

4. *Purpose finding*: Clarifying, articulating, and acting on one's personal mission in life.

5. *Creativity:* Allowing time and space to activate the imagination and engage in play.

6. *Accountability*: Holding oneself and others responsible for working toward defined goals.

These themes, interestingly, resonate deeply with the good life described in the narrative of Joel: finding ways to flourish when loss and trauma are intimate enemies, gathering and building community, nurturing one's spirituality, living a life with accountable boundaries, and making a positive difference in the lives of others and the world. The hope Joel's narrative awakes, however, towers over the hopefulness Thurston and ter Kuile find in the communities they identify, for Joel's hope envisions complete personal, social, and political restoration (see chapter 5). Still, Thurston and ter Kuile share powerful examples of alternative gathering.

How We Gather identifies The Dinner Party, a grassroots community "of 20- and 30-somethings who all have experienced a significant loss and who get together over homemade food to talk about it and how it impacts their lives." Building on historical twelve-step programs and support groups, The Dinner Party draws on candid conversations and community support as transformational forces after the experience of a significant loss. The mission statement of the organization, as stated on their website, is "to transform life after loss from an isolating experience into one marked by community support, candid conversation, and forward movement."[4] As we discussed in the previous chapter and the focus of this chapter, Joel commands us to gather in the face of the locusts of life. A conversation by Carla Fernandez, Lennon Flowers, and a few friends over a meal in Los Angeles in 2010 has grown into more than two hundred "tables" in eighty-five cities, with chapters being formed around the world. The Dinner Party is spreading across the world, indicating an unmet need.

Besides The Dinner Party, Thurston and ter Kuile discuss nine other mostly millennial communities, including SoulCycle and The Sanctuaries.[5] SoulCycle is a spin class where instructors facilitate inspiration, enjoyment, and empowerment as they encourage participants to go on "journeys," as a spinning session is called.[6] SoulCycle was founded in 2005 by millennials Elizabeth Cutler and Julie Rice and has a half-million active members in forty-six locations with fifteen hundred employees. The company's "mission is to bring Soul to the people. Our one of a kind, rock star instructors guide riders through an inspirational, meditative fitness experience that's designed to benefit the body, mind and soul. Set in a dark candlelit room to high-energy music, our riders move in unison as a pack to the beat and follow the signature choreography of our instructors. The experience is tribal. It's primal. It's fun."[7] The spiritual and religious overtones are obvious. Just as persons of faith would go on a pilgrimage, SoulCycle sends its followers on a journey. The language of inspiration, meditation, and the soul resonate deeply with thousands of young adults (but also others) who may have sought out the church for soul care in the past.

The Sanctuaries, in turn, is a diverse artist community in Washington, DC, promoting spiritual growth and social change through the creative arts. They host "Soul Slams" and "Community Huddles." In 2013 Rev. Erik Martínez Resly, a Unitarian Universalist minister, brought a group of neighbors together to build a new type of community that they couldn't find anywhere else. The Sanctuaries, with a mission to "empower people to live creative and soulful lives," celebrates creativity, spirituality, and diversity in the service of social change and justice.[8] Through a seven-month program, participants are empowered by artists of diverse religious and ethnic backgrounds to bring their artful soul to a city in need of change.

The allusions to traditional religious elements and rituals within the groups Thurston and ter Kuile identify are obvious. They conclude:

> Overwhelmingly, [millennial] organizations use secular language while mirroring many of the functions fulfilled by religious community. Examples include fellowship, personal reflection, pilgrimage, aesthetic discipline, liturgy, confession, and worship. Together, these groups encourage friendship, promote neighborhood welfare, and spread messages for the betterment of individuals and society.[9]

Some pastors and church leaders will be threatened by secular-but-spiritual groups co-opting what was once the possession and domain of the Christian church or mainline traditions:

- Just who owns the word *soul* or the gift of breaking bread together?

- How do you hear a diverse group say they are building the community they cannot find anywhere else if the church prides itself in *koinonia*/community?

- What attitude and skill do you need as a leader to learn from these vibrant groups?

- How do you listen to and build community with millennials as they long for belonging?

- What will happen to the church if spirituality is primarily nurtured outside its walls?

- The fear may be very personal and existential: "How will my salary and benefits be paid if people do not tithe to the church?"

Sociologist of religion Nancy Ammerman helps us to understand lived religion as described in *How We Gather*. In her *Sacred Stories, Spiritual Tribes: Finding Religion in Everyday Life*, Ammerman explores the spiritual lives of ordinary Americans.[10] Over a number of years, Ammerman and her colleagues interviewed persons of faith including Protestant, Catholic, Jewish, Mormon, Wiccan, an internet group and nonreligious individuals, spanning the conservative to liberal spectrum. Ammerman's subjects showed that for most of them, everyday activities, perceived as secular, were fused with a sense of spirituality. We can learn much from Ammerman's research: First, she shows that the typical distinction between "religious" (as the organized, institutional, public, and that which focuses on theological beliefs and traditions) and "spiritual" or "spiritual but not religious" (as the personal, individual, private, and experiential) does not reflect personal experience.[11] Furthermore, any practice can be imbued with spiritual meaning, not just prayer, scripture study, meditation, and communion. Tradition and the church may have given us the habits, vocabulary, and practices of faith, but many persons have made religious and spiritual practices their own even as they never set foot in a church.

A second takeaway from *Sacred Stories, Spiritual Tribes* is that not only beliefs and practices, but *place*, too, is important as persons seek spiritual nurture. By giving persons cameras to photograph places and spaces important to them and voice recorders to keep audio files, Ammerman discovered that church or traditional sacred spaces were seldom photographed. Secular settings and places in nature, however, were photographed. The work place, for example, had religious or spiritual meaning to her respondents as they found a community of care among their co-workers.

Third, persons for whom spirituality was very important often mentioned their spiritual and religious conversations in the context of community, some kind of "spiritual tribe." Regarding community, Ammerman found that members of churches practice their religion more often and have stronger relational ties than those not attending church or a spiritual community.

Fourth, Ammerman found that in times of crisis, such as an illness or "when things go wrong," many, but not all, still turn to their faith for support.[12] The locusts of life, as discussed in the previous chapter, cause existential crises. Furthermore, *Sacred Stories, Spiritual Tribes* reminds us that religious or sacred conscience is not limited to categories such as "spiritual" or "religious." Rather, "the everyday world remains enchanted."[13]

A final takeaway from Ammerman's work is that people live by "the Golden Rule," an ethical code crossing many religions: "No matter what you say you believe or how often you attend religious services, what matters is how you live your life."[14] Ammerman writes, "The one thing almost everyone agrees on is that real spirituality is about living a virtuous life, one characterized by helping others, transcending one's own selfish interests to seek what is right."[15] No surprise then that Ammerman's subjects fault religion when it comes to social, economic, and environmental issues, the very realities important to millennials. The worldview described in *Sacred Stories, Spiritual Tribes* supports the good life millennials long for. The book does have its limitations as its subjects were mostly Christian and Jewish and middle-class, yet the argument that the dichotomous tension often perceived between "religious" and "spiritual" does not reflect lived experience is persuasive.

Some church leaders may say, "Persons find community in the church, too," or "We do loss," or "Eating together is what we in the church do," or "The church has always been an advocate for social justice." Others may try to maintain a false dichotomy between the religious and the spiritual, valuing the former more than the latter. In their anxiety, they will not be able to listen to millennials and will attempt to shame or coax or worse, judge them into the church, when millennials already live full lives in what the church perceives as secular spaces. The tension is palpable: The way it should be (and has been historically) is that persons should find belonging and purpose and meaning in the church. The way it is, however, for the majority of millennials and an increasing number of persons in the West, is that people find belonging and meaning elsewhere. Joel, I believe, has something to say in support of millennials and to challenge the church.

In this chapter, we first explore Joel's command to gather. Besides lament, to gather and build community is an act of resistance to the reality of the locusts of life. Since Joel emphasizes ritual, we briefly look at the importance of ritual in life and explore the deepening of tribalism in society. The chapter then highlights one millennial who finds belonging in kitchens and around tables, rather than in the church. The chapter concludes by suggesting ways to listen to and gather with millennials.

Gather

Joel, recognizing the devastation left by the locusts, calls on the people to gather. Community, solidarity, and partaking in rituals are pastoral responses to tragedy and loss. As in the opening verses of the book, Joel continues instructing and commanding:

> Dress for a funeral and grieve, you priests;
>   lament, ministers of the altar.
>   Come, spend the night in funeral clothing, servants of my God,
>   because the grain offering and the drink offering
>   have gone from the temple of your God.
> Demand a fast,
>   request a special assembly.

Gather the elders
    and all the land's people
    to the temple of the Lord your God,
       and cry out to the Lord.
What a terrible day!
    The Day of the Lord is near;
       it comes like chaos from the Almighty.
Isn't the food cut off
    right before our eyes?
    Aren't joy and gladness also gone from our God's house?
The grain shrivels under the shovels;
    the barns are empty.
The granaries are in ruin
    because the grain has dried up.
How the animals groan!
    Herds of cattle are in distress
       because there is no pasture for them;
    even the flocks of sheep pant.
To you, Lord, I cry,
    for fire has completely destroyed
       the pastures of the wilderness;
    and flames have burned
       all the trees of the field.
Even the field's wild animals cry to you
       because the streams have dried up;
    the fire has completely destroyed
       the meadows of the wilderness. (Joel 1:13-20)

With "grain offering and the drink offering have gone from the temple of your God," "request a [sacred] assembly," and "gather the elders," Joel not only describes the temple practices of his day, but he calls a lamenting people together. Gathering and building community, Joel argues, is necessary, even if there is no temple to visit, for it has been destroyed. One cannot but wonder about the correlation of a millennial people—for whom there is no church and who gather in spinning classes, around tables, on yoga mats, and elsewhere—and the narrative of Joel.

Unlike other prophets exposing the sinful practices of Israel's priests—the prophet Malachi would be a good example (see Mal 2:6-14)—Joel is not bothered by the kind of sacrifices the people are to make, nor does he seek to improve the quality of those practices. He does resonate, however, with the book of Lamentations (see Lam 3), a book birthed in the despair that followed the temple's destruction. Still, Joel places himself in the prophet lineage and follows the older prophets as he brings the word of God to the people.

Joel merely commands: "Gather!" The Hebrew used, *korah,* suggests calling a sacred assembly. Here, Joel might have drawn on the cult of Baal and older Ugaritic traditions as he calls Judah into community.[16] This call went to a large group but was possibly heard with some confusion, since there was no physical temple where they could convene.[17] Joel reminds his people that they can pray to God and engage in religious practices despite God not having a house to live in. Commentator Elie Assis summarizes Joel's call as follows: "The prophet's central purpose was to imbue the people with the awareness that their connection with their Temple did not depend on sacrifices and that they could maintain their connection with God in the ruined Temple through prayer."[18] Assis sees Joel motivated in his command to gather "as one of strengthening the people's identity following their deep despair after the destruction of the temple."[19] For a people who had no temple to go to, Joel's message of assembling, fasting and praying, and observing the spiritual practices of his day was good news. The absence of the temple did not sever the people's relationship with God, for it is God's covenant with God's people that keeps their relationship with God alive. This relationship is not mediated by the temple.

Whereas Joel's first speech calls on the people to recognize the locust plague, which we explored in the first chapter, his second speech addresses primarily the priests. "The priesthood in Joel," commentator Christopher Seitz writes, "is without personal name or future specification, which may serve to make the text available for future generations."[20] *The Millennial Narrative* embraces the possibility Seitz envisions as it invites millennials to the good life. Joel's priests are to dress, lament, spend the night, and gather. Joel, as stated, does not join the other Minor Prophets who are very critical of the priests as the ones who led the people of God astray. The calamity the people are facing is not the result of priestly malfeasance. The mourning and fasting Joel demands bring the pain of the people to God. The "ministers of the altar," "servants of my God," and "the elders" show a progression, but speak of one group of people, the priests. It is the priests who model mourning, keeping their funeral clothing on, even at night.[21] Before they can put on their funeral clothing, however, they have to bare their chests. As ancient Near East funeral rituals dictated, they had to strike their chests while crying out, linking one's personal pain with the pain of another.[22] After gathering as priests, Joel tells them to widen the circle and bring the people together. The word *korah*, however, is ambiguous and can refer either to just a gathering of elders or a gathering of all the people in the land, as our translation says. The latter is the bigger possibility as it was the people's lives that were destroyed by the locusts. The priests and the people, joined in their common suffering, are no longer alienated by the locusts and cry out to God.

Joel thus contradicts his fellow prophets as he calls on God's people to gather, fast, and pray. Isaiah (1:13; 58:1-14), Amos (5:21), Jeremiah (14:12), and Zechariah (7:5-7) rebuked Israel when they engaged in these practices with sin on their hands. Joel, of course, has not mentioned sin yet and does not develop the theme of sin as the other prophets do.[23] Joel's focus is on the locusts, which devour like hungry lions and destroy like a raging fire. Such sharp vision takes sin out of focus. Our prophet is mindful that we witnessed extraordinary times, unlike those ever experienced, and that a communal response is yet lacking. Fasting—a ritual that usually lasted one day—is not seen by Joel as penitential (as compared to elsewhere in scripture: 1 Sam 7:6 or Neh 9:1-2, for example). Rather, fasting is an act of solidarity in the face of tragedy and an expression of religious seriousness.[24] Here too Joel taps into older traditions, as scripture does name fasting as a response to sorrow (see 1 Sam 20:34; 1 Kgs 21:27; Esth 4:3; and Neh 1:4). As the people gather, mourn, fast, and pray, they remember a future day—the Day of the Lord—when God's reign of justice and restoration will prevail on earth.[25] Joel plays with words, such as *Shadday* (Almighty; 1:15), which rhymes with *missadday* (devastation). He anticipates devastation worse than the one just experienced. In Joel, however, the Day of the Lord is not *only* something in the far-off future but a reality already being experienced. Furthermore, the Day of the

Lord is not brought on by people's sinful actions but by a natural disaster. Joel's linking of the Day with the locusts challenges the people's belief that their exile and the destruction of the temple were indicators of the Day of the Lord as final punishment (see Obad 11-14 or Lam 2:1, 22). (We'll explore the Day of the Lord further in chapter 5.) Strangely then, Joel finds God in the locusts, for God did not abandon the people of God when they entered exile.[26] This is the good news: God is present, in tragedy and when we gather.

Stating "the granaries are in ruin" (1:17), Joel faults those responsible to secure food for the people. For most of us in the West, imagining being without food is difficult. We live with tables of plenty. We do experience, however, leaders and politicians squandering their responsibilities and placing lives and the earth at risk with policies and practices through sins of omission and commission. Joel describes how the people, the priests, and even God are hungry. All await God's intervention and restoration as the plowed fields offer no yield. In light of devastated crops, Joel's call for a fast seems a bit ironic, yet fasting was an established response to loss in the ancient Near East. Even the animals suffer the horror of living through a locust plague that was possibly followed by a drought. Joel, assuming the role of priest, brings the people and the animals into God's presence as he calls out to God. The "herds of cattle are in distress" and the "flocks of sheep pant" (1:18), Joel writes. The natural world is united in a common plight, and gathering is a direct response to the catastrophe all face. Whereas God is experienced as absent, God, now addressed directly, cannot escape Joel. When those around Joel said God is no longer present in their lives, Joel believed differently.

Joel ends the opening verses with a personal prayer: "To you, Lord, I cry" (1:19). He models for the people that they can reach out to God, for God has not abandoned them. There is no request for restoration, no petition for a changed world as would be expected in a typical biblical lament (see chapter 1). Rather, Joel believes that the people gathering will stir God to take action on behalf of God's people who faced tragedy. The people, animals, and the earth wait upon God.

The book of Joel does not give us a clear picture of what gathering at that time looked like. One can imagine, however, a devastated people relying on their resilience to sustain themselves in the crisis, even as they draw on memory and ritual for strength and to process their losses. Maybe the people of God met in open spaces, a provocative image as they would seek God amid destroyed pastures and the smell of wildfires, with emaciated cattle and sheep panting for food and water. Or maybe they met in an empty barn or granary, seeking nurture as they fearfully wonder where the next meal would come from. As Joel calls us to gather, we are reminded that:

- God is there when the locusts of life seek to claim rule;

- we can maintain a connection with God in the absence of a church/ temple;

- gathering is an act of pastoral and prophetic protest in the face of tragedy;

- gathering is facilitated by "priests"—leaders who can empower a sense of belonging and who act as a bridge between the people and God;

- gathering instills identity when identity is eroded by crisis; and

- God, who persistently seeks ways to enter into relationship with us, remains faithful as the covenant God.

Joel calls a convocation (from the Latin *con* = together; *vocatio* - call), people coming together for a specific reason. The reason might be religious or social and today also academic or political. Here, the reason is lamenting a tragedy and practicing resilience. By bringing a people under a common plight or cause together, individuality (me, mine) takes a back seat to community (us, ours). Tragedy does awaken the longing for belonging, a dynamic that speaks deeply to the tribal impulses of millennials.

Believing in belonging

"Tribe," author Sebastian Junger writes, can be defined as "the people you feel compelled to share the last of your food with."[27] He uses "tribe" differently from the word's historic meaning, which has become problematic due to its ties to colonial powers and the othering and subjugation of traditional cultures. Today, social scientists are reintroducing tribe-language as they explore elements within contemporary American culture. Junger faults Americans, except those in the military, as having lost touch with a strong sense of belonging, making it difficult for especially war veterans to return home. The chase of affluence, rising cost of living, and the forces around urbanization, Junger contends, place us in a "desperate cycle of work, financial obligation and more work."[28] In this cycle there is little room for finding belonging. Many millennials are bucking this trend and may well restore to us the joy of gathering. We see this on college campuses.

In their study of American campus life, Arthur Levine and Diane Dean tell of the strong sense of community that remains unchanged from their previous studies:

> The last study found that student social life often occurred in packs, groups of men and women, rather than in couples, and it still does. But social media also allows each student to enlarge the pack to what amounts to a virtual tribe, consisting of friends, family, neighbors, acquaintances, and any other significant people in an undergraduate's life, past or present, and stay connected with that tribe twenty-four hours a day, seven days a week, in class and out.[29]

Levine and Dean describe young people as being deeply committed to a specific group they often created themselves.[30] Different groups do not tend to relate to one another. On college campuses, alcohol, drugs, and sexual experimentation inform the experience of many students, a reality Levine and Dean find troubling and dangerous. The practices we find on college campuses speak to loneliness, alienation, and the lack of belonging. Whereas the majority of millennial students were rooted in a group, 34 percent of the college students Levine and Dean surveyed were isolated with few personal relationships.

Elizabeth Drescher, who taught us about the "nones" and the "somes" in the introduction, deepens our understanding of the nones' proclivity for gathering. She sees them as "believing in belonging."[31] Belonging to a community becomes a spiritual practice, even if that community is void of anything overtly spiritual or religious or no belief in a supernatural being of force is sought or present. As one of her respondents told her, "Community *is* religion. Family *is* religion. All the rest of it—doctrines and rituals—I think those came about to help create tribes, communities, families, and so on."[32] Embracing The Pew Research Center's research on millennials (see the introduction), one can say that for the majority of millennials, religion is more anthropocentric than theocentric; it is about people, not God. Validating the community and sustaining power we witnessed within The Dinner Party, Drescher asserts that "preparing and sharing food" not only cultivates "intimacy, empathy, compassion, and connectedness" but defines "contemporary spirituality."[33] Drescher also discovered groups that originated in the workplace exploring restaurants and food as a practice of community, belonging, and spirituality. Here, Drescher's research and Ammerman's are in agreement.

Ammerman helps us to further understand the communal nature of millennial faith practices as she writes about "spiritual tribes"—the communities where personal and sacred meaning are discovered in relationships, practices, and shared ways of thinking.[34] In these communities, Ammerman was struck by the degree to which "caring for each other is not only a matter of mutual family responsibility but also a matter of religious virtue and community connection."[35] Ammerman's research shows that gathering, care, and ethical practices such as seeking justice or activism, more so than traditional practices such as attending a worship service, participating in prayer, or studying scripture, are defining many contemporary spiritual communities.[36] In Ammerman's study, persons who combined extra-theistic beliefs with more theistic beliefs mentioned spiritual practices more often, had a deeper sense of belonging, and found spiritual meaning in a wider range of places.[37] Extra-theistic beliefs speak to functioning outside tradition and seeking transcendence in nature. Also, such beliefs indicate seeking belonging in community and seeking meaning in life while being open to mystical truths. Theistic beliefs indicate traditional belief—doctrines and the religious practices that have shaped Christianity for millennia. Just where the secular ends and the sacred begins—or vice versa—however, is rarely clear. "In the world of everyday life," Ammerman concludes, "sacred stories can be found, for good and ill, throughout the social world."[38]

Millennial spirituality with its individualistic tones most often takes one into community and inescapably beyond traditional places of worship and spaces of devotion. Drescher reminds us that the preparation and sharing of food is important to millennials. Julian Galette, as we'll discover next, lives into this aspect of millennial life with creativity and passion. His ministry takes place in kitchens and around tables, spaces where he builds community, restores humanity, and nurtures spirituality.

Practicing table fellowship for spiritual nurture

(Cowritten with Julian Galette)[39]

Jules Galette was raised in a "very Haitian family." "The first plate of food I ever craved was my mother's scrambled eggs and sliced bananas," he remembers. Since his first memories he has loved this dish his mom introduced to him. Jules is the first to admit that others may find his favorite dish revolting, but "there is something perfect and life-giving about custardy, slightly salty eggs and the sweet but semi-firm texture of a just ripe banana. I realize that our relationship to food goes deeper than the ones we forge via our ethnic, racial, national, and even regional identities. My love of eggs and bananas is tied into my connection with my mother in ways I will never truly be able to articulate." Jules grew up with tables of plenty, tables he now shares with profound spirituality as he practices a form of sacred sensuality.

Jules invites friends and strangers to share their favorite recipe with him. In turn, he will share a recipe with them. He then invites the person or persons into his kitchen and together they make both recipes. Intimacy is cooked up amid savory smells and tastes. Jules finds the deeply spiritual practice of cooking a meal with and for someone else sacred. "It is a holy act to prepare food for the nourishment of another. It is communion and alchemy in perpetual motion. If I find any flaw in the Jesus we experience in the Gospels it is that he cooks only *one* meal [after his resurrection; described in John 21:1-14]." Through his practice and the dinner plates he creates, Jules states that he is not only nourished physically, but "the food enriches me spiritually in a way I could not have anticipated. Every scrap of dough, potato skin, knob of butter, and sprinkle of sugar involved in these recipes has connected me with the family histories and lives of the people who volunteered their time to help me with this effort."

Through the sharing of recipes and cooking together, Jules builds relationship, awakens intimacy, and gives new meaning to "soul food." The first time he tasted his friend's blueberry pie, he knew there was something special about the pie. He asked if she'd share the recipe with him and she entrusted him with a family recipe. Jules, however, is interested in much more. He explores the history of the recipe, asks about the faces and relationships that first used or created the recipe. He is curious of when and how the pie was consumed. In doing so, he invites his friend to remember herself as a person deeply connected to the women in her family, especially her grandmother. As she re-experiences love and care, a new relationship is deepening. Two souls not only unite, but are nurtured. A second friend grieves the death of a loved one and finds solace in Jules's kitchen. Her remembering is an act of resistance. A third friend, sharing a potato salad recipe, contemplates how the communion tables in our churches are privileged tables—every person is not welcome. This friend compares Jules's table with the ones he finds in the church. The latter is wanting. Another discovered the hospitality extended by a prisoner in a maximum-security prison who baked cheesecake in a setting restrictive and depriving in so many ways. Suddenly a recipe and eating together reflect creativity in baking a cheesecake with what's available and resist the industrial prison complex. For Jules, there are many friends, recipes, kitchen sessions, and tables.

As Jules gathers around recipe exchanges, he becomes a caregiver, a counselor, a confidant—a pastor, a priest—someone entrusted with much more than a recipe. He facilitates a ritual that awakens something deeply spiritual. "Food + God + Relationship = Eternal life," Jules concludes. He cultivates his own sourdough starters and bakes bread, to share with those who cross his path. Other times he'd leave bread in common spaces where people gather for them to enjoy. Many do not know the source, but enjoy freshly baked bread. Jules's call is to create tables around which deep sharing takes place through the simple practice of a recipe exchange. He invites persons to revisit life-giving relationships, moments of pain and trauma, and tables around which restoration occurs and belonging is discovered. Jules gives gathering new meaning.

Millennials: The priests of our time?

When people gather, they need facilitators or leaders. For Joel, who has been described as a "cultic prophet" due to his calling of the people of God to gather, such leadership is the responsibility of the priests and elders.[40] Joel might have been a priest himself as he references the *Tamid*, the daily temple offering that was a central ritual in Joel's time. The priesthood in Joel, we said, is somewhat vague, opening possibilities for us to reinterpret the nature and purposes of the priesthood.[41] The Reformation, of course, already did so by establishing the priesthood of all believers. Joel's priests portray specific tasks: they lament and lead the people in lament; they call people to gather; they bring offerings; they pray, encourage, and point the people back to God. In naming these tasks, Joel draws on the priestly tradition that has informed Israel's life since Moses's brother, Aaron, and Aaron's four sons were summoned to be priests (see Exod 28–29 and Lev 8–10). Set apart and identified by wearing a vest in bright colors of gold, blue, purple, and deep red, with gemstones, priests were called to facilitate rituals as the people of God gathered and sought God's presence. Hebrew Bible scholar Walter Brueggemann writes that "priests themselves do not mediate, but they supervise and attest the visual, material, physical acts of worship that do the mediation."[42] There was a time that practices, not persons (like Jesus), bridged to God. The priests, representing the holiness of God, reveal God's availability to be present in the lives of God's people as they facilitated order, coherence, and dignity in the face of disorder, alienation, and threat. "The priesthood is to protect and guarantee the maintenance of an alternative world, wherein Israel could 'see' God and see themselves differently in the world."[43] As such, priests, in gathering and through ritual, create moments of reconciliation with God, reparation of wounds received and restoration of relationships.

Ritual permeates the priestly life. Just as we need narratives to make sense of our world and ultimately thrive, we need practices and rituals.

Joel knows the wisdom that rituals communicate. Rituals are "structured sequence[s] of action that pay homage to some cultural ideal."[44] Some rituals point to a sacred *object*, but not all do, as others point to sacred values or ideals such as relationships, care, hospitality, or compassion. Furthermore, some rituals are public, whereas others are done in private. Rituals are typically found around important life events, such as a rite of passage, a traumatic event, when relationships change, and when hostility or disagreement sets in. Communications theorist Bradford Hall reminds us that rituals often evoke one of the following images: (1) they point to an action done repeatedly; (2) the action typically has meaning for those voluntarily participating; (3) rituals, which have an ordinariness to them, are often reserved for special moments (such as death, births, birthdays, and weddings) or settings (ranging from a building such as a church to a room with a table); and, (4) some rituals, despite their ordinariness, are reserved for special moments.[45] When rituals are absent or when the protocols around them are violated, Hall warns, such action can have negative effects on individuals, relationships, and communities, for rituals imbue meaning and without experiencing personal meaning in life, one cannot flourish. "Rituals," Hall concludes, "are a vital part of any community not only because they teach people what is good, and provide...a way to create and maintain important social relationships, but they serve a cohesive function for the larger community in general."[46]

Who are the priests for the millennial generation today? As *How We Gather* showed, millennials meet in groups and are congregating in many spaces for many reasons. One finds ritual, restoration, and healing. The lack of young adults in the church suggests that pastors and elders are priests to only a small number of millennials. I suggest that many millennial leaders are priests to their peers. They, like priests of old, find the sacred in the ordinary and call society to create and portray belonging, justice-seeking compassion, and care that touches all, especially the marginalized. Likewise, millennials find a deep connection between wholeness, spirituality, and ecological concerns (or nature). It is persons like Jules who embody the values once held by the priests of the ancient Near East and who invite persons overlooked by society into a covenant relationship, also with God. People in need or in emotional

43

and relational pain, our inner cities, the earth, and many other spaces and places are touched by millennials making a difference. Like Joel, millennial priests do not dichotomize the body and the soul, as Ammerman reminded us. Rather, body and spirit are interconnected and caring for one is not more important than the other.

There are however, also significant differences between ancient priests and their modern contemporaries. Whereas the priests of old kept ordinary people from the "most holy" spaces they identified and served, priestly millennials welcome all. In Joel's time, priests practiced a "one degree holier" ministry—ordinary people could access the holy, but not the most holy. The priests, already holy, could access the most holy. Anyone who acted two degrees holier died, for God's holiness would be offended.[47] Millennials disrupt this understanding of the priesthood, which included a prohibition against any person with any deformity from serving as a priest.[48] They redefine what wholeness and integrity means. No longer do grain and blood offerings define a sacred space; an ordinary table with a couple of recipes is sufficient. Proper conduct, once held dearly by priests, has lost its purity, perfectionism, and power. Here, Jesus showed us a different way. How often did Jesus gather and share a table with people to be called "a glutton and a drunk, a friend of tax collectors and sinners" (Matt 11:19)? Jesus, God Emmanuel—God with us—came close to us by joining a table. As one gathers and partakes in the ritual of eating together, a distant God can be an intimate, nearby presence.

By arguing that some millennial leaders are the priests of our time I do not imply that they all should be ordained or take up a church office. Rather, young adults exercise the priesthood of all believers as they follow their passion for a world where people are burdened by isolation to discover the blessing of belonging. Priesthood is thus not so much a role one plays, but a personal identity that drives actions and thoughts as it sees the world through spiritual and relational lenses. To live into this identity, millennials show that they are willing to accept especially financial sacrifices, but also relational and systemic sacrifices as they gather people with a compassion that transforms.

Gather: Five practices for significant leaders

Leaders seeking to practice gathering often feel uncertain or even paralyzed as they wonder how to proceed. Indeed, where to find the time and energy or the millennials to reach out to? The subtle and overt messages one receives as a leader is to bring young people into the church, preferably couples with young children. Reminders that in the past the nursery was filled with children, and that summer's vacation Bible school was once popular, are stifling. Meant as encouragement and support and also an expression of deep concern for the future of the church, these messages rarely empower new ways of leading or facilitate a changed reality. As we stated, to lament the reality of the church—*the way it is*—should complement a focus on *the way it should be*. Five leadership practices can assist you as you embrace Joel's call to gather:

Practice joining (before attempting gathering). Young adults are already meeting; they are experiencing deep belonging and life-changing community. Become curious and discover their current ways of being together. Rather than trying to start a new ministry or program or calling millennials to come to your church, ask a few about their relational lives. Your conversation partners will be those millennials God placed in your congregation, the children and grandchildren of existing members or possibly young folk you meet at the coffee shop, the CrossFit box, gym, or in other places in your walk of life. Invite these young adults to become your teacher. Your congregation can extend some financial support toward food or provide space if needed. Your grounds can be offered for ultimate Frisbee or flag football. Should your church have a café, open it to millennials. When a leader accepts the fact that one need not create something new—a small group ministry for young adults, for example—but rather has to discover what has been there all along, the responsibilities of leadership change. Invite a millennial to lunch and pay the tab.

Second, *practice witnessing*. Spread the word. Often tell about Joel's image of the good life. Be a witness. There is power in the irony that the good life begins with loss, invitation when called into community, grace to discover the compassionate God, empowerment to recognize the Spirit's indwelling, security in accountability, and joy and personal meaning in making a difference in this world. To be the bearer of the good news we find in Joel, you need to make Joel's narrative your own. How have the locusts touched your life? Where and with whom do you gather? How do you place yourself into places and relationships where you can discover God anew? In what ways do you recognize the Spirit within? How do you practice accountability? And, besides serving your church, how are you contributing to a better world? Inevitably, Joel's good life challenges the loneliness, isolation, burnout, and cynicism that can become intimate enemies of a pastoral leader. Be assured that the narrative we find in Joel is life-giving to all, you included. Spreading the word is a central task as we seek to gather.

Third, *practice warmth*, which also communicates welcome. Researchers Kara Powell, Jake Mulder, and Brad Griffin discovered that having "structures" to create authentic community is not enough. Assessing what young adults say about their churches, Powell and her colleagues discovered that in "the terms young people and adults use to describe their own churches or parishes, we noticed repeated words such as welcoming, accepting, belonging, authentic, hospitable and caring. We began to call this the *warmth cluster*."[49] Authenticity and warmth were stronger indicators than any other variable in those ministries already effective in reaching millennials. When a congregation had a youth group, small groups, or a special retreat for young adults, the nature and feel of those ministry moments were more important than the ministries themselves. The researchers recognize that structures are important, but they are fruitless in the absence of the warmth cluster. Warmth and welcome are rarely experienced if the activity is driven by monologues— one person dominating the conversation (think preaching) or a singular topic driving the interaction (think doctrine, tradition, or education)—for such activities inevitably exclude and set apart. As you might imagine, a busy programmatic life at your church can work against warmth. The uniqueness of the group will manifest in what they do together first—eating, serving, playing, conversing—before common beliefs will manifest. "Warmth," Powell and her colleagues conclude, "[is] the lifeblood coursing through the veins of your church body."[50] As your attention shifts to joining millennials where they are already meeting, you may have to deprogram your church or at least challenge expectations others may have on how to reach the younger generation. Warmth, indicating a place where a person can be authentic, is "like [being] family" and is the glue that helps millennials stick with church.[51]

In his book *Y: Christian Millennial Manifesto*, Joshua Best writes that "our desire for authentic experiences is more than a preference; it's a craving. You could say it's a need."[52] Best traces the need for authenticity not so much as seeking newness and moving away from what's familiar, but rather in "our empowered upbringing, it's enhanced by our empathetic tendencies, and it's brought to life by our creative thought process."[53] The search for authenticity, Best warns, should not be confused with being selfish, for millennials invest or give themselves for a cause or in a relationship, even as their sense of duty can be challenged at times. The desire for authenticity, Best believes, is the trait that will allow millennials to change the world. "Millennials have the guts to stand up for their beliefs and the boldness to be true to themselves. This is something that should be cultivated."[54]

Warmth certainly will change how your congregation welcomes visitors to your church. Empowering existing members to gather, to recognize a visitor, to reach out, to ask how someone new to them heard about your congregation, to offer directions, to invite the person(s) to the fellowship hour, and to decide what follow-up will take place and more are important should you desire visitors to return. When inviting millennials into the good life, always think personal relationships, not programs.

Fourth, *practice rites and rituals*. Rites of passage (such as transitions from high school to college or into marriage) and rituals (such as lamenting, eating together, fasting, or sharing) are powerful and transformative markers on the journey of life. Joel reminds us that gathering practices are key to being a sacred assembly. Hebrew Bible scholar Douglas Watson writes that Joel's rites and rituals have two primary purposes: they bring a people, scattered by the locusts of life, together; and they awaken the attention of the compassionate God, which we'll discover next. "By making external their misery the people hope to attract the attention of YHWH, a gracious and compassionate deity (2.13), and move him to action on their behalf."[55] Elizabeth Drescher, studying American religion, writes that four overlapping areas define the spirituality of the nones and somes: *family* (enjoying time with family), *friends* (enjoying time with friends), *Fido* (enjoying pets and other animals), and *food* (preparing and sharing food).[56] If we have "drinks" with strangers, acquaintances, and fellow employees, Drescher argues, meals are reserved for family, close friends, and honored guests. The anthropological and cultural history of food and place run deep in our veins, and millennials are reclaiming that heritage, preferring farm-to-table practices. Supporting our earlier question on who are the priests today, Drescher writes that in ancient Greece, the word for "cook," "butcher," and "priest" was the same—*mageiros*—and the word shares an etymological root with "magic."[57] Even the most ordinary dish follows a satisfying arc of transformation, magically becoming more than the sum of its ordinary parts. And in almost every dish you can find, besides the culinary ingredients, the ingredients of a story: a beginning, a middle, and an end.

The Dinner Party and Jules know that eating together is magical, that it transforms, even if the topic of conversation is loss, grief, and mourning or the relationships that provided a recipe. The meal itself, as the other content that fills the evening, becomes a larger story that invites you not only into belonging, but into transformation. Drescher's research on nones and somes shows that "preparing and sharing food" are among the top spiritually meaningful practices (23 percent of both groups), alongside "enjoying time with family" (32 percent of nones; 51 percent of somes), and "enjoying time with friends" (24 percent for both groups). Millennials feel most spiritual when family, friends, Fido, and food define the experience. "Relational unaffiliated spiritualities," finding community and meaning outside the church, even in a relationship with a pet, Drescher writes, is the "lived religion" of millennials.[58]

Lastly, *practice participatory leadership*. Millennials, even if they can lean toward being authoritarian, see authority figures as equals.[59] To practice a different kind of leadership is difficult if one is locked into hierarchies or if one has unconscious assumptions about millennials. *The Millennial Narrative* is deliberate in not strengthening the preconceived notions often assigned to this generation. Such projection will only bring distance between whoever seeks to invite a millennial into the good life and a person longing for a larger narrative to live into. As briefly shown in this chapter, millennials lead in many ways, taking the older generation into uncharted terrain. A courageous leader might even let millennials lead the way without feeling threatened. To practice participatory leadership requires involvement. Here, we have to divert from Joel. Merely saying to millennials, "Come to church"—or commanding them to gather as Joel did to his people—rarely, if ever, works. As stated in this chapter, joining millennials where they already are gathering—often around specific causes—is a more effective way in reaching this generation. Practicing participatory leadership anticipates robust conversation on the inevitable differences that are present when generations and traditions meet. Especially the Protestant tradition, built on speaking out, is challenged in this regard. We best heed the warning of theologian Dietrich Bonhoeffer who, as he reflected on "life together," stated,

> The first service that one owes to others consists in listening to them....Christians, and especially ministers, so often think they must always contribute something when they are in the company of others, that this is the one service they have to render. They forgot that listening can be a greater service than speaking. Many people are looking for an ear that will listen. They do not find it among Christians, for these Christians are talking where they should be listening.[60]

People long for someone who will listen to the damage the locusts of life have caused. Despite embracing the challenge to spread the word, to witness, we practice participatory leadership through our ears, not our mouths.

In his book *The Coming Post-Christian Tsunami: Connecting with an Increasingly Unchurched Culture*, Jon Perrin identifies six components to support an effective ministry in a post-Christian era: authenticity (practicing warmth), having aim (be clear where you are heading), accessibility (practicing welcome), alignment (practicing empowerment; see chapter 1), action (see chapter 6), and availability.[61] Addressing alignment, Perrin writes,

> We need to invite young leaders—even unproven ones—to sit at the decision making table with us. We need to give them meaningful leadership roles, sometimes even before they're ready. And we have to allow them to fail. If we can teach [millennials] the value of failure—to learn from their mistakes—they will see that failure isn't fatal or futile. This is how they

learn. And it's a much safer way to pay their dues than if they had to figure everything out.[62]

Perrin suggests that, once millennials join your congregation's leadership, asking the following questions as a regular leadership custom can cultivate the leadership skills of all:

- What went right?

- What went wrong?

- Was there anything you did not see coming?

- What was different than your expectations?

- What was the hardest part of this experience?

- From what you've learned, what is transferrable to other areas of leadership and ministry?

- What from this experience can you pass on to the people you will mentor?[63]

When collaborative leadership is practiced, your church system will change in ways unforeseen by the senior members of the congregation, the ones typically making the decisions. This change may be exactly what your congregation needs.

Toward gathering

The church can learn from millennials about gathering. Learning about something fundamental to the Christian tradition from persons who may not reflect that tradition in obvious ways is not easy and may even raise questions. Yet that is what the church may have to do to revitalize herself. A study of how generations work can be helpful. In her *Culture and Commitment: A Study of the Generation Gap*, published in 1970, anthropologist Margaret Mead writes, "It is true that the continuity of all cultures depends on the living presence of at least three generations."[64] Mead's three generations are

(1) the *post-figurative generation*—children learn about personhood and community primarily from their elders, the children's primary role models; (2) the *co-figurative generation*—children and adults learn from each other and peer learning is especially important; and (3) the *pre-figurative generation*—the youth creates a new culture that threatens tradition and the older generation learns from the younger generation.

Gathering, as described in this chapter, requires you to embrace the possibility of learning from millennials, with some co-figurative dynamics mixed into the fold. This is an uncomfortable, new role for many pastors, youth ministers, and lay leaders seeking to reach a younger generation. We find ourselves in a world where hierarchies, so common to ecclesial worlds, are not only challenged but are disappearing. Constructs developed by tradition that protect the rule of elders—personal sin and salvation, authority, theology, tradition and history, church and polity, education, method, ecumenism, and faith commitments in general—carry little influence. Rather, community, spirituality, ritual, meaning and purpose, but also embodiment (the pierced, tattooed, and modified body) and human sexuality are infused with new meaning.

Building gathering spaces where old rituals are wrapped in new skins is a sign of new creation in the midst of devastation. This, of course, is also the New Testament story centered around the person of Jesus. Joel, living a few hundred years before Jesus's ministry, seeks new social, religious, and even political life (see chapter 5) as a response to a catastrophe. He knows that when his people discovers the compassionate God that their restoration will begin.

Chapter Three

DISCOVER

The Compassionate God and the Promise of Personal Restoration

Millennials believe differently and gather in novel ways. They also live lives that rarely follow traditional trajectories. These facts are difficult for the church to digest and even for psychologists and sociologists to understand. The church and its leaders often approach millennials with programs and traditional criteria with various forms of normativity—specific ideas of what is right and wrong. When it comes to God and millennials, it should be no surprise that the older generations display much more reverence and protectiveness compared to millennials. The attitude of older generations is easily recognized in *Soul Searching: The Religious and Spiritual Lives of American Teenagers*, by sociologists of religion Christian Smith and Melinda Lundquist Denton.[1] Soul Searching describes young people's faith as "parasitic" and portraying "moralistic therapeutic deism."[2] Neither descriptors are inviting. Why would millennials seek out and join a religious community that might portray them in these ways? Descriptors such as these speak of anxiety, protectionism, judgment, and concern.

In a chapter called "God, Religion, Whatever: On Moralistic Therapeutic Deism," the authors fault teenagers for being conventional in their faith, "quite happy to go along and get along."[3] Mirroring the beliefs of their parents and culture's therapeutic individualism, Smith and Denton found that, for most teens, religion functions in the background and is not a primary aspect of their lives.[4] Religion is perceived as good for a person, in a general way, rather than revealing any truth or pointing to a deity, leading the authors to identify "moralistic, therapeutic deism" as the faith today's millennials bring. This faith is characterized by the following beliefs: a creator God exists ordering the world and watching over human life on earth; God seeks people to be loving, kind, and fair, as other religions also teach; happiness and feeling good about oneself is a goal in life; God need not be involved in one's life and is not demanding, but can assist in problem solving; and all good people go to heaven when they die.[5] The authors conclude that "it seems that [moralistic therapeutic deism] is simply colonizing many established religious traditions and congregations in the United States, that it is becoming the new spirit living in the old body. It's typical embrace and practice is *de facto*, functional, practical and tacit, not formal or acknowledged as a distinctive religion."[6] Their evaluation extends beyond the teenagers they surveyed to include the Christian tradition as it manifests in America: "We have come with some confidence to believe that a significant part of Christianity in the United States is actually only tenuously Christian in any sense that is seriously connected to the actual historical Christian tradition."[7]

Smith and Denton identify moralistic therapeutic deism as a "parasitic faith," feeding off Christianity, more so than being in competition with tradition. "It cannot sustain its integral, independent life; rather it must attach itself like an incubus to established historical traditions, feeding off their doctrines and sensibilities, and expanding by mutating their theological substance to resemble its own distinctive image."[8] Whether Christian, Jewish, or Muslim, the teenagers Smith and Denton surveyed presented with this parasitic faith. It is this faith, the researchers state, that explains why today's youth experience relatively little conflict if they encounter another tradition, as a "parasitic faith" is a "shared, harmonizing, interfaith religion."[9] Parasitic faith, we are informed, is not the same as secularism, for the latter would exclude having any faith, even if secularism too prides individualism and carries a general distrust in institutions of authority.

If the church comes to millennials with an attitude that reflects the judgments and concerns locked up in language of *moralistic therapeutic deism* and *parasitic faith*, I will be the first to join them in distancing from the carriers of the message and the traditions they bring. As we learned from Kara Powell

54

and her colleagues, thriving congregations are described in terms of "welcoming, accepting, belonging, authentic, hospitable, and caring. We began to call this the *warmth cluster*."[10] Programs, we said, can work against warmth. So too does judgment or perceived judgment. When millennials feel they cannot be themselves but need to be someone else to be accepted, they distance themselves from the church. The paths of millennials and especially church leaders can easily divert on this topic. Leaders, when feeling threatened or just deeply concerned about the church, often believe they need to reintroduce doctrine, that a return to orthodoxy (or neoorthodoxy) is what it will take to revitalize the church. These leaders, in their self-righteousness, do not know that they have become a new locust that devours the church, for the millennials have long since moved out of their reach.

Still, even as we question the normative and judgmental tone of *Soul Searching*, we agree with Smith and Denton that "very few teens seem to believe...that religion is about orienting people to the authoritative will and purposes of God or about serious life-changing participation in the practices of the community of people who inherit the religio-cultural and ethical tradition."[11] Stated differently, millennials—as probably many older adults in the United States—lack a narrative worth living into. When introducing millennials to the God of Joel, the narrative can be helpful, for it is neither individualistic nor parasitic. Rather, as the first two chapters indicated, Joel is communal: the locusts of life touch everyone and we respond to the devastation by gathering. Millennials are showing us creative and life-giving ways to grieve and to gather. Moreover, Joel introduces the compassionate God, a God that not only shows interest and involvement but also restores. It is this God that holds us accountable to a moral life.

This chapter is built around (re)discovering two powerful images of God the prophet Joel introduces to us: "God is merciful and compassionate, very patient, full of faithful love, and ready to forgive" (Joel 2:13) and "[God] will repay you for the years...the [locusts] have eaten" (Joel 2:25). Joel's God almost sounds therapeutic—imagine such audacity—a God who seeks the best for humanity; a God present and responsive to crisis. And where a parasitic faith draws life-giving energy from tradition and has little, if anything, to contribute, those who have been restored know they are now in relationship with a God who promised restoration, a promise that is millennia old. First, we revisit the images of God Joel introduces and argue that Joel is a true prophet, as Joel shows the *pathos* of God. To understand how we internalize an understanding of God, we have a brief excursus in asking how images of God function in our lives. Then we'll discover Kelsey Davis, a Vanderbilt University master of divinity student who knows the compassionate God intimately, to readily share that God with others. The chapter ends by identifying five practices leaders can follow to facilitate the discovery of the compassionate God and to introduce that God to millennials.

The compassionate, restorative God

Joel recognized the locusts and the damage they caused. Three times he called on the people to gather (Joel 1:13-14; 2:1-2, 16). As they lament, mourn, fast, and pray, Joel introduces and speaks on behalf of God. The context is darkness and danger, for Joel sees the Day of the Lord, like an approaching army, coming (to be discussed in more detail in chapter 5). For Joel, this day of accountability and reckoning is unlike anything ever experienced—similar to the locust plague. However, it is not this day that becomes the central plot for this third act in Joel's narrative. This spot is reserved for the compassionate God!

The prophets, Hebrew Bible scholar Abraham Joshua Heschel reminds us, acted from and communicated God's *pathos*—God's endearing love for humanity. "The central message of the prophets is the insistence that *the human situation can be understood only in conjunction with the divine situation,*" Heschel writes. "The pathos and judgment of God transcend the human dimension."[12] Heschel is emphatic:

> Sin, guilt, suffering, cannot be separated from the divine situation. . . . The life of sin is more than a failure of man; it is a frustration to God. Thus [humanity's] alienation from God is not the ultimate fact by which to measure [humanity's] situation. The divine pathos, the fact of God's participation in the predicament of [humanity], is the elemental fact.[13]

A basic feature of God's pathos is "divine attentiveness and concern," which drives and colors God's involvement with humanity and all of creation.[14] God perceives and apprehends. Pathos reveals a functional quality of God—it is enacted or experienced—more so than an essential attribute of God that never touches humanity and all of creation.[15] Acting with pathos, God is never neutral when engaging us. God is, however, always in relationship with us. It is absurdity for humanity to place itself above or disconnected from God, Heschel warns, a danger that easily manifests as humanity claims to be free, including freedom from God.

God's attentiveness, however, is hidden, to be exposed by the prophets, who are not merely mouthpieces for God but rather persons and partners reflecting the loving-kindness of God. Thus, prophets, old and modern, experience the very heart of God. Their speaking truth to power or their witness to destruction and injustice, as Joel shows us, is only as effective as their words and person are reflecting the love and passion of God. Heschel's vision of the prophets is also challenging the idea that we live primarily cognitively, emotionally, or even psychologically—we live relationally and theologically! That is, we live in the presence of God, who enters into a relationship with us characterized by pathos. Joel is a quintessential prophet, embodying a "theology of pathos," a way of looking at things he received through close communion with God.[16]

We should not confuse embodying God's pathos as merely *imitating* God—which is also a biblical motif—for pathos is much deeper than a mere repetition of a past act: "Pathos, [rather], is ever-changing, according to the circumstances of the given moment."[17] Heschel identifies a responsiveness and *response-ableness* in God's pathos, demanding self-reflection in us as we interpret persons, situations, and experiences. We cannot bring a generic pathos to people; it has been particularity determined by circumstances. If imitation is behaving in a pattern that reflects on a past event, pathos is creative and shines anew on others.

The pathos of God introduces a mystery and paradox we cannot solve: "[God] Who created All should be affected by what a tiny particle of [God's] creation does or fails to do?"[18] The paradox deepens as the God of loving-kindness holds humanity responsible for its choices. God withholds punishment because of God's pathos. "Divine pathos," Heschel reiterates, "maybe explains why justice is not meted out in the world."[19]

What news! "Above reward and punishment is the mystery of [God's] pathos."[20] It is through God's pathos that God freely enters into a just, reciprocal relationship with humanity, keeping the active link between God as creator and the God of history alive. God's pathos communicates: you are not alone when the locusts come. Or, in the words of Joel 2:18, "Then the LORD *became* passionate about this land, and *had* pity on [God's] people" (emphasis added). God is intimately involved in our lives and this world. God knows we are merely human, as the psalmist reflects (Ps 78:39). Heschel recognizes that the mystery of God's pathos does not make sense to us as we easily seek retribution. He reminds us of the prophet Isaiah, who said God's thoughts are not ours (Isa 55:8-9).[21]

The mystery regarding God deepens as most verbs in Joel indicate ongoing action (*yiqtol* verbs in Hebrew), whereas the verbs describing God's passion and pity for the people and the land are in the past tense, as a completed action (*wayyiqtol* verbs in Hebrew; see below). Scholars call this the "prophetic perfect," an event that happened in the past.[22] If God's pathos already manifested, what about the future? Is God's pathos available for us? Scholars struggle with how best to interpret an event that has taken place if most of Joel is future oriented. They point to the book of Jonah, which ends with an open-ended question regarding God's pity. Joel has an unfolding narrative and God's pathos is the central message. Heschel concludes his writing of God's pathos with a warning, especially for those judging how others experience or believe in God, a warning that is also an invitation: "Unless we share [God's] concern, we know nothing about the living God."[23]

Our text continues its peculiarity of raising more questions than providing answers. There is much disagreement among scholars whether Joel's second chapter is a continuation of the first or a separate chapter describing an invasion by an enemy army. Here, Elie Assis's argument, that Joel likens the locusts to a human enemy and thus uses military language metaphorically, is persuasive (see Joel 2:7-8).[24] Even as locusts are not mentioned, we remain in that opening scene, now metaphorically described for a second time as an approaching army that destroys its enemy. The third act of our narrative reaches a high point, after a third call to the people to gather and a description of the devastation, with the introduction of the compassionate God. Our narrative continues:

> Because the LORD utters his voice
>> at the head of his army.
> How numerous are his troops!
>> Mighty are those who obey his word.
> The day of the LORD is great;
>> it stirs up great fear—who can endure it?
> Yet even now, says the LORD,
>> return to me with all your hearts,
>>> with fasting, with weeping, and with sorrow;
> tear your hearts
>> and not your clothing.
>> *Return to the Lord your God,*
>>> *for he is merciful and compassionate,*
>>> *very patient, full of faithful love,*
>>> *and ready to forgive.*
> Who knows whether he will have a change of heart
>> and leave a blessing behind him,
>> a grain offering and a drink offering
>>> for the LORD your God?
> … Then the LORD became passionate about this land, and had pity on his people.
> The LORD responded to the people:
> See, I am sending you
>> the corn, new wine, and fresh oil,
>>> and you will be fully satisfied by it;
>> and I will no longer make you
>>> a disgrace among the nations.
> I will remove the northern army far from you
>> and drive it into a dried-up and desolate land,
>>> its front into the eastern sea,
>>> and its rear into the western sea.
> Its stench will rise up;
>> its stink will come to the surface.

The L<small>ORD</small> is about to do great things!
Don't fear, fertile land;
   rejoice and be glad,
   for the L<small>ORD</small> is about to do great things!
Don't be afraid, animals of the field,
     for the meadows of the wilderness will turn green;
   the tree will bear its fruit;
     the fig tree and grapevine will give their full yield.
Children of Zion,
     rejoice and be glad in the L<small>ORD</small> your God,
  because he will give you the early rain as a sign of righteousness;
     he will pour down abundant rain for you,
        the early and the late rain, as before.
The threshing floors will be full of grain;
     the vats will overflow with new wine and fresh oil.
I will repay you for the years
    that the cutting locust,
  the swarming locust, the hopping locust, and the devouring locust
  have eaten—
     my great army, which I sent against you.
You will eat abundantly and be satisfied,
     and you will praise the name of the L<small>ORD</small> your God,
  who has done wonders for you;
     and my people will never again be put to shame.
You will know that I am in the midst of Israel,
     and that I am the L<small>ORD</small> your God—no other exists;
     never again will my people be put to shame.
(Joel 2:11-14, 18-27, *emphasis added*)

Joel, concerned that the devastation caused by the locusts also damaged Judah's relationship with God, calls them to return to God. Verse 11, placing God "at the head of his army," links God and the natural disaster. Our narrative is not only about humanity's relationship with destructive locusts, but our relationship with God. The people now having to cope with the news that God was behind the locusts receive some comfort: "It means that 'even now,' even while God is injuring his people, it is possible to return in order that

God will have mercy on the people."[25] God remains free to act and the divine voice intrudes into the narrative just as the prophet announces God is behind the locusts. God, now speaking, is opening a way back to God that does not rely on the profession of guilt. Rather, the way includes being restored, an act of grace by God for the people and the land.

By calling the people to tear apart their hearts and not their clothes, Joel counters an age-old tradition first introduced by Reuben, Joseph's oldest brother and Jacob's son. Reuben tore his clothes when he discovered Joseph was not in the well they threw Joseph in and he was overcome with guilt and remorse that Joseph had been killed (see Gen 37:18-30). By following a demand ("tear") with a metaphor ("hearts and not your clothing," 2:13) Joel both draws upon but also diverts from a parallel text, his signature style.[26] The call to return to God follows a theme also found in Amos and Hosea and was a common understanding in the ancient Near East, that, in a time of crisis, one returns to one's God. Of course, little has changed as we also ask "Why God?" when crisis hits, even if we do not believe in God. To return to God should not be heard as repenting but rather as sadness, mourning, and lamenting and a willingness to hear God's voice.[27] For Joel, sin is not a primary focus. As one commentator writes, "Not the slightest casuistry and moral criticism can be felt."[28] The people are restored, not forgiven. Here, Joel distinguishes himself from the other prophets, who were very clear of the sins Israel committed and also of the fact that judgment could not be averted.

Returning to God furthermore reiterates that Judah should not turn elsewhere or to other gods. We do not know, however, whether the people believed in other gods or not.[29] Joel does not give the impression that the people worshipped other gods. The reference to "heart" evokes Deuteronomy 6:5, where Israel is instructed to love God "with all your heart," and Deuteronomy 30:2: "You must return to the LORD your God…you and your children—with all your mind and with all your being." In returning, the people have to incorporate rituals—fasting, weeping, mourning—despite the temple's destruction, tying the people to worship and the totality of their being; all their hearts. "Heart" here symbolizes a person's overall essence, the totality of who one is—it demands total commitment. Joel uses a repetitive and reverse (dual) structure (called a *chiasm*) to emphasize God's call, which includes an appreciation for ritual and practice:

1 2:12b: return to me

2. 2:12b: with all your hearts,

3. 2:12c: with fasting, with weeping and with sorrow;

2. 2:13a: tear your hearts and not your clothing.

1. 2:13b: Return to the Lord your God.[30]

For the ancient Judeans, the heart was the center of our thoughts and cognitive functioning (and the kidneys were home to our feelings).[31] The outward manifestations of religious life, fasting and weeping, indicate a wholehearted change. The turning of one's heart—also indicating the renewing of one's mind—for Joel, however, reflects an "internal change only God can bring about."[32] By placing his call to return to God in the context of the pending Day of the Lord, God is thrust into the narrative. The reality of the Day of the Lord, Joel believes, can be averted.

Joel reminds his people that God at Mount Sinai (Exod 33–34) was diverted from punishing them due to Moses's intercession. To return then is also to be renewed, held by the very nature of the covenant relationship between God and the people. The Lord passed by Moses after Israel played and prayed with their golden calf. In a moment when the covenant relationship with God was strained, we read,

> The Lord! The Lord!
> a God who is compassionate and merciful,
>> very patient,
>> full of great loyalty and faithfulness,
>> showing great loyalty to a thousand generations,
>> forgiving every kind of sin and rebellion,
>> yet by no means clearing the guilty,
>> punishing for their parents' sins

their children and their grandchildren,
as well as the third and the fourth generation.
(Exod 34:6-7)

The "mercy formula" is arguably one of the most evocative and genera-
tive texts of the Bible.[33] Biblical scholar Phyllis Trible shows us that the traits
used to describe God are *feminine* in nature. The word translated as "compassion" is "womb" in the Hebrew text (adjective *rahum*, compassion; *rehem*,
womb; plural *rahmim*, wombs or compassion).[34] God is womb-ish, and, as
the Creator God, not only loves with the intensity of a mother for her child
but selflessly participates in life! Trible reminds us that *rahum*-language in
scripture is used only pertaining to God, not people.[35] "In many and various
ways," Trible writes, "the maternal metaphor of *rahum* witnesses to God as
compassionate, merciful, loving."[36] God, beholden to no one, grants mercy
on whomever God sees fit, a fact Jonah found especially aggravating.

The God who renews has a long nose! The Hebrew describes God as "long
in nose," as patient or slow to anger.[37] The metaphor stems from the fact that
in anger, one's face becomes red or "burns." God's long nose is a negative
reassertion of God being compassionate; that God's love will not easily be
taken from people; that God holds back God's anger. God's compassion is
further affirmed by God's "great loyalty and faithfulness" (from the Hebrew
khesed), which indicates a moral quality given and received as a gift—"faithful
loving-kindness"—rather than a contractual agreement between two parties.[38]
The credo is building its argument with complementary statements presenting
God as unlike any other god in the ancient Near East. God's love (over)flows
to a thousand generations as forgiveness that covers any transgression. The
legacy impact of sin only carries to three or four generations. By stating that
God will "not [clear] the guilty," God's authority to hold accountable, judge,
and punish is placed over against God's love. The mercy formula is clear:
even if God's judgment is not inevitable, the people cannot abuse or take
advantage of God's mercy.

God is described as compassionate, merciful, patient, and faithful eight
times in scripture, with numerous other references highlighting some of
the attributes of God mentioned in Exodus 34.[39] Both Joel and Jonah
"reverse the order of the first two adjectives (this occurs also in Ps 145:8 and

Neh 9:17, 31), drop the noun 'faithfulness' ..., insert the phrase '(one) who relents from disaster' ..., and completely omit all subsequent material found in Exod 34:6–7" (see also in Numbers 14:18 and Nahum 1:3).[40] Joel's focus is on the covenant renewal, whereas Jonah's focus is on allowing other nations into God's covenant, perceived by Israel as once exclusive.[41] Joel draws directly on Moses for his mercy formula, though in truncated and rearranged form, most notably, leaving out God's wrath and the promise of punishment. A ravaged nation does not need to be reminded of sin. Joel does not name the third and fourth generation, but already included them as he commanded Judah to tell about the locusts—and the narrative contained in the book—to "your children, and have your children tell their children, and their children tell their children" (Joel 1:3). God's faithfulness and God holding us accountable (see chapter 5) span generations! It is this very faithfulness and gracious compassion that creates the possibility for Joel to call the people to return to God.[42] During Lent, Christian liturgies often use this text in Joel, for God's compassion and a people returning to God need each other. Joel's use of the formulaic way to describe God—"merciful and compassionate, very patient, full of faithful love, and ready to forgive" (2:13b)—suggests that Joel may have drawn on an old liturgy himself, as some commentators suggest.[43]

Even as the Day of our Lord is *expected*, it is a Day of Mercy that is *experienced*. As commentator Christopher Seitz writes: "The wrath of God is not in evidence in Joel."[44] Rather, because the people have experienced such destruction already, God will have "a change of heart" (Joel 2:14). Whereas other prophets, notably Amos and Zephaniah, saw no escape from God's wrath, Joel, through his "who knows..." (also translated as "perhaps" and implying "nobody knows"), opens a new possibility and announces "the character of God as wholly merciful."[45] "Joel," commentator James Crenshaw writes, provides "guarded optimism in perilous times."[46] God's mercy extends to providing all that is needed for table fellowship, ritual, and relationship with God—corn, new wine, and fresh oil (Joel 2:19). We can rest in the God who provides, the God who restores and renews. The actions of God awaken hope.

As the people return to God, God, like a caring parent, turns to the people. The mutual covenant relationship between God and Judah is clear. We hear the echo of Zechariah 1:3 ("Return to me...and I will return to you") and also Malachi 3:7 ("Return to me and I will return to you"). Joel uses the metaphor of marriage by using "passion" (or "jealous") to describe God's relationship with God's people. Did God-as-husband feel helpless and in pain when Judah-as-bride was ravaged by the locusts? Such is the power of a covenant relationship. When God says, "See, I am sending you the corn, new wine, and fresh oil, and you will be fully satisfied by it" (Joel 2:19), the reciprocal, covenantal relationship is honored. God will provide food, and the people will take food to God in worship and ritual. Joel, like the other prophets, is interested in Judah's weakened relationship with God as he remembers the covenant of Exodus 19:5-6: "So now, if you faithfully obey me and stay true to my covenant, you will be my most precious possession out of all the peoples, since the whole earth belongs to me. You will be a kingdom of priests for me and a holy nation."[47] The Dutch word for "covenant" is *levensgemeenschap*—the literal translation meaning "life-giving community." We are called into this community, with God and with each other. We return to God to renew this bond and to receive life.[48]

Witnessing the destruction of the locusts, "the nations" too wrestle with how to bring a compassionate God and the presence of locusts together. Why would a compassionate God allow locusts? The nations ask, "Where is their God? Couldn't God have prevented the locusts?" As stated in the first chapter, questions like these reflect on what is called "the theodicy." They reflect the existential crisis all people were in even witnessing the locusts. If we have a functional relationship with God—I believe in God for God does things for me, such as preventing the locusts of life—God is no more than an idol, serving our needs. Functional relationships rarely last as they inevitably disappoint. They do not reflect a life-giving community. Compassion and grace and being slow to anger indicate that God comes to us differently from what we would expect, with power and authority, dominance and judgment. Joel is clear, God has not forgotten those plagued by locusts.

As if the invitation to enter into a life-giving relationship with a gracious and compassionate God is not enough, God promises restoration: "I will repay you for the years that the [locusts] have eaten.... You will eat abundantly and be satisfied, and you will praise the name of the LORD your God, who has done wonders for you; and my people will never again be put to shame" (Joel 2:25-26).

The promise of *continual* restoration flows naturally from the gathering where the people prayed and lamented, practices that stirred God's compassion. Furthermore, the relationship between God and the people is restored through their actions. Scholars are divided about how to interpret the verses that lead up to God promising the restoration of lives and landscapes (Joel 2:19-24), as we do not have knowledge of who or what "the northern army" (Joel 2:20) refers to. Some commentators believe it is more a directional indicator, pointing to the four corners of the earth and the power of God, whereas other scholars think it might indicate a specific group of people.[49] It is clear, however, that the locusts are sent into oblivion—to drown in the sea—which opens the possibility for new abundance.

As Joel led the people in the opening chapter to internalize the devastation the locusts have caused, he now has to lead them to internalize their restoration. It is ironic that we do not naturally recognize the good that comes our way and the giver behind that good. God proclaims, "I will make up for you the years the locust has eaten, the grub, the consumer, and the cutter"—as commentator Elie Assis translates verse 25.[50] "[God] will pour down abundant rain for you, the early and the late rain, as before" (Joel 2:23). The land receives abundant rain and people receive food. Landscapes and lives are restored. That the creator God has an ecological mind should be expected. Joel suggests that the people can learn from the land—where the grasses come in first—and learn from the animals, for they will be the first recipients of the restoration received from God.[51] Yet again the fate of the people and the fate of the earth are closely tied together. With rain nurturing the earth and the animals satisfied because there is food to eat, we have the inverse of the opening verses of the book of Joel. This is what restoration is all about—the undoing of the loss and trauma that determined one's identity for so long. But the restoration is not just for the people. The land too experiences the gracious and compassionate God. Joel is asking the people: Do you see the rain in your life? Seeing rain and experiencing restoration after being touched by locusts is not easy. Being in a life-giving relationship with a compassionate God brings possibility for transformation.

Restoration leads to joy, an emotional experience that defines one's whole being, body, mind, and spirit. Once joy has set in, one cannot hide it. As nature shows rain has fallen, Joel sees joy bringing growth in the lives of the people. The people rejoice in a joy that has three "origins": they do so because Joel calls on them to do so, rejoicing wells up from the covenant relationship with God and from the rituals around worship, and joy wells up internally from the restoration received. We need to remind ourselves that the restoration and joy in Joel most probably come in a time when the temple was yet destroyed, a place many thought would be the only source for happiness and worship. Though ecological, personal, and economic restoration are clear for Joel, the political restoration lacks, as we'll discuss in chapter 5.

The restoration is complete when the shame (Hebrew: *yebosu*) the people carry is removed. Playing with words, Joel says that shame leaves one dry (Hebrew: *hobis*).[52] Since a people in shame may not be able to hear this good news, God reiterates, "My people will never again be put to shame.... Never again will my people be put to shame" (Joel 2:26-27).[53] Shame is that insidious feeling that one is not good enough, that there *is* something fundamentally wrong with oneself, not that one *did* something wrong, which would be guilt. Shame describes a personal state, guilt a certain kind of behavior. Every person knows shame intimately, for it is tied to an embodied existence. We know guilt too.

Arguably the most archetypal story in scripture, "the fall of humanity" in Genesis 3, can be read through three lenses. The first is the lens of guilt: Adam and Eve transgressed the rule placed by God. They were guilty, their punishment was being banned from Eden and their legacy was passing sin to all humanity. The second lens is one of transformation: Eve sought to gain knowledge; she wanted to be like God. Though she was led to believe that one can gain that transformation by merely eating (a fruit)—a tradition Joel draws upon as God provides food—the desire to be renewed and transformed drives every person. There is nothing "wrong" with this desire. The third lens through which we can read Genesis 3 is the lens of shame: Adam and Eve discovered they were naked, were ashamed, and went into hiding.

67

The people of God then and our contemporary culture remain ambivalent about shame. Shame easily becomes part of our identity and even the reflection on shame can induce shame. When we experience shame, we feel exposed, being looked at and vulnerable. Wanting to disappear and hide, as Adam and Eve did, is a natural response. So too is protecting ourselves with distancing, perfectionism, aloofness, rage, and by becoming controlling. Psychology has discovered that the only real cure for shame is being in an empathic relationship, where one is truly seen as worthy. In the language of Joel, empathy is experiencing grace, compassion, patience, love, and restoration in a relationship with God. A relationship with this God restores, as God sees us as worthy when we feel there is something existentially wrong with us. God affirms this deep covenant relationship in referring to Judah as "my people" (Joel 2:26). The compassionate, gracious God knows the locusts of life always induce shame and sees the disgrace, humiliation, and embarrassment we carry. From a place of hiding, we are restored. God reiterates the rain will come. We are watered and no longer dry in our shame.

Joel brings good news to people who know devastation, confusion, questioning, and despair. By emphasizing God's compassionate presence, Joel introduces a counter-narrative: we are not determined by the locusts, but by God's presence and restoration.[54] It is not divine abandonment, divine aggression, or divine judgment or punishment that describe the essence of God and determine the narrative of Joel. "Because YHWH is compassionate, kind, patient, infinitely loyal, and forgiving, the momentary anger may be an anomaly."[55] God's anger is not the last word. Rather, it is the covenant God's responsive passion and compassion that rule.[56] God remains responsive to our supplications. Meeting the God Joel introduces to us is transformative. It turns sorrow into joy and shame into esteem. It promises the possibility of a restored, flourishing life. As God says, "My people...," we say "My God...," not as a stop phrase, but to describe our renewed relationship with the living God. Embracing a compassionate image of God is a challenge since that God is rarely shared by parents, preachers, and philosophers. A religion of guilt such as Christianity speaks languages of sin and judgment much more easily than the languages of compassion and unconditional restoration. We seem to prefer the punitive God who judges people.

How we imagine and experience God

How we come to see God is a complex dynamic. Although theology would argue that we receive our images from tradition and that our images of God are formed around themes such as immanence and transcendence, how we see God is actually more *personal* and *internal*. Between one's inner subjectivity and what is presented as being objective (out there), our image of God is formed. In her book *The Birth of the Living God: A Psychoanalytic Study*, Ana-Maria Rizzuto explores how we form our God images: "God, psychologically speaking... is located *simultaneously* 'outside, inside and at the border.'... God is not a hallucination," she writes.[57] For Rizzuto, we internalize God based on the experiences we have and the messages we receive about God, especially in early childhood. We do not "create" God ex nihilo, Rizzuto argues. Also, we do not have direct access to God, even if tradition creates the illusion that it has access to that God. Language of *between* (subjectivity and objectivity), *internal,* and *personal* best describes how one sees God. These locations and dynamics counter the belief that one can give another person belief or God as if God is an objective Person (or truth). It also counters the belief that belief is relative—it is relational! The paradox is that we internalize God in complex ways even as God is an Objective Presence. Furthermore, as the next chapter will argue, God's Spirit is at work in people whether a millennial has some relationship with the church or not. Since we do receive part of our image of God from tradition, belonging and community can be formed where there is enough "overlap" between people. The lack of commonality explains why different traditions within Christianity can only maintain a loose connection.

We weave our image of God together from many experiences. "In the course of development," Rizzuto writes, "each individual produces an idiosyncratic and highly personalized representation of God derived from his object relations, his evolving self-representations and his environmental systems of belief. Once formed, that complex representation cannot be made to disappear; it can only be repressed, transformed or used."[58] Here, object relations refer to the internalization of relationships into one's psyche, a process that begins in early childhood where a child internalizes mother and father. This affords a parent the possibility of being out of view, while the toddler can keep a mental image of her parent alive. In a similar way, we internalize God. As Rizzuto indicates, changing these internalizations or representations is possible but not easy. An existential crisis, such as the ones caused by the locusts of life, can drive us to God even as it can be a catalyst to a spiritual crisis when we no longer find meaning between the God we believe in and the crisis we're facing. Joel reflects this moment of crisis when people say: "Have mercy, LORD, on your people, and don't make your inheritance a disgrace, an example of failure among the nations. Why should they say among the peoples, 'Where is their God?'" (Joel 2:17).

God is handy, Rizzuto writes, "always there for love, cold disdain, mistreatment, fear, hatred or any other human emotion that lends the object of God its usefulness."[59] Rizzuto tells of twenty-seven-year-old Bernadine, for whom God was generally good but also always critical of her—she was not good enough—and withholding. Bernadine would rather not believe in God, but she was convinced of God's existence and power.[60] Rizzuto met Bernadine as she was hospitalized for depression, anxiety, back pain, and a suicide attempt. From early childhood, Bernadine, as the oldest of seven children of teenage parents, was parentified—she accepted emotional and relational responsibilities beyond her chronological age. Her own emotional and relational needs went unmet as her mom reminded her she was a demanding baby. With unhappy, stressed parents, Bernadine tried hard to be a good girl, always failing to meet her own high standards. School, one place that could have recognized her, failed to do so. Her Catholic church, however, did become a shelter away from family. She heard about God's goodness but rarely experienced it. Bernadine is searching for a relationship that would "see" and restore her. To receive recognition, affirmation, and love—also for herself—is her biggest desire. With her needs unmet, Bernadine struggles to find hope in the face of despair. Rather, shame permeates her life. If only she were not such a worthless, inadequate person, she would be loved. She lives an isolated and alienated life. God, she believes, wants her to be someone else. "Bernadine Fisher's psychic life has remained as it was when she was a small child," Rizzuto writes. "She has continued searching for the approval of [her parents].... God, as a representation, has had no better luck with her. He too must respond [to her need for validation]. Until now he has failed."[61] The shame she carries has left her dry. "Hope," Rizzuto concludes, "remains for Bernadine, for the self longs to leave life-depriving places and relationships. Her symbol world longs for relief."[62]

Joel's narrative carries much invitation and can awaken hope for a person such as Bernadine. The opening act would recognize the devastation of locusts in her life. Joel will call on her to lament her childhood, and so state her longings and desires. The second act will beckon her into community and relationships where she can be seen. She will be placed in a position where she can discover that *her* God is "merciful and compassionate, very patient, full of faithful love, and ready to forgive." Many millennials have discovered this compassionate, restorative God. Kelsey Davis, a master of divinity student, has found a spiritual home in the Episcopal tradition. She is keenly aware of the locusts of life and the grace of God that come in relational form. She enters into life-giving relationships and creates welcoming communities. We can learn from her.

Millennials seek, know, and embody the compassionate God
(Cowritten with Kelsey L. Davis)[63]

Kelsey Davis is a graduate of Vanderbilt Divinity School ready to enter full-time ministry. The questions that drive her center around the experiences of human relationships. "As I imagine what ministry means," she says, "the images that come to mind are the moments when I received God's gifts of compassion, hospitality, and restoration from others along the journey. Sensing a call to ordination, Kelsey embraces ministry as an incarnational event that follows the life of Jesus. She resonates deeply with Jesus, who gave witness to and entered the totality of human experience: suffering, restoration, injustice, liberation, fragmentation, and redemption. In Jesus, she finds a compassionate God who not only advocates *for* us but accompanies and lives *with* us. For Kelsey, a meaningful and faithful life revolves around being with people, entering into the depth of their experiences, seeing and hearing people's stories, and offering a homeplace of belonging. "It's always been about God in and through people, even before I knew the words *imago Dei* or *Jesus Christ*. But now I have more language to articulate faith, and believe that the life of Jesus Christ reminds us that God's love and grace are incarnational realities. Jesus offered the world an alternative paradigm to live into—a way of being rooted in compassion and restoration. My prayer is to be transformed by God's love and to share that love with others." Arriving where she finds herself today, however, included valleys ravaged by locusts, friendships and communities that welcomed, relationships that nurtured and transformed, and grace that restored.

"I did not grow up in the church and only remember visiting Sunday school once with a friend's family," Kelsey remembers. "The canon that I was given as a child consisted of stories, poetry, philosophy, and virtuous tales." The stories that shaped her were neither explicitly Christian nor religious, but an array of literature that inspired her imagination and shaped a deep love of story-telling and meaning-making. Her parents struggled with alcoholism and mental illness. As such, she knew freedom by day and chaos by night. Soccer, at first an escape at age five, became something she was really good at; she was a natural athlete who worked hard at her craft. Rachel, a team-mate, wrapped her in friendship and Rachel's family gave her a second home with such love that Kelsey calls it "a sanctuary." Here, she found dinner most nights, a safe place to sleep, and shelter from the turmoil at home. Her adopted family allowed her the space for relationships and the joy of celebration while holding her deep sorrow. "Rachel's family welcomed me every day and at any hour of the night. Remembering this house as the first image of God's compassionate hospitality makes me tearful, as I am deeply grateful that their table always had a seat, the door was always open, and a warm bed was always ready to receive me—*just as I was.*"

To be her true self and experience belonging received new meaning and importance as Kelsey entered her teen years. "I came into Christianity in adolescence. . . . I was baptized at the deep hesitancy of my father. The reason for his hesitancy proved valid. At sixteen, I came out to my parents, or rather invited them into my love life. I shared that I loved women and was a lesbian." Her parents embraced their daughter, but wanted to protect her from the reaction of the nondenominational Christian church she attended and where she was moving toward baptism. "My father was worried that I would not find a welcoming place in Christianity, as many in the church deemed my sexual orientation sinful. He hoped that I would never feel the need to defend my sexual orientation and faith and that I would always know how deeply I was loved." Kelsey's father committed to walk *with* her, even converting to Christianity himself, so that she would always have someone on her side. Her parents' reaction and her father's decision to join her church, she says, "was one of my first memories of *knowing that the compassionate God walked with me.* My father accompanied me through a long, hard road of reconciling my faith and sexuality."

The locusts of life would visit Kelsey again, unexpectedly. "My father died by suicide when I was twenty-one. This was an unforeseeable, unimaginable blow to my reality. Processing my father's suicide meant entering into a season of deep spiritual questioning." Kelsey identified with Mary and Martha at the death of Lazarus (John 11), beating her fists at God, crying out, "If you had been here, my father would not have died, where *were you, where are you?*" Father Andrew, a Catholic priest and Kelsey's spiritual director, empowered her to lament and grieve. It was his presence and witness to her suffering, Kelsey states, that offered her assurance "that God was present amid the deep pain of losing my father." Father Andrew became God to Kelsey.

Heather, Kelsey's partner, is a witness, a supporter, an advocate, and a companion on Kelsey's life journey. Destruction and despair again appeared when Kelsey sought permission from Heather's family to receive her hand in marriage. A few family members, rather than welcoming another daughter, replied with deeply wounding words of judgment and rejection. Upon receiving the response, Kelsey, broken in her sorrow, sought sanctuary in St. Augustine's Episcopal Chapel in Nashville. Tears were streaming down her face. Praying was all she could do. Kelsey's priest, Rev. Becca Stevens, wrapped her arms around her, wiped her tears, grabbed her hand, and sat her down in a chair. In silence, Rev. Stevens began taking off Kelsey's socks and shoes while she pulled healing oils out of her pocket and began to rub Kelsey's feet with oil. "She anointed me, and as the oil spread messily over my feet, I felt the healing power of unconditional love," Kelsey remembers. "She said to me over and over: I am so sorry. You are loved. You are welcome here. Do you know you are welcome here? She finished rubbing my feet, redressed my socks and shoes, hugged me, and said, Go on your way. I love you." The compassionate God showed her face. As always, God came in the form of another person.

Kelsey has served as a chaplain with young adults at St. Augustine's Episcopal Chapel under the mentorship of Rev. Stevens. Rev. Stevens is also the founder of Thistle Farms, whose mission is "to heal, empower and employ women survivors of trafficking, prostitution and addiction through providing safe and supportive housing, the opportunity for economic independence and a strong community of advocates and partners."[64] The healing power of hospitality and compassion is surrounding Kelsey. "Becca's mantra will forever echo in my memory: *Welcome, Welcome, Welcome. We are so glad that you are here.*"

Kelsey is extending that welcome to others as she seeks to curate emerging communities in The Episcopal Church. Because God's love flows through communities like St. Augustine's Episcopal Chapel, Kelsey has experienced the shape that compassionate ministry takes: "Compassion feels like grace. It is a moment of relief that often comes through a cool drink of water, piece of bread, the gentle kindness of listening ears, and a warm embrace. Compassion acts like friendship and justice. It bears witness to the pain of others and seeks to alleviate the root of suffering through transforming unjust systems. Compassion sounds like hope, which calls us forth into communities of belonging and belovedness."

Kelsey sees radical compassion as choosing to see, hear, and bear witness to the suffering of her LGBTQ+ friends. "The whole world is in need of compassion and healing. And many of my LGBTQ+ friends are still facing various forms of exclusion in society and within some Christian circles. My prayer is that we will choose to find our way together, choose love, and choose to draw the circle wider, so that all may have a seat at the table of Love and Restoration. I am grateful to be home in The Episcopal Church, a place that invites me to share in the unconditional love of God through faith community, and we, like so many others, still have work to do in order to ensure the flourishing of LGBTQ+ people, and I am willing to join that work." Her hope is that "all churches will be places of sanctuary for those who are in need of friendship and healing that is full of God's love and kindness." For Kelsey, there is no other way of life or form of ministry.

Kelsey remembers Rachel's family, her spiritual director, Heather, Rev. Stevens, and others as persons and relationships "that have gifted me with the reality of the compassionate God, a God that is *with* us in the midst of suffering, that sees and hears our pain, that desires to restore us. Ministry is living the compassion and hospitality modeled by Jesus. It is ensuring that welcome means offering a space of sanctuary and flourishing for *all* people, especially those who experience marginalization and oppression. A ministry of compassion entails bearing witness to another so deeply that we allow ourselves to be transformed by what we hear."

Kelsey, with millions of her peers, is teaching the church deeper meanings of loss, trauma, gathering, inclusion, and restoration. They do so, as the next chapter will argue, because God's spirit dwells deeply in her and her millennial cohort.

Discover: Five practices for significant leaders

We live in an increasingly divisive world where both nationalism at the cost of a brother and sister and hateful speech seem to be tolerated, if not celebrated. The world longs to recognize the locusts of life in whatever form they come and seeks authentic belonging filled with intimacy. This world also hungers for a compassionate God. Whereas God is used to fuel division and hatred as opposing groups speak for the will of God and protect God—as if God needs our protection—Joel reminds us that compassion is a central part of God's self-revelation. Israel knew this God well, but often forgot that the God who heard their cries in Egypt is the God who called them into a covenant relationship. As a pastoral leader, you are challenged to introduce this compassionate God to millennials. It is a God that deeply resonates with all people, but millennials in particular. Of course, one person cannot "give" God to another. Rather, God can be discovered by a person, for God was there all along. The Spirit of God who dwells in us (explored in the next chapter) assists us in this discovery. Leaders can find relief in the fact that their task is not to "give" someone God and to make sure the person "accepts" the gift. *As leaders, we are responsible to create possibility for the discovering of the compassionate God.* We can enter into relationships, initiate conversations, and cultivate or join spaces where millennials can discover God as "merciful and compassionate, very patient, full of faithful love, and ready to forgive." Five practices can assist you as you listen to and travel with millennials:

First, *practice mirroring.* As a leader, present God's pathos—God's compassion—to others. Of course, this is a difficult task should one be anxious about the congregation's finances or uncertain as to where to find a young adult to relate to. As a parent mirrors a smile to an infant and the infant smiles in return, pastoral leaders mirror God to others. We incarnate the God who said, "The Lord bless you and protect you. The Lord make his face shine on you and be gracious to you. The Lord lift up his face to you and grant you peace" (Num 6:24-26). *Who is the God you are mirroring?* Some leaders mirror the God always mindful of sin, a God like that of Bernadine. They offer Jesus exclusively as a Savior, when Jesus also engaged women, children, sinners, lepers, tax collectors, and other marginalized persons. Leaders preoccupied with sin rarely reflect "the compassionate Father and God of all comfort. [The One] who comforts us in all our trouble so that we can comfort other people who are in every kind of trouble. We offer the same comfort that we ourselves received from God" (2 Cor 1:3-4). Other leaders take the awareness of sin one step further and proclaim the punitive and judgmental God. They shame others into submission. And then there are the leaders who say that God will make you wealthy and fill you with prosperity. Joel reminded his people of the compassionate God who restores. For his people, that God was enough—the only God they needed to know. Mirroring the compassionate God is sufficient for us today too.

Second, *practice memory.* Specifically, remember the stories in scripture of a gracious God who restores. God restored Israel from captivity and as a people. God restored normality after various plagues (Exod 8–10); bitter water became sweet; hunger and thirst were satisfied (Exod 15–17; 1 Kgs 17). Drawing on the act of restoration, now restitution, Moses stated that when an animal fell into a well, the owner of the well should reimburse the owner who lost an animal (Exod 21). A widow's finances were restored and her children saved from slavery when her oil kept on pouring (2 Kgs 4). Daniel and his friends' sense of safety were restored as fire wanted to consume and as he found himself in a lions' den (Dan 3, 6). Job received restoration after the death and devastation of his family and animals (Job 38–42). The temple was restored (book of Ezra). Jesus, of course, restored people's lives often: persons with leprosy, blind and deaf persons, persons with high fevers, a woman who had a hemorrhage, a man who had abnormal swelling—and then there was Lazarus. When have you experienced God's restoration? How do you tell of God as the Master Restorer?

Third, *practice invitation*. Be curious about the stories millennials can tell. Invite them to share their journey in life and with God. As previous chapters have shown, today's young people know loss and trauma, but also community, intimately. They are familiar with existential questions of meaning, purpose, and "Where is God?" Leaders often think they have to say something when they meet with another. This desire increases with anxiety. Practicing invitation is not about your words or vision, but rather listening to another. Even before listening becomes a challenge, leaders are frustrated in reaching young adults. They email or call, but do not receive a timely reply, if any reply at all. Millennials do not naturally use email or voice calls for their communication. They message and post, using platforms such as Twitter, Instagram, Facebook, Snapchat, and WhatsApp, to name but a few of the ever-evolving list of platforms. Practicing invitation can be frustrating if one's communication partner does not reply. Invitation is wrecked, however, if you as a leader give up on extending a listening ear. Arguably the most iconic CNN host, Larry King, taught us that one should best think of simple questions, not answers, when interviewing a person. Simple questions are often profound, not to be dismissed. Questions that practice invitation may include the following:

- You have lived a full life already at a relatively young age. What are some of the most significant moments of your life's journey?

- What have you learned about life already that we need to pass on to our children and teens?

- What are you most passionate about, those things that drive your way of being in the world?

- Who are the recipients or beneficiaries of your passion?

- (If partnered) How did the two of you meet?

- How did you decide upon your profession?

- How do you best build relationships?

- What are some of the communities you are a member of?

- What do best friends tell about you?

- What makes you *you*?

- How would you like others to remember you?

- What are the things you and your friends talk about that the church needs to know?

- What can we learn from you regarding [. . .]?

- What are the things in life you are most grateful for?

- I'm curious: What are your thoughts about a compassionate God? Where have you experienced this God?

- Should I want to serve you, what do I need to know about you?

- In what ways can we work together or can I support your work to make this world more just and peaceful?

These questions are not offered to you to take as a list to a millennial. One cannot discover and build intimacy if you have an agenda or if you are not authentic. Build your next question from the answer you received. Refrain from asking a question with a "yes/no" answer. Open-ended questions that invite a person to share a moment in a larger narrative are inviting and affirming. Use these sample questions to ignite your imagination while listening. Never ask questions if you are not ready to receive an answer.

Fourth, *practice appreciation*. Embedded in the practice of invitation is the ability to receive what you hear, to be a charitable listener. For pastoral leaders, trained in theology and serving a denomination or an elder board, upholding doctrine and following a shepherding tradition, and giving advice and guidance come easy, but so too judgment and the evaluation of beliefs. We can learn from David Cooperrider and his colleagues at Case Western

University, who taught us about appreciative inquiry.[65] As the name suggests, this approach to change draws on recognizing, valuing, affirming, prizing, and honoring persons and the stories they bring.

Appreciative inquiry finds that an emphasis on problems and problem-solving leads to less change in systems and people than a focus on possibility and a vision of manifested change. Persons and systems move in the direction questions indicate. The core principles of appreciative inquiry are the following: our thoughts and actions emerge from relationships (the constructionist principle); when we ask about people or systems, both the people and the system change—questions open new possibility (the principle of simultaneity); we arrange our lives and systems according to stories (the poetic principle); visions of a positive future guide the here-and-now (the anticipatory principle); and, positive feelings and gathering sustain momentum and change (the positive principle). Appreciative inquiry asks of you to *discover* a person or a system, *dream* together about a future, *design* possibilities where the dream can come true (a better world), and expect a changed *destiny* (lives and systems). Practicing appreciation and charity greatly support the life-giving community we seek to create as we live into our covenantal relationships. "Appreciative inquiry"—one way of engaging this practice—"begins an adventure," Cooperrider and his colleague, Donna Whitney, write.

A fifth and final practice in facilitating the discovery of the compassionate God is *practicing advocacy*. Religion is always political—politics literally meaning "the shape of the city."[66] Whether a congregation speaks out against injustices and advocates for the poor, oppressed, and marginalized or not, the congregation is shaping a city. Silence and omission do not save the accountability a congregation and we as a people carry. A pastoral leader can practice advocacy by getting involved in the neighborhood around the church. You will find millennials are already there. The possibilities for getting involved in existential concerns are endless: exposing and addressing injustices, fighting poverty, providing affordable housing, empowering persons with disabilities, reducing climate change, resisting gentrification, mentoring children, improving public transportation, expediting gender and sexual equality, and protecting civil rights and saving public lands, to name but a few. As we'll discover in the fifth chapter, the God of compassion holds us accountable as personal restoration has a political component. Here, millennials can teach pastoral leaders about advocacy and speaking into unjust worlds, for many are already actively involved in making a difference in the world. One way to live into Joel's call to tell the next generation this amazing narrative is to meet them where they already are! As Kelsey showed us, millennials are doing wonderful restorative work in places and ways the church rarely considers.

Toward meeting the compassionate God

Hebrew Bible scholar Nathan Lane argues that the mercy formula explored in this chapter—that God is merciful and compassionate, very patient, full of faithful love and ready to forgive—is not only "the fullest expression of an ancient Israelite cultic formula," but also "the most complete articulation [of God] in the Scriptures."[67] The "Credo of Adjectives" used to describe God—all feminine in nature as Trible showed us—elevates Joel as a narrative for our time.[68] Lane sees the recurrent use of the credo in scripture as indicating its normativity. God's love, as intense as a mother's love for her child, is, however, balanced with a proclivity to hold people accountable, as we'll explore in the fifth chapter. God's mercy, compassion, and love always run deeper than God's desire to punish, as God overcomes sin with forgiveness. With nine separate clauses, the credo Joel draws upon is clear: "The merciful attributes of YHWH are three times stronger than its wrathful counterpart."[69] In seeking justice, the loving God presents as a paradox, but in Joel, the mercy of God collapses the paradox, as restoration, forgiveness, and blessing triumphs (see chapter 6). Doing the work of restoration often comes at a cost, as many millennials already discovered.

Rob Lee, a millennial pastor, writes that "the prognosis [for the church] is grim; we must commend the institution we know as the church to the love and grace of God. Because the life and death of institutions are in the hand of God, we have to take seriously what the old Catholic liturgy says about the church being present until the end time."[70] Lee, who wrote his book while he was a student at Duke Divinity School, writes for those millennials who decided to remain in the church—stained glass millennials, those "exceptions to the rule."[71] He is such a millennial. Lee's concern is clear: "Churches are dying in numbers we hadn't conceived, and most millennials want nothing to do with a dying civic club or community organization."[72] His concern, however, also extends to the church not seeing millennials as "the very real present of the church and must be treated as such."[73] If the church sees millennials as the future of the church, the church will remain a "dying club."

Lee discovered painfully that not all churches can embrace a compassionate God. After a white supremacy meeting in Charlottesville, Virginia, Lee, a relative of General Robert E. Lee, spoke out against the white supremacy gathering during the MTV Video Music Awards.[74] Dressed in his collar, the unmistakable mark of a pastor, Lee said:

> My name is Robert Lee IV. I'm a descendant of Robert E. Lee, the Civil War general whose statue was at the center of violence in Charlottesville. We have made my ancestor an idol of white supremacy, racism, and hate. As a pastor, it is my moral duty to speak out against racism, America's original sin.... Today, I call on all of us with privilege and power to answer God's call to confront racism and white supremacy head-on. We can find inspiration in the Black Lives Matter movement, the women who marched in the Women's March in January, and, especially, Heather Heyer, who died fighting for her beliefs in Charlottesville.[75]

In a blog post, he also stated that Robert E. Lee's statue should be removed.[76] The church he served, Bethany United Church of Christ in Winston-Salem, became very uncomfortable with his compassion, advocacy, and visibility. His tenure at the church ended. Compassion comes at a cost, and millennials are not afraid to pay up. Indeed, the locusts of life take many forms, and we find ourselves in "precarious times" as Lee writes.[77] The compassionate God who restores longs to enter into relationship with us. The darkness and despair caused by the locusts of life fade as hope is awakened.

Lee can find himself in Joel's narrative, a story that awakens hope:

> There was a person who knew the locusts of life. The locusts caused devastation, loss, and trauma. He/she/they mourned the losses and sought healing for the traumas by building life-giving communities and nurturing

his/her/their spirituality. He/she/they discovered the compassionate God who promises restoration and pours the Spirit over all. The person embraced accountability, knowing that decisions made and actions taken have consequences. He/she/they participated in God's restorative work toward a just and sustainable world. The person lived the good life.

Chapter Four

RECEIVE

God's Spirit and the Promise of Spiritual Practice

Millennials often find spiritual meaning in ways that perplex older generations. Ask a millennial to share the significance of their sleeve of tattoos and you'll hear ink has significant meaning and can be spiritual because they are tied to transformative relationships or moments. Teaching a class on play, Anna shared with us her latest tattoo, a beautiful sea otter on her forearm. She named the playfulness otters are renowned for as a way of living she seeks for herself. The first thirty minutes of the class we learn how to juggle, not to become jugglers as much as learning that one can drop the ball and pick it up again. Juggling cuts through attitudes of perfectionism or competition and gives opportunity to recognize the accomplishments of others. As if the otter in Anna came out to juggle, her exuberance about life was evident as she chased balls in the air and across the room. For Anna, however, it was not just play, but engaging God, tradition, others. Mostly, she teaches young children, inviting them into a bigger, life-giving narrative.

Spirituality can be defined as experiencing transcendence, searching for and finding the sacred in the ordinary, and communicating deeply personal values and meanings as we reflect the image of God—the *imago Dei*—alive in every person. Things, spaces, places, and relationships witness to something bigger and beyond us. This definition of spirituality is closely tied to philosopher and psychologist William James's definition of personal religion as "the feelings, acts, and experiences of individual men in their solitude, so far as they apprehend themselves to stand in relation to whatever they may consider the divine."[1] In spirituality, we find that liminal experiences pointing to something or someone beyond ourselves and this world is a human need. When we use language of "spiritual but not religious" to describe a person or a group, we diminish both realms of existence. Spirituality is seen as lesser than religion, the latter seen by the person making the judgment that religion holds the keys to salvation. Religion, however, is diminished too, for it is presented as void of the spiritual. Spirituality may very well take one closer to God than what religion can accomplish. Religion, in turn, opens the possibility for the communal experience of transcendence, a need we also have. Gather, says Joel. Dichotomous living always leaves one diminished.

There is a myriad of ways one can assign spiritual meaning and experience transcendence. In tracing the spiritual lives of America's "nones," Elizabeth Drescher found that many of her interviewees had "spiritual things and places" in their lives.[2] Some had a special corner or table in their apartment or house with objects that had significance for them, others had special places they returned to often for spiritual nurture. Many of the sacred objects were gifts received from persons of importance: a parent, a grandparent, a favorite uncle or aunt, a friend. Other objects were acquired during a vacation or while traveling. She tells of Andy from Pittsburgh, who does not believe but keeps a hundred dollar bill in his desk. His dad, a machinist, gave him the bill when he went to art school. "I know the struggle for him to accept that the money he worked for so hard to get me through college was going for *art*. I pull it out when my confidence is flagging. It's like a kind of talisman."[3] Andy and others informed Drescher that the objects and the practices that surround them keep them connected to people and traditions. Moreover, the objects and practices are "the raw material for stories of the self that narrate what a person understands as her or his own identity, including spiritual or religious identity."[4] Regarding the spiritual things and places Dresher was introduced to, she says: "[they are] 'spiritual' because they connected with other parts of their lives—other people, mostly, and several pets."[5] The longing for spiritual experiences is inherent to human nature. Modern people of a world come of age cannot avoid this trait. Rather, it may very well have increased in intensity as the church is no longer the sole owner of spiritual truth.

The spiritual lives of others are often a mystery for no other reason than that spirituality, per definition, includes the unknown, the uncanny, the unanticipated, and the unconventional. Rudolf Otto was a Lutheran theologian and philosopher who, in his *Idea of the Holy* (first published in 1917), helps us understand core aspects of human spirituality. Otto identifies *the numinous* (or the liminal) as the central aspect of a spiritual experience.[6] Traveling throughout Africa, the Middle East, and Asia, Otto came to believe that all the world's religions awaken the numinous in their followers. The word *numinous*, Otto reminds his readers, come from the Latin *numen*, which means "divine power." It speaks to an unknowable reality and transformative power permeating persons and things.[7] Otto sees spiritual experiences as unique—sui generis—for they cannot be fully understood without personal involvement or by (science's) objectivist attitudes. He identifies the mysterious, the terrifying, and that which fascinates as the building blocks of a spiritual experience:

> The feeling of it may at times come sweeping like a gentle tide, pervading the mind with a tranquil mood of deepest worship. It may pass over into a more set and lasting attitude of the soul, continuing, as it were, thrillingly vibrant and resonant, until at last it dies away and the soul resumes its profane, nonreligious mood of everyday experience. It may burst in sudden eruption up from the depths of the soul with spasms and convulsions, or lead to the strangest excitements, to intoxicated frenzy, to transport, and to ecstasy. It has its wild and demonic forms and can sink to an almost grisly horror and shuddering. It has its crude, barbaric antecedents and early manifestations, and again it may be developed into something beautiful and pure and glorious. It may become the hushed, trembling, and speechless humility of the creature in the presence of—whom or what?—that which is a *mystery* inexpressible and above all creatures.[8]

Otto's *mysterium tremendum* [*et fascinans*] gives us another glimpse at lives devoured by locusts, who, as they gathered to mourn and grieve and build community, discover the compassionate God who restores.[9] Experiences of crisis and trauma can be "awe-full"—they awaken awe and wonder even as they awaken shock, horror, loss, and grief. Such experiences inevitably render one different—changed—as we discovered in facing the locusts of life. Individual differences and mystery then permeate our lives as both are fueled by not only the experiences that shaped us, but by God's spirit alive in each of us.

In this chapter, we follow the restoration promised by God as God's life force is poured out over all, especially the young and those at the margins of society. Our narrative takes a distinctive turn as we move beyond past destruction and a people presently gathering, to a future filled with potential and even ruminations on the end time. Through the embodiment of God's spirit every person can engage life differently, with prophetic power, which, as we stated, is embodying the compassion of God. We explore the meaning of God saying: "I will pour out my spirit upon everyone" and argue that God's spirit brings a dynamism and a new vitality to all receiving God's spirit. For the people of Judah, the difference was pronounced: they went from a beaten down people, literally chewed up by locusts and in grief and mourning, to a people restored and able to discern the will of God through the gift and blessing of God's spirit. Consistently the spirit does things differently and makes the old new. We meet A. Keller Hawkins, a spirit-filled leader with a wanderlust, seeking ordination in The United Methodist Church. Her ministry is strikingly different, inviting others into play spaces where persons can experience God anew. We explore the relationship between a millennial generation who does things differently and God's spirit driving difference. The chapter ends by identifying five practices for significant leaders who seek to witness the spirit of God alive in millennial lives and partake in the gifts that spirit brings. We identify a shift in spirituality to practices, away from spiritualities that require a specific place—a church for example—or spiritualities that are nomadic and seeking and incorporating truths from other religions.

Joel and the outpouring of God's vital life force

A shift is about to occur. Whereas "The Lord's word . . . came to Joel," (Joel 1:1) in the first half of the book, God's word now comes to all. Furthermore, where the previous verses were mostly preoccupied with agriculture, the land, and its people, the second half of Joel is sociopolitical—it is concerned with society, social justice, accountability, and the political restoration of Judah. The shift complements the focus of Joel, "to help the people renew their sense of connection with God."[10] Hebrew scholar Christopher Seitz states that Joel follows an indirect approach as he addresses his people. Joel, Seitz feels, knows that a people distanced from God and in despair will resist a direct message. The book of Joel warns us that when people are far removed from God or without a life-giving narrative, following traditional paths and calling persons out (versus calling them in or better yet, joining them) rarely succeeds.

A few verses earlier, the compassionate God affirmed that the devastation and shame caused by the locusts of life will be restored and removed. The people returned to God in their sadness and with repentance. With that promise still ringing in their ears, Judah receives a second gift, an invitation to a visionary life. Agricultural renewal opens the possibility for political and societal renewal. God continues to address Judah as if struck by an afterthought (Hebrew: *wehayah ahare-ken*; afterward), but possibly in response to the nations asking: "*Where is their God?*" (Joel 2:17). With a writing style and content different from the first part of the book of Joel, some commentators argue our text is a later addition. We follow those who see the problem of unity in Joel as "unresolved and unresolvable," if only because other arguments are not convincing.[11] The restoration of lives and landscapes God promised is seemingly incomplete. It lacked the vital power of divine origin that defines the essence of being a person reflecting the *imago Dei*. "No longer do we hear of the end of natural disaster and the restoration of fertility and fruitfulness, but instead we find a prediction of the coming transformation of human nature by the outpouring of YHWH's spirit, not on the land but the people."[12] Our narrative, in the form of an oracle, deepens as God states:

> After [I restored you and abundance reigns again] I will pour out my spirit upon everyone; your sons and your daughters will prophesy, your old men will dream dreams, and your young men will see visions. In those days, I will also pour out my spirit on the male and female slaves.
>
> I will give signs in the heavens and on the earth—blood and fire and columns of smoke. The sun will be turned to darkness, and the moon to blood before the great and dreadful day of the Lord comes. (Joel 2:28-31)

The outpouring of God's spirit was an established tradition in Israel (Hebrew: *espok et-ruhi*, to pour out; *ruah*, wind, vital life force): Moses finds God placing the spirit on God's people (Num 11:29); Isaiah (32:15) sees the spirit being poured out from on high; and Ezekiel (39:29) envisions the spirit of God poured out on the house of Israel. For Israel, the spirit represents God's creative power of life, the very power that spoke creation into existence, as Genesis 1–2 portrays. It is the very breath of God that gives life: "The Lord God formed the human from the topsoil of the fertile land and blew life's breath into his nostrils. The human came to life" (Gen 2:7). Commentator James Crenshaw translates the Hebrew text as: "Afterward I will endow all of you with my vital life force, so that your boys and girls will speak oracles on my behalf; your old people will discern my will through dreams, and your young adults will be visionaries."[13] The vital life source revitalizes and restores, even a heap of dry bones (Ezek 37). It awakens the prophet within.

Our text suggests that what is poured out is precious. Elsewhere in scripture, *shapak* is used for the spilling of water, blood, and even emotion (Pss 62:9; 79:10). This form of outpouring-as-blessing—or anointing—that includes "everyone" or "all flesh" (Hebrew: *kola basar*) is alien to our world for two reasons:[14] First, just as families do not teach their children how to grieve and mourn (see chapter 2), families rarely bless their children. Few have a memory of a moment where they were profoundly recognized by a parent or someone they looked up to. Cultures of shame does not do blessing well. Of course, many of us can express gratitude for growing up in a loving family, but that is not the blessing imagined here. We imagine a definitive moment witnessed by others. Like baptism in the presence of a community, families need to bless their members and especially children. Second, race, class, gender, and sexual orientation are often used in our society to bring division and to keep peoples suppressed. God upsets human-made hierarchies by gifting a powerless and hopeless people with God's vital life force. Privileges and dichotomies based on *gender* bias ("sons and daughters"), *ageism* ("old men…and your young men"), and *class* or social standing ("the male and female slaves") are obliterated. God's vision for reality was radical then as it is radical now. With God's vital life force poured out, all people, even the socially marginalized ones, are empowered to see, do, and speak things unheard. The embodiment of God's life force creates an instant prophetic community with an egalitarian authority structure. When a pastor or professional colleague laments the lack of professionalism, often seen as a sign of disrespect in millennials, I'm reminded how we do like and seek to protect our hierarchies. The paternalistic, sexist, and colonial roots of the church run deep.[15]

Joel is clear that the spirit-blessing and its charismatic impact are more powerful than rain on a parched earth. Compared to the rain, this outpouring is a more precious gift.[16] It shows on a graceful God that restores body, heart, and soul as well as the people's relationship with God alongside the land. Finding themselves in a place of spiritual deprivation, Judah is called into spiritual vitality. It may be that Joel lived in a time such as the one described in 1 Samuel 3:1 when few heard the word of God for "the LORD's word was rare at that time, and visions weren't widely known." Flesh, which is fragile and fallible, is placed in a relationship with God through God's vital life force. The spirit makes the transcendent God immanent as God now speaks and works through ordinary people. Dreams (Hebrew: *halomot*) and visions (Hebrew: *hezyonot*), the pathways of revelation and modes of communication God relies upon, are now unlocked. Joel, with his positive interpretation of dreams, differs from Jeremiah, who was critical of dreamers (Jer 23:25-32).[17]

Whereas the locust plague and the accompanying drought are now events of the past, the outpouring of God's vital life force is placed in the future, or as one commentator states, in "a more distant time."[18] Moving the narrative into the future, God's signs and wonders instill "hope more by their assurance that God is ultimately in control of the world's fate than by an immediate prospect of fulfillment."[19] For Joel, the future is "open," creating the possibility for every generation to claim it anew as God is not held to a single moment of blessing. Rather, we can anticipate every generation blessed by God's vital life force. As Joel continues to play with time, he also envisioned the end of time, as we'll explore in the next chapter.

Some commentators note that the promise of the spirit belongs to Judah only and we had to wait until the early New Testament church before Gentiles were included (Acts 10:44-47).[20] This is one way of reading salvation history. Other commentators disagree and state that what first was meant for the Judeans, through God's divine generosity, becomes a message for everybody.[21]

Hebrew scholar Ronald Troxel writes that "*all flesh* may mean all mankind, and we should interpret if thus."[22] Commentator Elie Assis follows Troxel and writes that even as Joel was thinking of his people, Judah, "all flesh" means all people.[23] "[God]," Jewish commentator, Mordecai Schreiber, writes, "is informing us that true prophecy is latent in every human being, Jew and non-Jew alike. This should not be taken to mean clairvoyance or even the ability to relate messages from God. *It actually means the divine inspiration which leads one to an enlightened and uplifted state....* One is reminded of the Latin saying, *Vox populi vox Dei*—the voice of the people is the voice of God."[24] In Joel, the question of who receives God's life force is "finely balanced. Perhaps the restriction to '*your* sons...' does swing the argument in favor of restricting the oracle to Judeans, but the universalist note should not be ignored."[25] We can say with strong confidence that Joel democratizes prophecy.[26]

That *all* people receive this blessing has been a problem especially for religious leadership since Peter showed he could not fully understand the vision of Cornelius in Acts 10:23-48. *That God's redemptive actions flow to all people—and not just some—offends.* Later the apostle Paul would write that "there is neither Jew nor Greek; there is neither slave nor free; nor is there male and female, for you are all one in Christ Jesus" (Gal 3:28). Before Jesus brought in the other, however, God did so repeatedly. Joel informs us that the blessings of God are never limited to select few only. Through God's vital life force, all people are connected with God. As the Argentinian theologian Norberto Saracco, reminds us, God cannot be contained by "structures, dogmas, customs, and precepts."[27] Having visions and being spirit-filled are no longer the privilege of the priests and the prophets or those who call themselves church members. The vital life force of God lives in the millennial generation.

Even as God destroys the demographic divisions, it does seem as if God's spirit manifests differently for white and black millennials. As study by Loyola University Chicago found that white young adults easily moved between belonging to a community and disengaging, holding personal needs as a core criterion for maintaining involvement. They had strong individualized understandings of religion. Black and Hispanic young adults, in turn, described their involvement with faith communities in terms of "family" and "home" language and metaphors. They were more likely to describe a sense of "calling" in belonging to a community and less likely to leave or change communities.[28] The researchers state that cultural forces have a powerful influence on how religion is lived. "The legacy of race-based oppression and privilege has helped to fuel differences in black and white Christians' religious sensibilities... blacks and whites not only approach faith matters differently, but faith matters differently to blacks and whites."[29] The researchers also found that young adults see religion as social and spirituality as individualized, with "the church as an institution as irrelevant to them or sometimes as an actual hindrance to spiritual development."[30]

The vital life force brings dignity, purpose, a calling—even as a spiritually informed notion of vocation is not common among millennials. It is not purely for personal or subjective experiences or for private consumption. No, as our next two chapters will argue, Joel envisions using the gifts or restoration received from God and the empowerment the spirit brings to enrich lives and lands. The vital life force takes one to others, into community, and toward a world in need of change and restoration. As the millennials introduced here show us, they have a profound sense of being the very change they would like to see in the world. Furthermore, the spirit brings the ability to read the times: "I will give signs in the heavens and on the earth—blood and fire and columns of smoke. The sun will be turned to darkness, and the moon to blood before the great and dreadful day of the LORD comes," says the Lord (Joel 2:30). For the Judeans, a solar eclipse and atmospheric abnormalities—wonders (Hebrew: *mofetim*)—were uncanny moments speaking of divine intention and intervention. They were signs sent to communicate something. What is being communicated is often referred to as "The Day of the Lord"—a day of profound accountability. We'll address this act in the narrative of Joel in the next chapter. Suffice here to say that the extreme signs God mentions here—fire, darkness, smoke, fog, and blood—are tied to that day. Whereas this is a day of dread for Judah's enemies, Joel sees the day as less threatening for Judah, for it is the God who is "merciful and compassionate, very patient, full of faithful love, and ready to forgive" who rules over it (Joel 2:13). Judah has a special relationship with God that the nations lack.

We already mentioned Peter and those familiar with Pentecost in the New Testament (described in Acts 2) will immediately recognize Peter quoting

Joel 2 to assign meaning to people who suddenly could speak languages new to them. One more time God's vital life force is poured out over *all* people. Here, Joel is more thorough and universal compared to Luke's Acts. The people gathered in Jerusalem were Jews. We have to wait until Acts 8 before a first Gentile, an Ethiopian proselyte, confesses Christ is Lord and only in Acts 10 does the spirit descend on Gentiles. As God links the Spirit's outpouring to a day of accountability, so too does Luke tie the spirit to the end of time and the fulfillment of history. For Luke, the spirit leads to inspired speech as Peter and others spoke the word of God into the world.

The section on the "supernatural blessings" from God ends with Joel speaking again as he seeks to reassure his people: "But everyone who calls on the LORD's name will be saved; for on Mount Zion and in Jerusalem there will be security, as the LORD has promised; and in Jerusalem, the LORD will summon those who survive" (Joel 2:32).[31] Where previously there was no escape from the locusts and especially the day of accountability, "God's grace averted [the catastrophe of judgement], now escape is guaranteed."[32] The people need not fear; they will be kept safe. In the interim, all can dream dreams and see visions.

How would one discern whether a person has God's life force or not? The book of Joel gives us some indications, such as dreaming, seeing visions, and reading the signs of the time. Also by being accountable (see the next chapter) and by being a blessing to others (see chapter 6). Embodying God's spirit, however, impacts all of one's life. Eugene Peterson, a seasoned pastor, gives us a clearer view in his translation of Galatians 5:22-23, a text often referred to as "The Fruit of the Spirit." Peterson asks: "But what happens when we live God's way?" (MSG). His answer, steeped in the tradition of Joel, might surprise:[33]

> God brings gifts into our lives, much the same way that fruit appears in an orchard—things like:
> affection for others,
> exuberance about life,
> serenity.
> We develop a willingness to stick with things,
> a sense of compassion in the heart,

and a conviction that a basic holiness permeates things and people. We find
ourselves involved in loyal commitments,
not needing to force our way in life,
able to marshal and direct our energies wisely.

In the midst of affection for others, exuberance, peace, endurance, love, and grace one recognizes God's spirit. Peterson concludes saying that "Legalism is helpless in bringing this about; it only gets in the way" (v. 24 MSG).

If Peterson's translation is a mirror in which one can recognize the vital life force of God within a person, it is clear that not every person embodies the spirit of God, even if all people reflect the *imago Dei*. Joel does not proclaim universal salvation, even if he does say Jew and Gentile are gifted with God's spirit. Frankly, it seems as if the majority of those who claim leadership are far removed from God's spirit. The younger generation is noticing this and the people in power should shudder in the knowledge that their days of power are numbered. God's vital life force is always available to be discovered, for the promises contained in Joel remain.

Doing things differently

Possessing the vital life force of God in the Hebrew scriptures implies that the person has access to God's revelation and can communicate that to others. Prophesying, seeing visions, and having dreams, which God identifies as core functions of being a prophet, are complemented with being able to embody and communicate the *pathos* of God (see chapter 3). "The spirit enables charismatic activity in terms of both speech and actions, word and sign," one commentator writes.[34] Practices, we'll shortly argue, are key to the spirituality ignited and fueled by God's spirit. Embodying the spirit meant doing things differently. A brief internet search indicates that many industries are concerned about millennials doing things differently, or in journalistic attention-grabbing language, "millennials are killing [many industries and customs]!"[35]

Business Insider reports that millennials are "killing" casual chain restaurants and fast food, for they prefer to cook at home (see chapter 2); they are "killing" the idea of the starter home and home ownership, since they rent longer and then buy more expensive homes. This impact is extended to napkins, for paper towels are more hygienic; cereal, because they eat on the go or prefer Greek yogurt and muesli or avocado and toast; golf, while personal fitness is flourishing; bar soap, for it is filled with germs; diamonds, for being too expensive; department stores, as online shopping is the millennial choice; and the oil industry, as it fuels climate change.[36] Other lists include marriage being killed, and also gambling, travel marketing, credit, consumerism, patriotism, motorcycles, beer, banks, and even the car industry.[37] Even as these lists are often drafted by a late boomer journalist or concerned Gen X researcher, millennials *are* doing things differently, disrupting industries and defying customs and traditions. The church knows this intimately too.

Disrupting the church should not be confused with the fact that many young adults are the prophets of the day and are building faithful lives in nontraditional ways. They embody God's life-force and are "forward think-ing," not in the traditional sense of being eschatologically minded, but rather in being intentional in their actions and mindful how we impact lives, com-munities, and the earth. Still, millennials are changing the church as they are clear about what they seek in a community of faith:[38]

- being accepted and not being judged according to stereotypes, such as millennials being narcissistic or having little resilience, or for being gay, queer, or transgender;

- having a theological degree or denominational sanctioning to be a leader or minister is optional;

- joining the church is a possibility in time;

- gathering in smaller venues, such as a section of a strip mall, is prefer-able to large worship spaces;

- participating in visible acts of leadership—such as leading worship or preaching—recognizes, affirms, and indicates a breakdown of pater-nalistic hierarchies;

- discipling is individualized *and* collaborative—each need to find their own way, but they can do so together;

- seeking excellence in all that is offered;

94

- being authentic and transparent, addressing real-life issues and wrestling with one's imperfections, rather than keeping up appearances;

- needing a clear vision of what this community is all about;

- influencing and shaping culture, being tolerant, is more important than judging or opposing culture;

- respecting and working with others, including other religious traditions, is expected;

- fighting worship wars is a deal breaker;

- keeping sermons short and simple;

- including visuals in worship, including short movies will keep short attention spans focused;

- assembling in small groups is necessary;

- meeting at odd hours and when convenient, rather than having set schedules, supports their calendars;

- questioning leadership decisions, tradition, how scripture is interpreted, and more is a sign of intellectual skepticism only (not a sign of disloyalty or unbelief);

- embracing technology is cool (Why fill out a visitor's card if I can text you or add my name on a web-form?);

- creating the possibility to serve their immediate community is mandatory; and

- returning to communities that have moved beyond desperation and a survivalist mentality (due to the lack of membership or resources).

Millennials are doing things differently. Either the church and its leadership embrace this fact, or it runs the risk of alienating a whole generation and their children, Generation Z (also called the iGeneration, Net Gen, or post-millennials; born 1995–2014). Doing things differently does not necessarily means "killing [a specific industry]" as is reported in popular media. Some industries die under their own weight and the church is not excluded from this.

The spirit of God and a life of holy playfulness

(Cowritten with A. Keller Hawkins)

Keller Hawkins, a graduate of Vanderbilt Divinity School, has a Trinity knot tattoo on her right wrist. Under the symbol is the word *shekinah*, a difficult to translate Hebrew word meaning *God's dwelling place* or *Divine presence*. "I had read theologian Jürgen Moltmann's description of *shekinah* in his book *The Spirit of Life*," Keller states, "and immediately felt it necessary to get this ancient word tattooed on my body as a holy reminder." Regarding the *shekinah*, Moltmann writes:

> The *Shekinah* does not leave us. Even in our most frightful errors, it accompanies us with its great sense of yearning for God, its homesickness to be with God. [It is being reunited with God] when we encounter overwhelming joy: we become selflessly happy and come wholly to ourselves...if we become one with ourselves, the Shekinah comes to rest....We expect the mystical union of the Shekinah with God in every true encounter [with another]....We encounter every other created being in the expectation of meeting God.[39]

Responding to Moltmann, Keller states: "I've come to know God as playful, imaginative, and creative. What's more imaginative than a God who put on flesh, saw society's unseen, feed thousands with a small amount of food, healed the ailing sometimes with his own spit (i.e., Mark 8:22-25), preached good news to the poor, and challenged the powerful? What's more creative than instituting a ritual using the stuff of everyday (bread and wine) and washing his own disciples' feet as if *he* was *their* servant? What's more absurd than a God who is resurrected after being dead for three days and reunites with his disciples on a beach with a fish breakfast (Luke 24:42-43)?" Keller sees God inviting us to live playful, imaginative, and creative lives that reflect the very heart (or spirit) of God. "Instead of trying to capture God, I think we are to play alongside God, inhaling God's *ruah* (spirit) in our lungs as we dance, skip, sing, juggle, and play to God's beat."

Keller discovered the unconventional God through personal experience: she recalls encountering God on labyrinth walks; in swimming pools; at picnic potlucks; at political protests; during theological conversations; at Ping-Pong tables, in bars and pubs, coffee shops, and kitchens; on bus rides; in learning to unicycle with friends; juggling during worship services; and in the joy and healing she feels in her body when she plays and moves and laughs and subverts norms. "God is co-creative, always inviting, prompting, hinting, and nudging us to join in Holy Playfulness, in Holy Mischief (a concept I received from Shane Claiborne)," Keller witnesses. "God invites us into a life of Holiness that ignites rather than settles us, inspires rather than dulls, awakens rather than sedates—a way of life where we are to be fully *alive* and call others into the joy of living."

As she practices Holy Playfulness and participates in Holy Mischief, Keller's life and ministry cannot be anything but unconventional. "God's spirit urges me to go beyond convention so that we are reminded of God's playful, creative, and inventive Spirit that dwells in, among, and around us," she states. Compelled by the Spirit, Keller writes papers sitting outside; plays Ping-Pong in a city park while encountering others who challenge her to be open and curious; travels to places unknown; listens to the pain and grief hiding behind hostility and dives deep into community living; dwells in ritual while being receptive to transgression and subversion; chooses people over rules; and *practices resurrection*, with all its absurdity and hopefulness. She is called beyond the walls of the sanctuary or fellowship hall. Reflecting on her ministry, Keller states that "God's spirit guides me to be present with my fellow humans as we all try to figure out this thing called life. I have learned that I am not an expert. My goal should never be to convince or convert or save souls. Instead, I have found that I am merely a fellow pilgrim on a journey. Authentic ministry requires mutuality and continued learning and growing in God's Holy Playfulness. We all have wisdom to share." Keller is drawn to persons who exude the playfulness of God. She sees their playfulness dripping on her like nurturing water (see chapter 6). Watered and wet, she can drip the life offered by the Spirit on others.

Like many of her contemporaries, Keller loves travel. In her final year of study, she spent her summer with the Iona Community in the Scottish

Highlands.[40] The Isle of Iona is drenched with monasticism. She now knows why Iona is called a "thin place"—a term from Celtic Christianity that describes a place where the boundary between earth and heaven is particularly thin, where the Holy is somehow more radiant. There is the bright blue of the sea on a sunny day, the stark beauty of the Iona Abbey on a cloudy day, the sunsets on the west side of the island. The place vibrates with God's glory. "I followed a rhythm of life with my momentary community, eating, cooking, laughing and cleaning together. Central to our rhythm was worship three times a day in the centuries-old Iona Abbey. Service itself was anything but ordinary. In this ancient stone abbey, we would splash color on the communion table, sit on the floor, sing songs in languages not our own, and create interactive worship spaces. Sometimes there were balloons. Other times shells and rocks. Always candles. Twice we juggled during service. Even in a conventional space, we ushered in our unconventional God. We left drenched in curiosity, creativity, openness, and hope."

At the Iona Community, sacred moments surprised Keller: it was exploring life around a table at the pub and finding delight, the surprise when a pod of dolphins traveled through the Sound of Iona and newly formed friends braced each other for better views and against the cold, it was drawing a labyrinth with stone lines on the beach and walking in slow silence after a chilly swim. "It was as if we were recognizing the Holy in the midst of the creation," Keller reflects. "None of us would have been able to build such a large labyrinth by ourselves, and that was the beauty of it. It was as if the corners of the world met in this tangible yet transcendent space." After they walked the labyrinth, filled with exuberance and giggling with delight, they left it intact on the shore, wordlessly inviting other beachgoers to engage in Holy Playfulness. It reminded Keller that God's presence knows no bounds; that God still walks with us on the path of life, even if we feel lost.

Keller's Iona experience reflects her call to find places that are seemingly barren or bare; gather in community; illuminate the fruitfulness already present; and invite others into joy, engagement, and practicing resurrection. She finds God's Spirit contagious: "Holy Playfulness inspires, urges, and challenges. It awakens us to what is and gives us a vision of what could be. It pushes us outside the church and into the world full of God's creation, a gift for us to honor, steward, and cherish. I trust that God shows up in places where I am not expecting God. I trust that God loves us enough to invite us, challenge us, and work within us as we radiate the Spirit of God's Holy Playfulness. I trust that God's *shekinah* will guide us into newness and a flourishing life where we can recognize we are God's beloved as would be our neighbors. I trust that labyrinths will be built, that Ping-Pong matches will be transformational, that juggling continues to be a spiritual practice, and that the absurd will open us to the promise and hope of God."

Keller Hawkins lives a spiritual life close to God's dwelling place.

Receive: Five practices for significant leaders

Being a leader with people who have been blessed by God's spirit redefines the nature of collaborative leadership. The promises contained in Joel speak of an empowered community, one where all discern the presence of God in their midst. Effective leaders are called to recognize the vital life force of God at work in others. Dominant forms of leadership, easily recognized in poor listening, claiming authority, and control; superficial relationships; and being threatened will lead a community and their leader nowhere. Drawing on the same spirit that is alive in men and women, young and old, as well as those closer to the center of the power structures and those at its margins can allow a leader to be a significant presence in the lives of others and a faith community. Five practices can assist you as you listen to and travel with millennials:

First, *practice openheartedness and heartfulness*. Pastoral leaders are more defensive and shame prone than most others. We receive this "gift" from an elevated narcissistic trait we need to lead the people of God. Leading with others gifted by God's spirit can be threatening and being shown our own inadequacies or experiencing the competence of others can lead to self-shame.[41] Leaders defend against these uncomfortable feelings by claiming power and control, a strategy that rarely, if ever, succeeds. *Openheartedness* is a cultivated state of being in which feelings of care, warmth, compassion, and trust inform a mutual relationship between two persons. It is a stance that defies defensiveness and feeling threatened. Being openhearted assists one in naming and grieving the locusts of life. It opens one for the need for community and restoration and is closely related to heartfulness. *Heartfulness*, in turn, can be defined as "an internal set of skills such as clarity of mind, self-confidence, empathy, awareness and focus."[42] It reflects a meditative and mindful state that can be open to the experience of the moment. We do not naturally end up being openhearted or having heartfulness. These traits of mature leadership will assure that you will not be a stumbling block as God's spirit moves young and old toward a new community and reality.

Second, *practice spirituality* (or engage in spiritual practices). "[*Spirituality* refers] to people's subjective practice and experience of their religion, or to the spiritual exercises and beliefs which individuals or groups have with regard to their personal relationship with God."[43] It is a multidimensional construct with *intra*personal (e.g., personal prayer, reading scripture, meditation, yoga, and other practices) and *inter*personal aspects (e.g., involvement with others, church, 12-step programs, and service). Pastoral leaders with a vibrant spirituality lead differently from those who rarely engage in these life-giving practices. Research indicates that reduced life satisfaction often leads to a diminished spirituality.[44] As especially mainline Christianity experiences declining membership and expectations placed on pastoral leaders increase, one can expect their spiritual health to decline. When a leader reads scripture for others (such as in preparing for a sermon) or prays for others (such as in a pastoral prayer), but rarely does so personally, the leader is in trouble. Practice what you preach, for millennials appreciate authenticity. They deserve to be met by a leader with a vibrant spirituality.

Third, *practice bracketing* and *holding. Bracketing* is a philosophical concept and life skill, first proposed by Edmund Husserl, whereby one suspends judgment about others (or things) awakened by what one sees. It allows one to be open to and be surprised by experiences, even familiar ones. When a young adult walks in with dreadlocks, a nose ring, a pierced tongue, or a sleeve of tattoos, what are the first thoughts that go through your mind? Only by bracketing those thoughts, often tied to deep-seated prejudices on gender, race, class, sexual orientation, and age as they are, can a leader partner with a younger generation that does things differently. *Holding* is a psychological construct closely related to bracketing. It speaks to the capacity to contain emotion within oneself. Strong feelings not held, whether frustration, anger, fear, or sexual desire, spill over to typically hurt others. When millennials feel that a church and its leadership prefer to have a financial relationship with them as they promote tithing or stewardship, they will avoid the church. This is a fine line to walk, as the tithes and offerings of members assure a salary can be paid. Significant leaders can hold the expectation for increased membership—imagine young families—or else risking coming across as being desperate or needy. Holding, of course, also speaks to confidentiality and holding juicy bits of information in confidence.

Fourth, *practice vision catching*. Joel is clear that God's spirit is poured over all people and they dream dreams and see visions. Effective leaders then are vision *catchers*, not vision *casters*. As church leaders emulate charismatic business leaders, called to turn around a struggling church-as-organization, they often see themselves as vision casters. A powerful leader, safe in his power and hierarchy—vision casters are almost always male   tells others what to do. Congregations love such leaders, for in following they resign their functioning as the community. Denominations love dominant leaders too, as it creates the illusion of excellence. Joel would not only criticize the idea of being a vision caster, he would say that it is inherently against the order of things God created. Vision catching requires a leader to spend time with all who have received God's vital life force. It is only in relationship with an empowered generation that a leader can flourish and a congregation can grow.

A fifth *practice of clarity* is to embrace people of all genders, ages, and social standings as receiving God's spirit. This practice asks that you are clear about who you are as a community. If loss changes one's identity, as we said in the first chapter, then the likelihood that a congregation knows who it is is rather slim, particularly if loss is seen as an intimate enemy. Millennials seek a clear vision of the mission, values, and nature of community your church has. Moreover, they want to know and see how your congregation is active in its immediate surroundings. Working collaboratively with the church members to redefine its identity and empowering them to be active outside the church are perpetual tasks of significant leaders.

101

Leaders can find rest in these practices since God's vital life force also lives in them. One need not lead by one's own strength or natural gifts. Rather, being acutely aware of the fact that one is merely a part of a larger body can be a relief. Knowing one's strengths and weakness in reflexive mindfulness opens the possibility of not being unbecoming or a hindrance for a faith community to partner with the millennial generation. There are many relationships to be formed with an open heart, many visions to catch, and lives and a world in desperate need of restoration.

Toward a practice-oriented spirituality

One of the gifts millennials give society is that they are doing things differently. They truly are redefining established industries by the choices they make and the interests they have. The roots of the gifts millennials carry are spiritual, yes, but also cultural. Business research indicates that corporations remain challenged by millennials. Their talent management strategies fail and many millennials leave their jobs within two years of being hired. A study by PricewaterhouseCoopers recommended that corporations create a flexible work culture that recognizes the unique gifts in each millennial, increase collaboration, have transparent performance and reward decisions, build effective teams (with excellent managers), improve conditions for part-time workers, support play at work, increase connection with millennials, and know that one size does not fit all.[45]

Behind this experience one finds three powerful cultural drivers that shaped millennials: *positive psychology* (with positive self-image as one of its foci, alongside what makes life worth living; the good life), *information technology* (with computers, the internet, smartphones, and Apple products), and *innovation*. Millennial youth were treated as peers (or at least mini-adults), became data oriented, and were encouraged to be self-starters and entrepreneurs and to think outside the box.[46] Doing things differently is fueled by mobile, social, cloud, and information technologies. Trained well by culture, millennials want to feel good, do well, and be different. Even if a church is willing to embrace the spirit poured out over millennials, few church systems are able to accommodate the demands placed on them by millennials.

Millennial spirituality is awakened by God's spirit, fueled by culture, and stimulated by what sociologist Robert Wuthnow calls a spirituality of seeking with diverse spiritual practices. In his *After Heaven: Spirituality in America since the 1950s*, Wuthnow describes how American spirituality has been shifting from "a spirituality of dwelling" to a "spirituality of seeking." Both spiritualties envision a specific "habitation." We have moved, however, from a garden of Eden, a promised land, and a specific church to an infinite number of places with sacred meaning, for they are tied to personal presence.

In a spirituality of dwelling,

> God occupies a definite place in the universe and creates a sacred space in which humans too can dwell; to inhabit sacred space is to know its territory and to feel secure. A spirituality of seeking emphasizes negotiation: individuals search for sacred moments that reinforce their conviction that the divine exists, but these moments are fleeting; rather than knowing the territory, people explore new spiritual vistas, and they may have to negotiate among complex and confusing meanings of spirituality.[47]

The book of Joel, written in a time when no temple dominated Israel's life, anticipates and actively promotes this shift. In Western religion, spiritual dwelling anticipates traditional religion and envisions a specific faith community—a group of people—a particular tradition, and patriarchal systems. There will be the studying of scripture, well-defined rituals, liturgy, and the differences brought by a specific tradition. A particular social order that delineates religion from other spheres of life holds it all together, instilling a sense of security. Spiritual seeking, in turn, finds an individual on an open quest in search of new spiritual experiences. This pilgrimage is not necessarily void of scripture or tradition, but may assign less authority to them as an individual explores many alternative sources and practices to inform their spirituality. In spiritual seeking, there is no social order to keep things together or to instill a sense of security. Symbols are varied and can come from many sources. Even the meaning of "spiritual" shifts in a move to spiritual seeking: "Faith is no longer something people inherit but something for which they strive. It provides security not by protecting them with high walls but by giving them resources, by plugging them into the right networks, and by instilling the confidence to bargain for what they need."[48]

103

Throughout human history, Wuthnow asserts, the world's religions have always had components of both forms of doing spirituality. As stated, the book of Joel certainly entertains both. Nearly a thousand years after Joel, for example, the sixth-century Rule of Saint Benedict required vows of stability, obedience, and *conversatio*. *Conversatio* is difficult to translate, but Wuthnow sees it indicating "the changeable life of the spirit, especially the ephemeral qualities of the Holy Spirit as opposed to the enduring character of God the Father. *Conversatio* is a commitment to live faithfully in unsettled times and to keep one's life sufficiently unsettled to respond to the changing voice of God. It emphasizes vulnerability as a basic fact of the human condition and mystery as a characteristic of the sacred."[49] Today, our world is described as VUCA—volatile, uncertain, complex, and ambiguous—and the need for a personal identity and self-definition increases. So too does subjective, personal spirituality grow in the absence of rulers or rules that inform, protect, or persecute. Defining spirituality is thus increasingly difficult.

As Wuthnow concludes his chapter on spiritual dwelling and seeking, he sees a third alternative beyond dwelling and seeking: *practice-oriented spirituality*. "Spiritual practices put responsibility squarely on individuals to spend time on a regular basis worshipping, communing with, listening to, and attempting to understand the ultimate source of sacredness in their lives."[50] Practices include prayer and meditation, breathing techniques, yoga, massage, reading texts, journaling, communing with nature, eating, serving, attending retreats, worship, and more. Core themes within these practices are discernment or deep reflection; personal reward; social connections; they have a moral dimension; they compel duty, obligation, and service; have ties to tradition; and they allow for self-interpretation.[51] Spiritual practices are increasingly individual practices, even if performed in a group. Wuthnow finds the practices help their practitioners reflectively engage their past, present, and future. He identifies a moral character in especially individual practices, "encouraging people to walk each day with partial knowledge and in cautious hope."

Wuthnow introduces Avery Fielding, a thirty-something expecting her first child with her partner. Her spiritual search has taken her far beyond the Christian tradition (Catholic and Lutheran) that shaped her. Rather, she states she follows her own personal religion. Avery grew up in a home where her parents were disillusioned by the church and did not attend, though she was confirmed in the Lutheran Church, a process she hated. Still, God intrigued Avery and from an early age she can recall mystical experiences, "that there was a oneness with everything, whether it was the tree or it was a bug on the ground; there was no separation, there was no right or wrong, there was no better or less than."[52] No one she spoke to, but her grandmother, understood or affirmed these experiences. Her grandmother encouraged Avery to seek meaning deeper than pleasure or material wealth and existence. Avery explored metaphysics, yoga, the occult, and spirituality.

The death of her seventeen-year-old brother was traumatic, deepening her path into spirituality. She changed careers from being a business owner to doing massage therapy. She married, divorced, and after gaining training in hospitals, opened her own clinic. She also discovered that she was abused as a child. These moments came wrapped in spiritual anguish and a deliberate focus on her spiritual needs. In emotional and spiritual anguish, she stopped eating. One night, feeling she was going to die, she dreamed of a golden tunnel of warm, radiating light and heard a voice encouraging her not to die. Fully awake after what she describes as a wonderful, healing experience, she got up and made a meal to eat as she started a long path back to wellness. She sees surrendering to her pain as a key aspect of her experience. Avery's journey into health continued as she attended spiritual retreats and cultivated her spirituality through meditation and prayer, shifting from relationships and spaces of fear to systems based on love. "It's learning how to look at life differently," she says. "I may not be able to change what I see, but being able to see it differently helps me to respond to it much differently."[53] Avery describes profound personal transformation due to her intentional journey. "Spirituality is the way I live my life, the way I relate with people, the way I choose to see the world."

Avery is not unique. Many a millennial has a similar story and journey in life. How might the church reach out to a person such as Avery? Why would she be interested in a faith community after her experiences of church in childhood? How has God been at work in her life? Wuthnow summarizes his argument for a practice-oriented spirituality alongside spiritualities of dwelling and seeking as follows: "Practice-oriented spirituality is thus different from seeker-oriented spirituality chiefly in providing a more orderly, disciplined, and focused approach to the sacred. The people we talked to…tended to settle into a routine that permitted them to cultivate a deep spirituality rather than being influenced by their moods, circumstances, or exposure to constantly changing ideas."[54] Spiritual practice has taken a step or two beyond spiritual seeking and is far removed from spiritual dwelling. Where the latter requires a leader or guide for spirituality, practice-oriented spirituality can flourish without such a presence.

Dwelling and seeking and practicing are inherent parts of being human. We seek attachment to special places and would return to them, in fantasy or in person. In these spaces, we find peace and can experience solitude. Along the way we engage in practices, including prophesying, dreaming, and visioning. Continually we seek newness and difference as we easily tire of what's familiar. Always we want to feel alive. Today we live between many sacred spaces, which is a challenge for the church as faith communities are inherently more dwelling than seeking and practicing. If corporations actively seek to keep millennials on staff and struggle to do so, it should not surprise that churches also find attracting millennials and meeting their needs a challenge. Joining millennials where they are dwelling, seeking, and especially practicing is deepened when they have discovered a life-giving narrative worth living into. The human need for relationship, community, spiritual nurture, and also accountability—as we'll discuss next—remain.

Chapter Five

BE ACCOUNTABLE

A Just God and the Promise of Personal and Political Restoration

In cities around the world you will find them: YIMBYs (pronounced "yim-bees")! They are millennials, but not exclusively so, who mostly coalesce around fighting for affordable housing. YIMBY is an acronym for Yes In My Backyard![1] The acronym's place and date of origin is uncertain, but in 2006, people in Toronto created a YIMBY group in response to extensive, unrestrained real estate development in certain areas of the city. At the same time, community activists in San Francisco united to address expansion of Silicon Valley that was creating rent burdens young people especially could not carry. A group opposing the YIMBYs is the NIMBYs—Not In My Back Yard—"a pejorative characterization of opposition by residents to a proposal for a new development because it is close to them (or, in some cases, because the development involves controversial or potentially dangerous technology) often with the connotation that such residents believe that the developments are needed in society but should be further away."[2] NIMBY dates to the 1980s (and possibly earlier to the 1950s), and present groups band together around a number of issues: housing developments, homeless shelters, bike lanes, rapid transport, chemical plants, airports, wind turbines, landfill sites, prisons, nuclear waste sites, and even recreational cannabis shops. A NIMBY, generally, is not against the particular development per se and might even argue that it is needed for a society at large, just "Not in my back yard!"

The Sierra Club, founded in 1892 by John Muir, is the largest and most influential environmental organization in the United States and finds an ally in YIMBYs. The club's magazine, *Sierra*, reports "Pro-Housing Urban Millennials Say, 'Yes in My Backyard.'"[3] "A new movement," the *Sierra* writes, "composed largely of millennials, is pushing hard on city leaders to make their cities denser and more walkable and bikeable, with green infill development, more affordable housing, and transit-oriented centers."[4] The Sierra Club and many millennials see equitable housing as a justice issue, which includes protecting the environment. Dense populations, as one finds in urban centers where work and life can be more closely integrated, reduce carbon emissions. *Sierra* writes that policies of mixed-income housing in urban settings frequently lead to tension with more affluent residents—often older and whiter—who don't want the traffic, congestion, and other effects of urban density, such as shadows or obscuring views from high-rise buildings.[5] The conflicts play out before zoning boards, city councils, and other public bodies where young YIMBYs turn out to support large housing projects. The NIMBYs who oppose them are often progressive, environmentally minded individuals who believe in climate action and recognize that sprawl is unsustainable; they just want to preserve the look and feel of the neighborhoods they call home.

In June 2017, a woman at a City of Berkeley council meeting petitioned against a housing development to secure sunlight for her zucchini garden will receive no sun should a planned housing development be approved. She seemed confident she had her community's support behind her and requests like hers have derailed development in the past. And then the YIMBYs spoke. "You're talking about zucchinis? Really? Because I'm struggling to pay rent," an indignant Victoria Fierce, a millennial, said at the meeting.[6] Fierce continued, naming failed policies in the past that led to the housing and rental crisis San Francisco is facing. Rather than retreating and suffering in silence, young adults in their twenties and thirties are rallying and attending planning meetings to argue for affordable housing. Soon the zucchini became an online meme and something to joke about.

YIMBYs and their impact on affordable housing represent one example of the political impact of millennials. They are true politicians—politics meaning "the shape of the city."[7] Jesus scholar Marcus Borg writes that Jesus shaped his "city" around the value of compassion imitating God's compassion, when the Jewish religious leaders sought to structure society around holiness codes. "The Jewish social world and its wisdom became increasingly structured around the polarities of holiness as separation: clean and unclean, purity and defilement, sacred and profane, Jew and Gentile, righteous and sinner," Borg writes. "What distinguished him from most of his contemporaries as well as from us, from their conventional wisdom as well as from ours," Borg continues, "was his vivid sense that reality was ultimately gracious and compassionate." Here, YIMBYs and millennials reflect Jesus's ministry closely (see chapter 3 for the God of Compassion).

Two factors drive YIMBYs as changemakers. First, they have half the accumulated wealth of their parents at a similar age. They rent more than own, making them vulnerable to rent increases, greedy landlords, and market forces. Second, millennials have a profound moral sense of right and wrong. Whether the issue is affordable housing, ecological concerns, or contingent labor, millennials often lead the way. Their sense of right and wrong, however, is ambiguous. Researchers Arthur Levine and Diane Dean found that of undergraduates, 60 percent approve of deporting undocumented immigrants, 70 percent state they should not get in-state tuition, and 74 percent would deny them any federal aid programs. Only 55 percent supported guest worker visas.[8] From an early age millennials were reminded by parents and teachers to keep to the rules, for "three strikes and you're out." Levine and Arthur also found that college students often lack a complex understanding of the world affairs and power dynamics that can inform careful ethical discernment. Still, this picture of millennials is not the final one, as we'll discover in this chapter.

To understand the concerned views YIMBYs hold regarding affordable housing and climate change or society's engagement relationship with undocumented immigrants, transgender persons, or those resisting heteronormativity, the *framework of accountability* is helpful. Accountability can be defined as "the quality of being accountable; liability to account for and answer for one's conduct, performance of duties, etc."; it is "to answer for responsibilities and conduct; required or expected to justify one's actions, decisions, etc.; answerable, responsible."[9] Accountability speaks to taking ownership of something and being able to justify one's behavior. Millennials are often accountable to themselves, when especially late boomers would be accountable to organizations. Gen Xers and boomers can be surprised by a millennial's decision that seemingly comes out of the blue, with no advance notice. Millennials often do better in groups than working individually and should a better opportunity arrive, they will embrace that opportunity, even if that means changing jobs often. Millennials find boomers untrustworthy, for boomers believe in the good of organizations and often sacrifice work-life balance.[10] Boomers, in turn, often view millennials as not being accountable. Accountability is closely tied to whoever has the (perceived) power.

It is around accountability that *The Millennial Narrative* and the book of Joel find another touch point. God, merciful and compassionate, very patient, full of faithful love and ready to forgive, is also the God who holds Israel and the nations accountable. In Joel's world, there is no ultimate personal choice and freedom—a vision of life often promoted by culture—but only a life of living response-able. Our prophet imagines a specific moment where the call to justify one's actions will occur: a day Joel identifies as "the Day of the Lord." This day speaks beyond the social restoration of Joel, which occurred earlier in the narrative, to include the political restoration too. Cities, destroyed by the locusts of life, including foreign armies as locusts, will be reclaimed and rebuilt. Judah, finding itself in exile, will return and have Jerusalem as its restored capital. This chapter begins by reframing the Day of the Lord as a Day of Accountability. It is a day that envisions consequences for some, but affirmation for those who know the compassionate God. After looking at what biblical scholars write about this Day of Accountability, we look at the cause ministry of Rj Robles, a changemaker holding society accountable to the violence that especially trans persons experience. The chapter concludes by identifying five practices pastoral leaders can embrace as they partner with millennials seeking political restoration. But first, we need to reckon with the fact that "crowd after crowd fills the valley of judgment, for the day of the LORD is near in the valley of judgment" (Joel 3:14).

A day of accountability

Elizabeth Drescher's research on "nones" and "somes" shows that they fault Christianity and especially religious leaders, for "hypocrisy, greed, judgmentalism, sexual abuse, sexism, homophobia, [and] anti-scientific ignorance."[11] Millennials are not as concerned with inner sin—an emphasis of tradition—as they are with outward sins. Hebrew Bible scholar Aaron Schart names this tendency when he writes, "A Christian understanding of sin often has a tendency to be understood as something restricted to the individual and to one's inner life before God."[12] Whereas the Christian tradition sees the admittance of personal sin and the expressed need for salvation as an entry point into the tradition, millennials, in general, reject such an understanding. They do not have a moralistic understanding of sin nor do they believe there is only a single path to salvation. With their outward focus on sin, millennials will find a supportive conversation partner in Joel, where "foreign policy, juridical matters, economic exchange and social behavior are fields where God wants God's people to act according to [their] covenant relationship with God."[13] It should thus not surprise that millennials generally do join congregations "in working together, in addressing issues such as poverty, hunger, and homelessness."[14] The latter concerns speak to a restored humanity, a political correction, and building a just society. This social, political, economic, and ecological accountability reflects millennial righteousness before others and ties them intimately to Joel's narrative.

In the book of Joel, the Day of the Lord—*yom YHWH*—a day of God's political and social restoration of Israel and judgment over nations, features prominently.[15] Historically, the Day of the Lord was not consistently understood as a future event, as many today would interpret it, but rather an invitation to live responsibly and with accountability in the present.[16] The day, spanning both Testaments of scripture, is a contested concept holding different meanings. It appears nineteen times in the Old Testament and four times in the New Testament.[17] After God promised agricultural restoration, which also restored the families and communities in Judah, God continues and promises political restoration in Judah's relationship with its neighbors. The shame the people of Judah (Hebrew: *ammi*, "my people") experienced was not just tied to their lack of food and not being able to give food to their children and to God in worship. Shame burdened them as a people in exile. "Once the idea of agricultural redemption is introduced and theological implications of the relations between the people and God have been raised, the skeptical people can believe in the possibility of a political salvation."[18]

Joel comforts the people by saying that in the Day of the Lord, they will be brought back out of exile.

As with other parts of the book of Joel, the book's depiction of the Day of the Lord is another contested theme. Some argue it is a day that already happened, while others see it as a day in the present, and yet others a day in the distant (or eschatological) future. Furthermore, some see the day as one of final judgment that will end life as we know it, whereas others, including the Reformers, Martin Luther and John Calvin, do not hold that belief.[19] A contemporary Hebrew Bible scholar, Mordecai Schreiber, holds the view that the Day of the Lord is unfolding in our midst. He writes,

> There are today social protests that have begun to effect profound changes in certain countries and which will probably have their impact on the rest of the world. This, indeed, may be the ultimate meaning of "the Day of Adonai," a time when the divine spirit is awakened among people, inducing them to take action and thus "perfect the world through the sovereignty of God" (le-takken olam be-malkhut Shaddai).[20]

Traditionally seen as a day of judgment and vengeance by a righteous God, we will argue that it is a Day of Accountability, opening new possibilities of engaging Joel and the Day of the Lord for a contemporary people.

God's afterthought, in which God promises the outpouring of the Spirit (Joel 2:28), continues:

> Truly, in those days and in that time, I will bring back to Judah and Jerusalem those who were sent away. I will gather all the nations, and I will bring them to the Jehoshaphat Valley. There I will enter into judgment with them in support of my people and my possession, Israel, which they have scattered among the nations. They have divided my land, and have cast lots for my people. They have traded boys for prostitutes, and sold girls for wine, which they drank down. What are you to me, Tyre and Sidon, and all the regions of Philistia? Are you paying me back for something? If you are paying me back, then in a flash I will turn your deeds back upon your own heads. You have taken my silver and my gold, and have carried my rich treasures into your temples. You have sold the people of Judah and Jerusalem

to the Greeks, removing them far from their own border. But now
I am calling them from the places where you have sold them, and I
will repay you for your deeds. I will sell your sons and your daughters
as a possession of the people of Judah, and they will sell them to the
Sabeans, to a nation far away; for the LORD has spoken.

Announce this among the nations:
>   Prepare a holy war,
>   wake up the warriors;
>   let all the soldiers draw near,
>   let them come up!
Beat the iron tips of your plows into swords
>   and your pruning tools into spears;
>   let the weakling say, "I am mighty."
Come quickly,
>   all you surrounding nations;
>   gather yourselves there;
>   bring your mighty ones, LORD.
Let the nations prepare themselves,
>   and come up to the Jehoshaphat Valley;
>   for there I will sit to judge
>   all the surrounding nations.
Cut with the sickle,
>   for the harvest is ripe.
>   Go and crush grapes,
>   for the winepress is full.
>   The jars overflow with wine,
>   for their wickedness is great.
Crowd after crowd fills the valley of judgment,
>   for the day of the LORD is near
>   in the valley of judgment.
The sun and the moon are darkened;
>   the stars have ceased shining.
The LORD roars from Zion,
>   and utters his voice from Jerusalem;
>   the heavens and the earth quake.
>   But the LORD is a refuge for his people,

> a shelter for the people of Israel.
> So you will know that I am the Lord your God,
>   settle down in Zion, my holy mountain.
> Jerusalem will be holy,
>   and never again will strangers pass through it. (Joel 3:1-17)

Oracles of salvation were common to the people of the ancient Near East, including Israel, yet we know very little about their origins. They most likely were produced in scribal classes, rather than by ecstatic prophets.[21] As God speaks, cosmic events unfold: there will be "blood and fire and columns of smoke. The sun will be turned to darkness, and the moon to blood before the great and dreadful day of the Lord comes" (Joel 2:31). The people of the ancient Near East would study signs and wonders (Hebrew: *mofetim*, portents) to interpret godly sanction. Now the sun and the moon will be disfigured. During a solar eclipse, the moon appears red, thus the reference to blood. Blood also awakens the imagination to the warlike scenarios Joel prophesies. Blood evokes memories on doorposts as Israel was about to embark on the exodus out of Egypt (Exod 12). For a prescientific people, a bloody moon was a curse indicating great pending calamity. As the nations (Hebrew: *goyim*) gather, Judah need not fear, for they are gathered in the sanctuary under the protection of the compassionate God. They will be kept safe; others should be concerned about being held accountable.

Following Zephaniah (3:8ff.), Obadiah (15-17), Ezekiel (38:7), and Isaiah (66:18), Joel sees God assembling the nations to await judgment. Joel may actually see two judgments, one against Tyre and Sidon and all the regions of Philistia, the immediate neighbors and enemies of Judah and one against "the nations"—a general judgment.[22] To be secure in Zion—which speaks to Jerusalem's eternal nature—Judah's enemies had to be removed.[23] "Jehoshaphat," meaning "Yahweh judges," implies that Joel did not have a specific place in mind even as he imagines a valley wide enough for a large number of people. There is no known place in the Bible with the name Jehoshaphat.[24] Rather, it is a symbolic place. By the fourth century BCE, interpreters believed it was the Kidron wadi, a dry riverbed and not even a valley—such is the power of making scripture one's own.[25] In laying a claim against the people, God confirms, "Hurt my people and you are hurting me."[26] Acting against God's people is acting against God. The Phoenicians and Philistines, Israel's long-standing enemies—including the great commercial Phoenician city of Tyre and its sister seaport, Sidon, with Philistia, controlling the South Arabian trade routes—are implicated.

The charges are fourfold: the scattering of Judah and breaking up of families, taking possession of the land, enslaving the people, and stealing the silver and gold sacred objects that belonged to God's temple (Hebrew: *hekelekem*).[27] Silver and gold can also metaphorically refer to the people of God, as Ezekiel (38:13) and the book of Lamentations (2:41 and 4:1) indicate. God condemns a practice common in Joel's time—selling people into slavery—even as God indicates that the perpetrators will become slaves themselves. With poetic justice, "the land-loving Judahites [will be sold] to sea peoples, the seafaring Phoenicians and Philistines will be sold by Judahites to desert dwellers (Sabeans)."[28] The wickedness of the nations is great. Slavery was an existential crisis for a people living in exile, as the Judeans knew intimately. We can imagine a group of soldiers, drunk in celebrating their victory over Judah, gratifying their most basic desires and seeing no value in human life. God, as plaintiff and judge, rises as the champion for war victims and refugees. Justice is the virtue as God sides with the oppressed, the dispossessed, and economically marginalized. Justice has restorative purpose. The choices the nations made are returning to them with interest as God protects the land, the temple, and the people. About two hundred years after God spoke these words through Joel, the people of Sidon found themselves enslaved by Antiochus III (345 BCE) and Tyre by Alexander the Great (332 BCE).

The people of God need not fear this day, for "everyone who calls on the Lord's name will be saved; for on Mount Zion and in Jerusalem there will be security" (Joel 2:32). Some commentators see calling on God meaning prayer, others see it as those serving God out of respect, and others yet see it as only those trusting in God will be saved.[29] The last does have some support in scripture. The phrase "calling on the Lord" refers almost exclusively to entering into a covenant relationship with God and being loyal to God.[30] What differentiates the people of God from the other nations is that they call upon God's name, for that reflects the unique nature of their relationship with God. "Calling on the Lord" also has a legal component, as in Joel's time "proclaiming a name over something was a legal act that meant an establishment of ownership."[31] Joel reminds us that the locusts of life come to all, but that those in relationship with God meet the locusts differently, knowing they do not have the last say. Neither the safety of Jerusalem nor the universal salvation of all people is guaranteed by Joel. Likewise, the Day of Accountability is different for those who know the God of compassion. In the final chapter we'll argue that being in relationship with God is participating in God's work of personal and political renewal and restoration. It is not merely a personal confession, a practice such as attending church or joining another spiritual and/or religious gathering.

As God enters into judgment, visions of a holy war (Hebrew: *qaddesu*) arise. It is unclear just who does the calling and who might be called into this war. Some scholars see God calling the nations into war whereas others see the nations organizing themselves.[32] It is the nations, not Judah, who are hungry for war. Here Joel follows the Hebrew Bible thought that judgment and war go hand in hand. Joel, with grim irony, reverses Micah 4:3, which state: "God will judge between the nations and settle disputes of mighty nations, which are far away. They will beat their swords into iron plows and their spears into pruning tools. Nation will not take up sword against nation; they will no longer learn how to make war." Likewise, Isaiah 2:4 states: "God will judge between the nations, and settle disputes of mighty nations. Then they will beat their swords into iron plows and their spears into pruning tools. Nation will not take up sword against nation; they will no longer learn how to make war." The book of Joel does not accept this utopian vision; rather, it envisions war before justice and peace can be secured. The nations do not go to Jerusalem to confess God's reign, as in Isaiah and Micah; here they go to resist God's sovereignty and judgment. "Thus are the nations presented as warmongers who prefer military violence over the agricultural labor with which they were occupied."[33] Beating plows into swords, however, will be futile. The nations' military power will not save them. "Joel's parody puts a choice before the nations. Isaiah had promised peace; Joel affirms that peace will indeed come, whether the nations oppose it or not.... The phrase 'plowshares into swords' makes a blunt mockery of the world powers, who think that by completely arming themselves with much effort they will have power and superiority over the people of God."[34] Some commentators see an Israelite army who will fight the nations, whereas other commentators believe angels and the heavenly host will fight on behalf of Israel. Others yet see the references to holy war as metaphoric only.[35] Regardless, God determines the outcome as God seeks "the principle of *lex talionis*, an exact retribution for every offence."[36] If Judah was sold into slavery, the perpetrators would become slaves themselves.

The experience Judah had with the devouring locusts is nothing in comparison to God's judgment. The locusts, at best, were but a precursor to the Day of Accountability. In the Jehoshaphat Valley—the valley of judgement (v. 14; Hebrew: *emeq heharus*)—the enemies of Judah will be harvested like grain or grapes in the fullness of the season as judgment comes upon their wickedness. By establishing the Day of the Lord, Joel echoes the Day's introduction in Joel 1:15 ("What a terrible day! The day of the LORD is near; it comes like chaos from the Almighty") and Joel 2:2 ("a day of darkness and no light)." It is both a chaotic day of judgment and a great day establishing God as the compassionate and just God who protects God's people. No doubt the people recited Psalm 46:1: "God is our refuge and strength, a help always near in times of great trouble." Jerusalem will be secured as holy, says God, "and never again will strangers pass through it" (Joel 3:17).

The Day of the Lord is important to the Book of the Twelve, even if the books do not give us any indication of how they know the day is coming. No prophet, however, describes the day as vividly as Joel. Whereas modern readers read about judgment and punishment and are filled with dread, the Day of the Lord also carries connotations of hope.[37] For Joel, the Day of the Lord implies the restoration of people and lands and nations. It is also the conviction of all who devise and participate in injustice. As a Day of Accountability, the Day of the Lord is a hopeful day one need not fear, unless one partakes in practices and policies that dehumanize persons, as the enemies of Judah did.

The hope in Joel is fueled by Joel's primary goal: to reconnect the people with God. Whereas the first part of the book focuses on agricultural restoration—which for an agrarian people meant personal restoration—the second part of the book focuses on political salvation. For Joel, the political is spiritual. The two are intricately linked. Without political salvation—how communities, cities, and nations function—the people's connection with God will be incomplete.[38] Agricultural restoration is now in sight—the locusts moved on and died out—and the possibility of political restoration can be believed. "From a psychological perspective," commentator Elie Assis asserts, "agricultural salvation is easier for the people to accept at this stage and prepares them to hear about salvation on a national level."[39] Now they can hear that in the Valley of Judgment (or Decision), their enemies and the wicked will be destroyed. God is like a lion, fiercely protective yet ominously dangerous. The roar of nations attacking in war is thundered out by the roar of God holding them accountable. Judah will "know" God reigns, indicating a close relationship between God and Judah. For Joel, the knowledge that God reigns over nations and will restore the agricultural and political worlds of Judah is enough to secure the people's return to God. The question the nations asked, "Where is [your] God?" (Joel 2:17), has been answered. An exiled people's hope is awakened. They have a new story to tell. No longer is their story one of being exiled because of their sin. Now they can tell of agricultural and political restoration and a God that holds them accountable.

There is much reason to support reading the second half of Joel through the lens of accountability. Drawing on the narrative material in Joel, *The Millennial Narrative* reframes the Day of the Lord as a call to live with responsibility before God and with care toward one's neighbors. The emphasis in the Day of the Lord is not only on what God will do, it is also on how one should best live one's life, the everyday decisions we make that impact our world. As commentator Christopher Seitz writes, the way the Day of the Lord is depicted in Joel "is intended to serve as exemplary for future generations."[40] Seitz reminds us that "all interpretation involves a degree of circularity in that the reader brings some kind of hunch to the task of line-by-line reading based upon a larger grid into which that will finally (it is hoped) fit."[41] Good readers, he believes, can change their "hunch" based on what they read. Today, language of accountability and consequences, rather than sin and punishment, resonates with millennials. In systems where patriarchy rules, the latter language might be the only language one can use. Patriarchy, however, has been exposed for the abusive power it is, denying and exploiting women, children, the elderly and all who are not close to the power structure—the immigrant—or who are not masculine enough. Stated differently, today we do not have a power endowed with enough trust to punish, especially the church that often uses language of sin and guilt. Partnership is always better than patriarchy. Of course, a person can grow into a relationship with God that recognizes the creator God's power and authority. The narrative of Joel invites one into that relationship with the compassionate God. The entry point is recognizing the locusts of life and recognizing the gifts of gathering and the promise of restoration. Sin, the threat of eternal damnation, and the need for personal salvation are themes and a language whose time may have passed.

Joel's Day of Accountability envisions a person making an *individual* decision, even if the day also holds nations (groups) accountable. The choices individuals make have unprecedented consequences that may not be survivable, not by the individual or the group exposed to the individual's decision. Whereas linear, cause-and-effect thinking falls apart most often, here it remains in place. One's decision can have direct, if unforeseen, consequences. Climate change is but one reality that is teaching us this. Between cause and effect, accountability brings forth immediacy—it has a local focus and is important for the here-and-now first, before its long-term effect becomes clear. Joel is adamant that Judah has to decide now; it cannot wait. It is thus no surprise that "the overall pattern of Joel's theology strikes many a chord for those conversant with New Testament teaching: turning to God from sin—a call to be obeyed 'now'—sovereign grace, the covenant community and its security under God, judgment to come and future bliss."[42] The narrative of Joel does not indicate an awareness of a future savior for Israel, although we can assume that, being Jewish, the author was familiar with Isaiah's vision of a woman giving birth to a son called Immanuel—"God with us" (Isa 7:13-14).[43] Joel, of course, is concerned with the land, devoured as it is and awaiting restoration, in ways the New Testament rarely portrays. As Joel writes of locusts and drought, it is not far-fetched to argue that Joel-for-today reminds us that our decisions have consequences, whether our decisions are relational, spiritual, economic, or environmental in nature. Ways of being and leading that are sexist, racist, homophobic, classist, and xenophobic will be judged harshly by God.

119

Accountability in the Hebrew Bible flows from the universal to the particular and vice versa.[44] It moves from calling Israel and other nations to task to focusing on the individual, a theme that evolved especially around the prophet Hosea marrying the prostitute Gomer. After Hosea, adultery and its individual unfaithfulness was a metaphor describing Israel's relationship with God. Joel does not receive his particular and personal focus from Hosea's theology. Rather, Joel's accountability stems from the fact that the locusts of life devour an individual's life first, before it becomes a communal tragedy. When Joel writes that "[they] have divided my land, and have cast lots for my people. They have traded boys for prostitutes, and sold girls for wine, which they drank down" (Joel 3:2), he implicates individual behavior. Individuals still make decisions that divide lands, play dice with people's lives, and place the next generation in a precarious ecological and financial position. Politicians, individuals in power, and those nostalgically reaching back to patriarchy, especially, can benefit from discovering the narrative of Joel.

Joel's accountability resists the facelessness and lack of community so common in our world, where the rich get richer while the poor are getting poorer; where we prefer not to see the homeless person standing with a sign at the crossing; where politicians consistently create laws and remove funding that assures human flourishing; where international decisions are made without care of what happens to communities on the other side of the globe. Knowing that one's thoughts and actions carry accountability is frightening, especially for those living in privilege and with power.

Fear can be used to sustain the status quo and keep us from seeking a just society. Transgender persons, more so than possibly any other marginalized group, know this reality. Thank God that there are persons like Rj Robles who can teach us a different way of living and being the people of God.

Resisting fear and embracing radical love
(Cowritten with Rj Robles)

Rj Robles, whose gender pronouns are *they*, *them*, and *theirs*, are transgender and genderqueer. They do not identify nor adhere to dichotomous categories of gender, binaries with deep patriarchal and colonial roots. In the church, we can learn much from Rj—about lives that too often are cut short due to violence and murder, faith that seeks transformation, the transness of God, and the impact of abusive cultural values. Rj consistently call us to see the injustices trans people, persons of color, immigrants, and other marginalized communities experience. We are invited to join them in their cause ministry as together we seek justice and practice accountability. We follow Rj as they join Joel in weaving together the personal and the political.

My first recollection of Rj is us worshipping together. It was the spring semester of 2015, and we were in a Vanderbilt Divinity School chapel service. As the worship leader solicited prayer requests to lead the people of God in prayer, Rj named Taja DeJesus, Penny Proud, Bri Golec, Kristina Gomez Reinwald, Keyshia Blige, and Vanessa Santillan among others—trans persons beaten, stabbed, and shot to death between February and April 2015.[45] According to the Human Rights Campaign, violence against trans persons is on the increase, with twenty-three persons murdered in 2016 and twenty-eight in 2017.[46] As the current United States presidency and administration reject the civil rights complaints of trans students and violent rhetoric permeates Washington, DC, we can expect violence against trans people to increase. The church, through its silence, participates in this violence. Rj reminded us that day that we have trans persons in our community too, persons intimately familiar with the violence others direct toward them. As silence set in, Rj reminded us that the majority of trans murders are rarely solved. For many, if not the majority of trans persons, justice does not roll down like waters and righteousness does not become an ever-flowing stream (see chapter 6).[47]

Rj's prayer request reflects their deep faith as queer, trans, and Latinx activists. They are currently completing their master of divinity degree, enriched by studies of the intersections of trans, pastoral, and Latinx theologies. Their inspiration for this embodied work comes from the strong legacy of the trans liberation of especially Sylvia Rivera and Marsha P. Johnson. As graduation approaches, Rj anticipate seeking ordination in the Disciples of Christ Christian Church.

Reflecting on their activism and cause ministry, Rj state that "my activism is deeply rooted in my embodied presence in the universe. My activism is pro-Black, pro-immigrant, pro-queer and trans, and anti-colonial. I am an active member of Southerners on New Ground (SONG), seeking to continue the strong legacy of trans people of color. I join the struggle for the liberation of queer and trans people of color in the South."[48] SONG is a regional queer liberation organization made up of persons of color, immigrants, people with disabilities, working-class and rural and small towns citizens, and LGBTQ+ people in the South. In Nashville, Rj also work to improve trans healthcare, to offer pastoral care, and to attain racial and healing justice. Their activism, however, never drifts too far from immigration reform.

Rj's calling to cause activism (see chapter 6) is rooted not only in their deep faith and belief in God but also in their family or origin. "I believe I have an ancestral calling on my activism," Rj state. "All of my family is from Lares, Puerto Rico. This town is known for El Grito de Lares, also known as the Lares Uprising, one of the first major revolts against Spanish colonial rule in 1868." As a child, Rj heard exciting and radical stories about their family's resistance. "I wished to someday be a similar activist that stood up against empire and colonial structures of oppression." They started their vocation of activism in Chicago's West Side Puerto Rican neighborhood of Humboldt Park. Through spoken word, youth justice movements, and joining in reproductive justice, Rj formed their prophetic identity. Mentored by Jose Lopez, a Puerto Rican elder with deep roots of struggle and political resistance, they discovered the long history of the Puerto Rican struggle for liberation from the US. "I became invested in learning about my people, our long history of colonization, and marginalization." Hungry for knowledge, they read materials not prescribed in school, discovering the histories of social movements across the US. "Through my family, stories and lessons passed down from community elders, and politicized books my activism developed over time."

Rj's vision for a just society has a specific focus: "I am committed to making changes that will guarantee that every person of color is worthy of dignity and respect. I am trying to make room for queer and trans people of color to have the right to exist and thrive in this country." Rj work toward this just society through community organizing and are learning that oppressed persons can be empowered. "I support organizing that builds collective power and leadership among all involved and I think this begins with people who are most targeted in this society. I am attempting to center the leadership and voices of people of color and queer and trans folks, with the hope that we can bring people together in multi-issue, multicultural community organizing. Our liberation depends on coming together across and within our differences."

As a person called into church leadership, Rj's cause ministry and activism never drift too far from the church. "I firmly believe that every form of activism is faith in action," they state. "The church is not just simply held on Sundays or locked up in church buildings. Church happens every day, at every protest and action, down every street where the cry for liberation can be heard. My activism is my ministry." Despite the fact that mainline Christianity is most often mute to the challenges, prejudices, and violence trans people face, Rj maintains hope in the church as an agent of change. "The church must be a place that speaks truth to power. I believe that Jesus had a street ministry. He constantly moved in between places preaching the good news, and that good news was and still is liberation. My work in the trans movement, the LGBTQ+ movement, the immigrant movement, and Black Lives Matter is deeply spiritual/faith justice work. Activism and ministry are not separate for me. I understand that my activism is me doing the work that is necessary to see the Kin-Dom of God realized in this life and on this world."

As a trans and genderqueer person, Rj—a contemporary priest and prophet (see chapter 2)—experience life and the church in ways many of us are finding difficult to imagine. What they experience can help society and the people of God in naming the dynamics that may lie behind confusion, silence, and dangerous apathy. "I am learning that what fuels hatred, bigotry, white supremacy, and what hinders change is fear. I have learned that fear is oftentimes *the* factor that is holding us back from embracing another human being. I have learned that both oppressor and oppressed carry fear in their bodies." Rj's activism exposes a fear that places individual persons but also society at risk. "When fear is not unlearned or debunked, it can have a serious impact on the lives of others. I have seen fear in the eyes of people who are standing on the wrong side of justice. I have seen fear in the eyes of the powerful that fear the rising of the marginalized. I have smelled fear from pastors and ministers who profess the Christian faith, yet fill the pulpit with hate. I am learning that fear will not get us free."

Despite identifying fear, Rj remains hopeful, for when we let go of our fear and build relationships, systems and structures of oppression can be dismantled. Rj's hope is infectious despite them being very familiar with the locusts of life that fuel fear, a fear that initiates the violence often directed at trans persons, immigrants, and persons of color. "I am reminded every day that love is love is love. My hope is that any difference that I make is rooted in radical love of self and radical love of my neighbor."

It's a safe assumption to say that the vast majority of church leaders do not have a trans person in their lives who can educate them on using pronouns of they, them, theirs, or who can invite them into a ministry of justice where a flourishing life is sought for trans persons. This might be true to a ministry serving immigrants or persons of color too. As one of the most marginalized populations in our society, trans persons can find hope in the voice of God saying: "I will repay you for the years that the cutting locust, the swarming locust, the hopping locust, and the devouring locust have eaten" (Joel 2:25). This voice, however, also calls on us to practice accountability. As Rj stated when they quoted Jesus, we need to love our neighbor as we love ourselves (Matt 19:19).

Leaders can join Rj in their work by being accountable and practicing leadership skills that initiate social and political restoration.

Be accountable: Five practices for significant leaders

The Millennial Narrative is an invitation for pastoral leaders to envision a life of faith and doing ministry differently by partnering with millennials outside the church. It seeks to empower the *restoration* of a pastor's call to the ministry—which is difficult to sustain in the presence of the locusts of ministry. The stress of "saving the church" is real and debilitating, fueling pathways to burnout. We also seek to *revitalize* faith communities. We said that dominant leadership will assume all responsibility for the success or failure of a church. Significant leadership activates a congregation and awakens hope in belonging to something bigger than what an individual brings. Five practices can assist you in becoming and remaining significant as you embrace God's promise of social and political restoration and partner with millennials. The practices are the following: practice accountability—take responsibility; practice transparency—allow others to "look into" your ministry; practice non-defensiveness—be openhearted and resist shame-responses; practice responsiveness—address the needs of those in your neighborhood; and practice paradox—see the world as complex while holding unsolvable tensions and managing polarities.

First, *practice accountability.* In *Millennials Matter: Proven Strategies for Building Your Next-Gen Leader*, Danita Bye, a consultant familiar with Christian communities, identifies accountability as one of seven character traits leaders should exhibit and cultivate in millennials.[49] Earlier we defined accountability as "the quality of being accountable; liability to account for and answer for one's conduct, performance of duties, etc."[50] Bye describes accountability as "having the emotional maturity and internal backbone to take responsibility for your own actions and choices, and not shift blame to external factors. Accountability is an expression of the virtues of fortitude, prudence, justice, temperance, and faith."[51] Bye acknowledges that many millennials are good at the blame-game, carefully groomed by an entitled and victim-oriented culture. Locusts, I imagine, can awaken the same attitudes. Yet millennials also yearn for growth and self-correction, aspects of life anticipated by accountability. First and foremost, accountability demands introspection by a leader. These questions can assist in reflexivity:

- What are my responsibilities?

- What responsibilities need clarification?

- What responsibilities am I neglecting?

- What are the ways that I am underperforming—in self-care, my spirituality, my job expectations, toward others?

- When do I tend to shift blame onto others or retreat in shame?

- When do I slip into a victim mentality—a past event is determining my present actions?

125

- Where do I tend to confuse boundaries in ways that undermine my excellence in ministry?

- To whom should I give account?

- What goals and outcomes do I have or seek but do not reach?

- What can I do differently that will increase my effectiveness as a leader?

- What incentives do I have to change the way I perceive my leadership?

- How will others know that I am accountable in my leadership?

- What responsibilities can I give over to someone else/others?

Bye suggests that leaders should cultivate accountability in the lives of the millennials they mentor. Although we seek to learn from and work with millennials, the questions above can also inform a mentoring relationship built through critical listening and trust.[52] Millennials are great at sniffing out hypocrisy and have charged the church with this vice. Before you ask a millennial to practice accountability, witness it in your life and leadership first.

Second, *practice transparency*. Transparency complements accountability. It anticipates an intentionality through which you share your work and decisions with others, allowing them to assess whether you are keeping to covenants made or expectations placed. Transparency is a challenge for religious leaders, for they present with a superlative self, always having things under control. This self avoids conflict and likes to be liked. Should others find something absent or "wrong" in what a leader does, especially if conflict ensues, the leader may feel exposed, even disliked, and easily fall into shame. Transparency should not be understood as one airing one's laundry in public or offering disclosures that put others in a precarious position. That would suggest poor boundary keeping and even the abuse of power. For personal matters, seek a confidential conversation partner. Rather, we are speaking of disclosing professional *responsibilities* and *processes*: how decisions were made; what some of the anxieties and uncertainties are; what might be strengths, weaknesses, opportunities, and threats; how money is spent, and so on.

Practicing openheartedness, as the previous chapter encouraged, will speak to the fear and resistance one may have in practicing transparency. So too would being part of shared leadership and collaboration (see chapter 6). Inviting millennials and others to transparency will fail if you do not invite them into some of the decision-making processes central to your ministry. Inevitably that implies inviting millennials into your leadership. As I meet congregations and their leadership, I am struck that millennial leadership is seldom recognized. Transparency asks that you make the invisible visible. Remember, God said, "Never again will my people be put to shame" (Joel 2:27). You need not fear.

Third, *practice non-defensiveness*, for it supports transparency. One of the most common weaknesses pastoral leaders carry is defensiveness. We do not like to be seen as incompetent and disempowered or being called out for mistakes we made. We are thus quick to explain or give reasons for decisions made as others experience us as poor listeners or defensive. Being called on our mistakes feels like a personal attack. Research by The Center for Creative Leadership indicates that defensiveness in leaders make them less effective.[53] Effective leaders may be innovative, remain calm in anxious moments, proactive, reflective, and able to take risks, but when defensiveness creeps in, the effectiveness of their leadership diminishes. To be non-defensive goes one step beyond transparency in that it invites feedback. "High learning-agile individuals seek feedback, process it, and adapt themselves based on their newfound understanding of themselves, situations, and problems. . . . They are open to new experiences, seek challenges, and are willing to introduce new ideas and question 'norms.'"[54] Non-defensiveness also asks leaders to take time to reflect and seek why and how dynamics and processes unfold. The Center's research found that "defensive individuals were more likely to be rated as less effective by their managers on a number of competencies, including self-awareness, communication, ability to respond to complexity, ability to adapt, and ability to meet business objectives."[55] Furthermore, their research showed that the more successful one becomes, the less one is open to feedback. Considering one's role in successes and failures, being willing to receive new information or learn new approaches, and opening oneself to novel experience can take one beyond being defensive.

Fourth, *practice responsiveness*. Embedded in the practices mentioned—accountability, transparency, and non-defensiveness—is the ability to be responsive to what life and leadership bring you. The loss of ability to be responsive or psychologically flexible is the fast track to burnout. Still addressing accountability in her *Millennials Matter*, Danita Bye recommends "positive action rather than reaction" to leaders and their millennial mentees.[56] "What you do when you don't have to," she continues, "will determine what you will do when you can't help it."[57] Since reactivity comes naturally to a person in crisis, few leaders can avoid it when the message is clear: get more young people into the church, especially young families! As one's anxiety increases, so too one's reactivity, with self-reflection, discernment, and collaboration decreasing. Being responsive anticipates that one prepares for situations or events as much as possible.

Responsiveness is illuminated when we look into its conflicting practice: reactivity. Robert Anderson and Williams Adams help us understand reactive leadership, which they discuss in their *Mastering Leadership*. Anderson and Adams state that leaders tend to operate out of one of three stances: egocentric, reactive, or creative.[58] Seventy-five percent of leaders are reactive in their leadership! This leadership style is built around being compliant to outside forces, behavior first discovered and praised in childhood. "We are not aware of what is happening, we are simply breathing in the surrounding self-defining messages and constructing ourselves accordingly. We define ourselves, not from the inside out, but from the outside in," the authors write.[59] The reactive self is fused with its surroundings and, as a result, has poor work-life balance. *Mastering Leadership* identifies three types of reactivity: complying, protecting, and controlling.[60] *Complying types* are kind, caring, and supportive, vulnerable to reactivity in relationships where they seek acceptance and affirmation. In doing so, they'll give their power to others to be liked. *Protecting types* are naturally good at what they do and tend to be rational. Seeing themselves as intellectually superior to others, they maintain emotional distance from people, limiting their ability to influence and bring change. *Controlling types* are leaders whose accomplishments determine their sense of self. They use their power to beef up a vulnerable self and in doing so, are ineffective in working with others or toward a common goal.

What the three types of reactive leaders share is that their sense of self is externally defined. Overdetermined by a strength, the self manifests with weakness. Anderson and Adams encourage creative leadership, which we called significant leadership: leaders who operate from a creative mind, who learn not to be compliant to outside forces and draw on the inner strengths of themselves and others.[61]

A fifth practice that supports accountability is to *practice paradox*. Paradox is "a seemingly absurd or contradictory statement or proposition which when investigated may prove to be well founded or true."[62] A merciful, loving God who holds one accountable, judges, and punishes nations inevitably induces tension, inconsistency, and contradiction. So too a narrative around an omnipotent God who loves people and locusts that devour landscapes and lives. The tension or contradiction within paradox cannot be solved. Rather, one has to manage the polarities contained in the paradox. Denying the tension inherent to paradox by choosing one polarity over the other, thereby splitting reality, actually increases our existential anxiety, for we no longer honor the complexity of our experience. Paradox demands "double vision," the ability to hold onto two seemingly opposed realities or possibilities.[63] Splitting, seeing the world in opposites where one has to choose one of the two poles—right and wrong, black and white, rich and poor, saint and sinner, or the compassionate God who restores and the God who judges and punishes—leads to poor leadership at best.

Ministry contains many paradoxes: It is for profit *and* it's not for profit (it's about money vs. serving a larger purpose), it's about individuals *and* the organization (or denomination), it engages the sacred *and* the profane (serving God vs. committees, cleaning, etc.), it is inclusive *and* exclusive (members and those who are not members), it sees truth as timely *and* timeless (reinterpreting Scripture for today vs. eternal wisdom and truth), and it seeks products *and* is mindful to processes (increased membership or people saved vs. traveling with people through life).[64] The urge to dissolve a paradox is strong, as our culture thrives on such a way of looking at things. We forget that splitting is a defense mechanism; it is helpful in the short term for a moment of crisis, but not meant to become permanent behavior or an orientation to life. The ability to hold the tension awakened by paradox is an achievement not all leaders reach.[65] Avoiding critical inquiry on difficult topics or resisting the exploration of the moral nature of our universe (which will show reality in tones of gray, not black or white) comes naturally to leaders who defy accountability, transparency, non-defensiveness, and responsiveness. Such leaders disappoint themselves and fail those they lead. Without holding on to paradox, there is no possibility of accountability. Wise leaders know that.

Toward practicing accountability

Both YIMBYs and NIMBYs are concerned about what's happening in their own backyards. Each group's concern, however, is motivated by very different values. As Joel envisions a Day of Accountability, where all will face the choices they made, YIMBYs and NIMBYs may find themselves on opposite sides of the verdict to come. God is clear that self-protection, the exploitation of people, and stealing from lands and what is deemed sacred have consequences. Even power in the form of a mighty army will not be able to protect against the verdict. Joel might suggest another acronym: AIMBY—Accountability In My Back Yard! Like the Day of the Lord, which is a recurrent day and also one anticipated in the future, AIMBY anticipates daily discernment and accountability. Without AIMBY, there is no good life, not for oneself or one's neighbors! Without accountability, relationships, communities, cities, nations, but also the earth—"our blue boat home"—are increasingly at risk.[66] As water levels rise in some parts of the world, droughts plague other areas, and storms are more violent than ever, we will discover Joel's locusts in new ways. These forces will unleash a mass migration of peoples. A day of reckoning is coming.

In discovering the God who restores, we named *practicing advocacy* a key habit. We said that religion and doing ministry are always political for they shape cities. We are always partaking in either creating relationships and places where persons and the earth can thrive and flourish or we are destroying the gifts we have in others or have received. Those who practice accountability recognize a world in peril. The world suffers under

- food and water scarcity;
- housing too expensive for many;

- a lack of opportunities to be educated;
- corrupt leaders and dictators;
- mass human migration;
- the emotional and sexual exploitation of women, children, and the elderly;
- trans persons killed and living in fear;
- poverty;
- addictions;
- class struggles;
- religious extremism;
- wars and ethnic cleansing;
- climate change;
- and...

The valley of Jehoshaphat is getting crowded—we will be held accountable and face the consequences of our decisions.

Surprisingly—or maybe not—the book of Joel does not end with individuals and nations in a precarious place. An evocative image appears that speaks to the faithfulness of God, merciful and compassionate, very patient, full of faithful love and ready to forgive. The image deepens the hope already awakened and empowers persons to participate in God's restorative work. We discuss that image, contained in the following verse, next: "A spring will come forth from the Lord's house and water the Shittim Valley" (Joel 3.18).

Chapter Six
RESTORE

The God Who Nurtures and the Promise of Renewal

We have been looking at the book of Joel as a narrative that has six acts, each unfolding like waves on a beach. We have reached the final act, which we'll identify in a few verses only. Joel's conclusion is open-ended and suggests an ending that repeats itself with never-ending faithfulness. Once again one can find oneself in an age-old narrative. Media theorist Douglas Rushkoff reminded us in the introduction that having a narrative to live into is "comforting and orienting. It helps smooth out obstacles and impediments by recasting them as bumps along the way to some better place—or at least the end of the journey."[1] Joel is an "along the way" kind of book; it meets you where you are on the road of life and wants to comfort and empower you for the journey that continues. Along the way you encounter locusts, gather with others, discover a compassionate God, see visions, remain accountable, and discover the joy of being a positive difference in the world.

The 2017 Millennial Impact Report—a report researching millennial cause engagement annually since 2009—is a hopeful read.[2] The current report, surveying three thousand millennials and released in three phases, found that "millennials [are] quietly redefining terms long accepted in the cause and philanthropy space: Activist. Cause. Social issue. Ideology."[3] The researchers were interested in the social issues attracting millennials, measuring their level of engagement, and looking at the traits of millennial social involvement. We learn that millennials describe their social engagement using unique language (they do not identify being "activists"), that the greater good drives them to engagement and that they are more socially involved than ever, a fact attributed to the divisive 2016 presidential election in the United States. The report distinguishes between social issues and causes. A *social issue* is "a problem that affects a considerable number of individuals within a society. Examples include racism and sexism." A *cause*, in turn, is "a common action-oriented behavior aimed at a service-based or philanthropic end, generally one helping people and communities. Examples of causes include Black Lives Matter and the Women's March."[4] Millennials have been motivated and galvanized by many social issues, which they address with concrete behavior.

The researchers found that millennials care especially about the following social issues: racial discrimination, civil rights, and social justice; employment, poverty, and homelessness; education and literacy; children (mentoring and early education); higher education (access to and payment for); women's health and reproductive issues; healthcare reform; environmental issues; mental health and social services; criminal justice reform; and immigration. When ranked, racial discrimination, civil rights, and social justice, followed by employment, healthcare reform, climate change, and immigration came in as the most important concerns, with at least 20 percent of all respondents indicating the particular issue.[5]

The researchers were surprised to learn that millennials are hesitant to embrace the label "activist," finding the word militant in nature and implying a deeply personal involvement or commitment, which they may not feel toward a particular social issue.[6] Rather, they prefer being "an advocate," "an ally," or "a supporter" of a social cause. Forty-nine percent of the respondents saw themselves as supporters, 21 percent as activists, 17 percent as advocates, and 11 percent saw themselves as allies to specific causes.[7] A male respondent wrote, "I don't consider myself an activist, [just] someone who cares. 'Activist' can have a negative connotation to it, that it controls my life and it certainly doesn't do that. If it's a cause I care about, I don't mind donating my time and money to help." A woman replied, "I don't think I am an activist [because] I've always been very averse to protesting an issue. I'd rather help organize the protest than participate in it. But for me, activism doesn't have to be marching in the streets. . . . I can [be an activist] with what I do professionally and in my volunteering life." A third respondent said, "For me, by making a donation and talking to my friends about it, I might be inspiring action in others. I pay attention to where I spend my money too, [which is] the biggest impact you can have in certain areas. So, I would say I am [an activist], but not in the same way other people might think." Millennials may prefer being advocates, supporters, and allies, but their desire and actions to dismantle unjust systems and build just communities reflect some of the activism of the past.

A central trait in the social involvement millennials seek is "liberty and justice for all." The report maintains that the interviewees "wanted to give all people—but especially marginalized or disenfranchised individuals or groups—early interventions and opportunities that would ensure increased prosperity later in life."[8] One respondent stated, "The public education in [my city] is awful. Volunteering at the book bank was so eye-opening. A lot of these kids don't have books and if they don't have books, how are they going to read? If they can't read, how are they going to better themselves? It's one thing to say, 'Go better yourself.' But, you have to put the boots on the ground to do it." Another said, "Issues of immigration and especially fair treatment of our Latino neighbors, both those that come to the US and those outside the US, have been an interest of mine since high school. How I've been able to engage in that over the years has changed pretty significantly. I'd not been involved in political conversations revolving around immigration until more recently...and that has been a change." A third replied: "The intensity or level of commitment I now plan to assume is an awareness that we are going to have to re-litigate some of the issues we thought were put to bed. It's an acknowledgment that these [issues] are now open for change and shouldn't be, and it's a commitment [to ensuring] we don't go backward."

The key findings of the 2017 Millennial Impact Report showed that the millennial generation is maturing as changemakers. Specifically, the report found that, besides being mindful of how to label their activity, the vast majority—71 percent of the respondents—were unsatisfied or uncertain about the direction toward which the USA is moving; 73 percent were unsatisfied with the 2017 White House; 66 percent stated voting is really important to initiate change; and 77 percent saw voting as a civic duty.[9] Furthermore, the *Report* showed that the millennial generation prefer to be active locally and they recognize that slacktivism (action taken through social media) is important, but not the best way to bring about lasting change. A female respondent reflected a common theme among her peers: "I think it's inevitable that each person has a responsibility now to take care of our country... not just with infrastructure and things like that, but on a personal level. I don't want my kids growing up in this kind of environment."[10] Between voting, signing petitions, engaging social media, changing consumer practices, contacting political representatives, participating in marches and protests, and donating, millennials are making a difference.[11] The findings of the 2017 Millennial Impact Report do instill hope. As the time of boomer leadership is fading, a new social and political reality will dawn.

Making a difference in the world is the final touchpoint between the lives of millennials and the book of Joel. In this chapter, we reflect on an evocative and pervasive image from scripture, of water flowing forth from God's house or throne to nurture parched lands. We are invited to join in that work of restoration. Lindsey Krinks, a millennial making a difference in her city, introduces us to her street ministry. She embodies the spirit of Joel. Her pathos and imaginative approach can teach pastoral leaders and their congregations much. The chapter ends by identifying five practices significant leaders can embrace as they join the millennials around them to make a difference in their immediate communities.

Joel and flowing, renewing water

There are many themes that permeate scripture: creation and re-creation, God's enduring presence and grace, human brokenness, sacrifice and sin, the reign of God, the need for Sabbath, the need for justice, blessing, covenant, circumcision, the promised land, baptism, the life and ministry of Jesus, and the Spirit being poured out, to name but a few. There are also enduring images or moments: a garden, slavery, plagues; the exodus, wilderness wanderings; the temple; mountains; the Tower of Babel; miracles; the cross; and resurrection. A relatively unknown but pervasive image in scripture is water that flows, most often from God's temple, throne, or house—a sign of blessing. We find the image in the very first pages of scripture and it appears on the very last, as if bookends to the witness of God's relationship with humanity and all of creation.

Genesis 2, a creation narrative, tells of "a river [that] flows from Eden to water the garden, and from there it divides into four headwaters" (v. 10). The narrator of the creation myth draws on an ancient Egyptian belief that rivers flow from King Nun's mouth to nurture the earth. Eden, from an Aramaic word meaning "fruitful" or "watered," is marked by the Tigris and Euphrates Rivers where they meet the Persian Gulf, as well as by the Pishon and Gihon Rivers (they may have been mountain streams). The flowing water that nourishes the garden suggests abundance and life-giving power. As we begin to read of humanity's relationship with the creator, blessing and the gift of life define the story.

The psalmist picks up the theme of Eden's rivers and tells of a specific river. Psalm 36, attributed to David, praises God's unfailing protection and provision in the context of a person being persecuted. The people, David writes, "feast on the bounty of your house; you let them drink from your river of pure joy. Within you is the spring of life. In your light, we see light" (vv. 8-9). God, as the only "spring of life," overflows to all of creation, so that we too can have life. Since God lives in the temple, God's house and the spring or fountain that flows are inseparably linked. God's temple thus waters and sustains. Psalm 46, a communal psalm sung in the temple and used liturgically, continues this theme. After identifying God as "[a] refuge and strength" (v. 1)—a Mighty Fortress as Martin Luther would sing in his famous hymn—and naming the fear of chaotic waters of a storm at sea, the psalmist names a place that is safe with calm water that secures and renews: "There is a river whose streams gladden God's city, the holiest dwelling of the Most High" (v. 4). The Khorahites, those who sang in the temple and the creators of Psalm 46, use metaphoric language as they envision this river, for Jerusalem does not have a river. However, without water a city cannot be secure, thus the Khorahites envision a river flowing through Jerusalem.

The prophets were familiar with this river too. Drawing on the psalmist, Zechariah envisions the Day of the Lord and sees "running water [flowing] out from Jerusalem" (14:8). The water has healing and protective qualities securing the city when the surrounding nations succumb to a plague. The prophet Ezekiel has arguably the most vivid image of a river that flowed from beneath the temple's doors. Ezekiel is shown the river by God (or God's angel). It measured six thousand feet (or 1.13 miles) wide! Ezekiel inched in, first ankle deep, then knee deep, and when the water reached his waist he finally recognized it as a river too high to cross. He returned to shore to see the river flowing eastward to give new life to the lifeless water of the Dead Sea. Then he heard God speaking:

> Wherever the river flows, every living thing that moves will thrive. There will be great schools of fish, because when these waters enter the sea, it will be fresh. Wherever the river flows, everything will live. People will stand fishing beside it, from En-gedi to En-eglayim, and it will become a place for spreading nets. It will be like the Mediterranean Sea, having all kinds of fish in it. Its marshes and swamps won't be made fresh (they are left for salt), but on both banks of the river will grow up all kinds of fruit-bearing trees. Their leaves won't wither, and their fruitfulness won't wane. They will produce fruit in every month, because their water comes from the sanctuary. Their fruit will be for eating, their leaves for healing. (Ezek 47:9-12)

The river that flows from the temple gives life, provides food, and heals. Still, God keeps the people's salt source intact, as life without salt was not possible in the ancient Near East. The water's flow indicated the boundaries for Israel's territory, received as their inheritance. God, always looking out for the stranger and marginalized, commands Ezekiel, "When you distribute the land as an inheritance, the immigrants who reside with you and raise families among you are considered full citizens along with the Israelites. They will receive an inheritance along with you among the tribes of Israel. You will assign the immigrants' inheritance with the tribe with whom they reside. This is what the LORD God says" (Ezek 47:22-23).

Before we look at Joel's conclusion, one more "river text" comes to us via the Apostle John while in exile on the island of Patmos. We read about his vision in Revelation 22, the last chapter of the Bible. With echoes of Ezekiel's vision, John sees a river:

Then the angel showed me the river of life-giving water, shining like crystal, flowing from the throne of God and the Lamb through the middle of the city's main street. On each side of the river is the tree of life, which produces twelve crops of fruit, bearing its fruit each month. The tree's leaves are for the healing of the nations. (vv. 1-2)

John's vision proclaims the reign of Christ. Its sole purpose is to instill hope for a persecuted people. Revelation's heavenly river of life-giving, crystal-clear water carries the same themes as all the "river texts" in scripture: it indicates a source of life; it proclaims God's presence; it is central to all of salvation history; it flows outward, away from the temple in undefined ways; it gives power to trees, their leaves now able to heal; there is abundance— the river or fountain never runs dry; it connects God, the people, and the land in intimate ways; and the water that flows from God's throne or temple promises and works well-being and renewal.

Joel's vision came to him nearly six hundred years before John received his, and it seems unlikely that Joel relied directly on Ezekiel for his reference to "a spring will come forth from the LORD's house" (3:18). Still, the witness of God's Spirit in and through all the "river texts" is clear. After holding the nations accountable in the Day of the Lord, Joel envisions God settled in Zion and the people, now having a refuge, returned from exile. He concludes his book with two interacting messages, one for Judah and the other for their archenemies, Egypt and Edom:

In that day
> the mountains will drip sweet wine,
> the hills will flow with milk,
> and all the streambeds of Judah
>> will flow with water;
> a spring will come forth from the LORD's house
>> and water the Shittim Valley.
Egypt will become desolate
> and Edom a desolate wilderness.
This is because of the violence done to the people of Judah,
> in whose land they have shed innocent blood.

But Judah will be inhabited forever,
>> and Jerusalem for all generations.
I will forgive their bloodguilt,
>> which I had not forgiven.
I will act on their account;
>> I will not pardon the guilty.

The LORD dwells in Zion. (Joel 3:18-21)

Our narrative has a provocative ending, though not without controversy. Using "in that day," as Joel opens this last act, was a common way for the prophets to introduce new material to their oracles.[12] Some scholars feel the verses are a later addition, whereas Elie Assis and others—as we do—"see[s] unity between these verses and the rest of the book."[13] Previously, Assyria and Babylon had to face reckoning and be accountable for their actions. Now it is Egypt and Edom, rounding out the major enemies of Israel. As the Day of Accountability (see chapter 5) continues for the nations that rallied against Judah, those nations that had blood guilt on their hands face the consequences of their actions. Judah, in turn, discovers a new era is about to dawn. The land will erupt in abundance and fertility as water reaches desert soil.[14] Joel echoes the ending of Amos: "The mountains will drip wine, and all the hills will flow with it" (9:13). He refers to food stuff to metaphorically show the richness of God's renewal.[15] Upon hearing God speak through Joel, Judah, no doubt, would recall the promised land and the milk and honey discovered there.[16]

Joel's conclusion has two integrated parts, contrasting the difference between having been restored by God and living under the consequences of one's actions. Where mountains (Hebrew: *harim*) will drip with sweet wine (Hebrew: *asis*), Egypt and Edom will face desolation because of their violent treatment of Judah; where milk (Hebrew: *halab*) and water (Hebrew: *mayim*) will flow plentifully, violence (Hebrew: *mehamas*) and blood (Hebrew: *damam*) will flow for Judah's enemies. In both parts God resides in Zion (Hebrew: *mibbet*, from *bayith*).[17] Here Joel follows ancient Ugaritic lore that a god's dwelling place is next to a river.[18] We descend from mountains on high to hills and valleys with deep gorges (Hebrew: *nahal*) and on to streambeds and finally into the city. Every place humanity resides or works is covered by bounty because water from the temple flows there. Along the way, the drunkards who have been warned in the opening verses (1:5) receive sweet wine. Commentator Elie Assis writes that "the closing describes a new, rectified situation, completely different from what it has been."[19] In a reversal of fortunes, Judah and its wine drinkers, who knew desolation and shortage after the locusts, now experience abundance. Egypt and Edom, once renowned for their might, are now desolated.

As we follow the flow of the water from God's house, we enter the Valley of Shittim (or the Valley of Acacias). The valley has an ambivalent history for Israel. Here they had illicit sex with Moabite women and worshipped Baal of Peor (Num 25:1-3). It was also from the Valley of Shittim that Joshua sent his spies to explore the potential of Jericho and the promised land (Josh 2:1). Joel's Wadi Shittim, however, may not be the one Israel frequented on their sojourning. Joel's valley cannot be clearly identified, as that would mean that the spring or fountain that flows from God's house runs right through the Jordan River.[20] Rather, we assume a wadi in the Kidron Valley, possibly Wadi en-Nar, a dry gorge that runs into the Dead Sea. Since acacias prefer to grow in dry riverbeds, as we find on Africa's savannah, the reference to acacias makes sense.[21] Joel sees a barren valley and envisions it as a place of promise and potential, for the renewal God offers is complete.

A pastoral reading of our text is both challenging and hopeful. Simply stated, as we seek to live into the narrative of Joel, we are called to "flow" to our neighbors, to our communities and cities, to all of creation, in mercy and compassion, with patience and love, always ready to forgive. It takes but one look around us and our neighborhoods to recognize those persons and places ravaged by the locusts of life. After all, we have been devoured too. We have lamented and gathered, we've discovered the God who restores and we are now empowered by God's Spirit. We know that we will be held accountable for our choices and that not getting involved is not a wise choice. Being in relationship with God, we can participate in God's work of personal and political renewal and restoration. We thus saturate those we meet and the places we frequent with the waters that baptized some of us but is now flowing through all of us. We meet others where they are and without judgment, as "the Book of Joel is characterized by the absence of reproach to the people;

there is not even a mention of any sin."[22] As we participate in the world's personal, social, political, and ecological renewal, we need not fear, for our choices and actions will be kept in mind on the Day of Accountability. It is not easy work, but we can remind ourselves that we will not be shamed. Having tasted the abundance of God, we have plenty to share. God's economy is not a closed economy such that if we share God's abundance with others we'd have less to ourselves. Rather, the opposite is true. The more one gives, the more one receives.

The narrative of Joel has a strong internal movement of encouragement and rejuvenation. Where it began in despair, it ends with hope. Many millennials have joined a similar movement from despair to hope by being changemakers. In each chapter we've discovered a special young adult. Lindsey Krinks, another remarkable millennial, has quenched her thirst from the waters that flow from God's house. She now flows with loving-kindness to the people who live on the streets of Nashville, a city whose injustices and struggles cannot be drowned out by its great music.

Flowing into the streets
(Cowritten with Lindsey Krinks)[23]

Lindsey is a pastor and a street chaplain, but also an advocate, community builder, and changemaker. In 2010, Lindsey cofounded Open Table Nashville (OTN) with her friend and colleague Rev. Ingrid McIntyre. OTN is an interfaith homeless outreach nonprofit that disrupts cycles of poverty, journeys with the marginalized, and educates on issues of homelessness.[24] In 2008, Lindsey began serving Tent City, Nashville's largest homeless encampment, located on the banks of the Cumberland River. As Lindsey and Ingrid befriended the 140-plus residents, advocated for their rights, and partook in their lives, they were met with hospitality and discovered a vibrant community where people shared what they had, looked out for one another, and cared for their pets. After a flood in 2010 pushed the inhabitants of Tent City into a Red Cross shelter, the city of Nashville condemned Tent City. The struggle Lindsey and the inhabitants of Tent City had in the wake of the flood—depicted in the documentary *Tent City, U.S.A.* (available online)—led to OTN's incorporation as a nonprofit . The name "Open Table," Lindsay says, "means a place where everyone is welcome. It signifies fellowship, community and radical inclusion. In other words, we're not here just to make sure our friends on the streets get crumbs from the table. That is no more than charity. We're here to make sure our friends have a place at the table and that is about justice."[25] Participating in collective liberation, OTN also collaborates with other organizations on issues of race, health care, food justice, workers' rights, environmental justice, and the rights of immigrants, refugees, and the LGBTQ community.

Lindsey and OTN meet their friends who are un-housed on the streets as they serve those "invisible" in a growing tourist destination. Lindsey's typical day is filled with meeting persons where they are. "We go beneath bridges, trek through woods to carry supplies to homeless encampments, and visit families in roach-infested hotels. We build relationships, care for untended wounds, and help people navigate the resources they need to move from the streets into housing. We go to the people who have been forgotten and discarded by our society and seek to build community in the margins of empire."

People are met regardless of their physical, emotional, mental, or spiritual place. They are assisted to access support services and in acquiring permanent housing. Consistently, OTN claims a presence in the political sphere, advocating at Nashville Metro Council and Commission meetings. "People experiencing homelessness," Lindsey says, "are not problems to be solved or cases to be managed," attitudes often found in churches and in society. Rather, OTN works toward a community where all are welcome and nourished. This community goes beyond *charity*, the crumbs *of* the table, as it seeks *justice*, providing a place *at* the table. As OTN pursues "Housing, Healing, Hope," Lindsey and her volunteers are building a community beyond church walls where all can flourish.

Before the un-housed and precariously housed are helped, they are invited into caring and supportive relationships and even leadership roles at OTN. It is the strength of the community Lindsey and OTN build that supports OTN's friends as they receive and access life-changing and often life-saving care. Many come with histories of trauma, abuse, neglect, exploitation, addiction, and mental, emotional, and physical health issues that only now can be addressed. Lindsey and her coworkers also accompany people who are at the end of their lives, awaiting death.

At the heart of OTN's mission is building a community where people are respected and loved. "They also need to know that they are not alone, that someone cares for them and knows their name and story, and that they have a voice in their own process of healing and recovery," Lindsey believes. Building this community often begins on the streets with interfaith chaplaincy, but extends to camps, hospitals, prisons, and in providing end-of-life care. Through presence, accompaniment, and radical love and hospitality, persons are resurrected even as systems that discard, displace, and dehumanize seek to hold on to their power. Working alongside the very people society prefers to render invisible, Lindsey and OTN make a difference that benefits all who call Nashville home.

OTN's vision is not to plant churches or to point persons to faith communities. Still, Lindsey is quick to admit, "We would not exist without our partnerships with churches and faith communities. We are highly relational with the people we serve and also with the congregations we partner with in a symbiotic relationship." Congregations support OTN's work financially or with donation drives and OTN comes alongside churches by offering educational opportunities and trainings, introducing them to the friends on the streets, and better equipping faith communities "to do justice, embrace faithful love, and walk humbly with your God" (Mic 6:8). Churches who want to be involved in issues of homelessness in meaningful and sustainable ways, but often don't know how to do so, find in OTN a wonderful partner.

Lindsey has learned much from her friends: she has discovered that doing this work alone and isolated is not possible, that working in a team (or as a member of a community) sustains when the burden can be heavy. Furthermore, Lindsey realized early on not to be a "voice for the voiceless"—for her friends have their own voices, even if those voices need amplification at times. Her experience working alongside friends who are un-housed and precariously housed has given Lindsey a glimpse of what a life-giving ministry can look like. "I truly feel like this kind of community is like the 'beloved community' that Martin Luther King Jr. spoke so eloquently about," Lindsey says.

The work Lindsey and OTN do affirms four repetitive themes within *The Millennial Narrative*: Church leaders need to partner with someone like Lindsey whose place of ministry is on the streets and rarely in a church building unless she leads an education event. Millennials are reframing belonging and where belonging is found. They are changemakers, flowing in justice through their cities and into the world, and millennials are the priests of today.

RESTORE: Five practices for significant leaders

There is an inherent risk in being a religious or pastoral leader. One can have the illusion that in merely doing one's work, one is flowing with the grace and blessings to others. Such an understanding confuses one's call or vocation with the intentionality required to participate in God's renewal of humanity and creation. How ideal it would be to merely go through the motions of ministry and thereby do great work. The problem is this: the water that flows from God's throne always leaves the temple. An individual or a congregation can flow as life-giving water, unless, of course, they place themselves in a dam or build levees around them and soon become stagnant water. Such water does not give life, even to the one hoarding it. It seems as if building levees comes naturally to those who encounter locusts and receive God's promises. Or as a fountain we become a flash flood of judgment upon others as we erode made-of-topsoil-but-the-image-of-God persons and leave deep scars on the landscape of their souls. Flash floods never nurture the earth, that valley of acacias Joel calls us to. Sadly, flash floods in the public area, in politics, in the Twitterverse, and also in the church abound. Kelsey's story earlier warned us against this danger (see chapter 3).

Five practices can assist those leaders who want to flow as life-giving water and join God in the work of restoration and renewal:

First, *practice participation*. A popular theological theme is *participation*. It has a long history in ethics and religion, dating back to the thought of Plato. Participation "is the human counterpart of, or correlative to, God's activity in relation to humans and their involvement in not only society but nature."[26] Ethicist James Gustafson writes that participation is "a 'root metaphor,' a 'hermeneutical principle,' a 'template,' which comprehensively and coherently may help to integrate our intellectual and personal lives."[27] To practice participation thus speaks to the very essence of what it means to be a fulfilled person as one shares in co-creating the world God envisions for us. It is the foundation of an incarnational life: in loving one's neighbor, our neighbor experiences God's grace and we fade into the background. All participation stems from our being in a restored relationship with God, for we have returned to God, as Joel beckoned us. Practicing participation is driven by the question, what is God doing in my neighborhood and in the world? Joel and all the prophets participated in the actions of God. So too did Jesus and the twelve apostles. We participate too. Participation always moves toward a restored creation. We are continually called to join in that life-giving work. God is pleased when we do so. When we try to do that work of restoration ourselves, our effort will be greatly diminished, at best.

Through participation one discovers "a way of telling a story of a human life...and a story of life in general, but also a story of religious and moral experience insofar as it is grounded in and ultimately ordered by the Divine, by God."[28] Feeling that one is participating in God's life and ordering of our world—sharing something significant with God—instills passion, gives meaning, and provides a sense of having a moral compass. Participation shapes one's person, one's relationships, one's places of belonging, and also the world in general. When we do nothing or resist the work of renewal, it opens the possibility of participating in evil, for which one will be held accountable.[29] Participation, Gustafson concludes, demands commitment, "a special act of self-determination; obligations to oneself and to others follow from it in various forms of participation. One's moral integrity is at stake in keeping it."[30] There is no authenticity without participation and commitment.

Second, *practice volunteerism*. The easiest way to partake in the restorative work of God is to volunteer and to empower your congregation to do the same. Originally a word that implies signing up for military service, modern volunteering almost always anticipates community service. Opportunities to volunteer are boundless, including doing disaster relief work. Joel would recommend that you start local, there where the water that flows from your sanctuary first meets a dry, parched earth. A colleague, sent by the Red Cross to be a counselor when many were killed in Las Vegas by a gunman who shot at them while they attended a music concert, shared that those he spoke with resonated with Joel's warning of the fast-moving locusts that appear from nowhere. He reminded them of healing found within community and the God who restores.

Service-learning is part of American higher education and, as such, almost all millennials have volunteered. The Millennial Impact Report confirms that 70 percent of young adults are donating time and finances.[31] By volunteering you are joining the largest generation in an activity they know intimately. The gifts of volunteering are plentiful, ranging from living your faith outside your church, meeting people you'll rarely meet in your daily life, and learning new skills, to participating in the restorative work of God.

Third, *practice generativity*. Generativity speaks to living a creative and productive life, not because you partake in the market economy or climb the corporate ladder, but because you invest in the lives of others—especially the lives of the younger generation or persons marginalized in society. It asks, "How can you contribute to this world?" Psychologist Erik Erikson first pointed us to the importance of generativity for our emotional well-being. We engage it when we do acts of care.[32] Caring, however, is not such an easy task. It takes self-confidence, feeling secure in yourself. You need to have a sense of autonomy, the belief that *you* can do things because you have overcome any shame and doubt that plague you. Caring calls for initiative, that you can *do* things, gain new skills, and experience a sense of mastery. And caring is best done in relationships of mutuality, which requires a capacity for intimacy and vulnerability. Generativity contributes to society and includes the maintenance and rejuvenation of institutions—such as schools, churches, hospitals, prisons, and more, for without institutional health, personal flourishing is compromised. When we refuse to engage generativity, we become self-absorbed, selfish, and stuck in life. This, in turn, leads to despair, assessing your life negatively, regretting the decisions you have made, and wondering if you could have done better with your life.

Fourth, *practice collaboration*. Inherent to volunteering is working with others. *The Millennial Narrative* has been consistent in encouraging pastoral leaders to join millennials and partner with them where they are active in the world, rather than inviting or calling them to your church. Collaboration asks that you not replicate what others are already doing. So often we want to do our own thing, a trait most pastors have, spreading limited resources when those pooled resources can make a bigger difference. Faith communities often do not work together, finding doctrinal and other differences unbridgeable. This unfortunate reality is contrasted by the millennial experience. From *kindergarten*, millennials have been taught to get along with all and to work together. The older generations, for whom divisiveness comes naturally (baby boomers) or for whom doing things alone is more appealing (Gen Xers), can learn from them. Collaboration is deeper than merely working with other people toward a common cause. It includes collaborative leadership and welcoming millennials into the decision-making process (see chapter 2).

Finally, *practice self-care*. Participating in the work of God by restoring and bringing renewal to persons, communities, cities, and the earth demands much physical, emotional, relational, and spiritual output (or energy). Self-care is the wisdom that one cannot extend more energy than one is replenishing. Research indicates that between 40 and 50 percent of clergy have symptoms of burnout.[33] "Burnout is a psychological syndrome emerging as a prolonged response to chronic interpersonal stressors on the job. The three key dimensions of this response are an overwhelming exhaustion, feelings of cynicism and detachment from the job, and a sense of ineffectiveness and lack of accomplishment."[34] Comparing eighty-four studies on burnout, Christopher Adams and his colleagues name ten stressors accelerating burnout among clergy: role ambiguity; role conflict; and role overload; boundary violations; emotional triangulation; emotional isolation; exposure to crises; interpersonal attack; parishioners' need for help; and administrative demands.[35] As one participates in God's work of restoration, as one volunteers and collaborates with others, and as one practices generativity, nurturing self and soul, one's relationships and personal communities increase in importance. Without a physical body healthy and vital enough, without a vibrant spirit secure in itself and in relationships, the call to partake in God's restorative work is greatly weakened and may even fall on deaf ears.

Toward practicing restoration

Lindsey Krinks is a changemaker fully engaged in "the cause economy." So too is Jordan Somer, CEO of the Miss Amazing Pageant for persons with disabilities.[36] Likewise, Dream Rockwell, founder of the nonprofit called Cuddle the World, is bringing the arts, creativity, and hope to disadvantaged children all over the world.[37] Gabrielle Magid, founder of Stronger than Stigma, leads a movement that helps millennials with mental health concerns by actively working in making their and our emotional and mental world a better place.[38] There are thousands of millennials making a difference in this world, flowing with love and care and passion to others. Living in a multicultural, connected world, millennials have a deep awareness of what is happening locally and abroad.

The image of a fountain that constantly flows from God's house and restores communities small and large has parallel narratives in scripture. An unnamed man, follower of the prophet Elisha, died, leaving his unnamed wife with significant debt.[39] The debt collectors came knocking at her door. The widow, bitter in her grief and her uncertain financial future, asked, "Why God? Why did he have to die? My husband worked for the prophet Elisha, why am I on the brink of financial ruin? Who is going to care for me and my two children?" About to see her children taken from her to be sold into slavery, she visited with Elisha, half-blaming him and his God. Elisha, seemingly unaware of her grief, asked the widow what she had of value. She answered that she had only a small jar of olive oil. Olive oil was precious in those days, used for food; medicinal purposes; for religious rituals; and oil lamps, soap and skin care. It was a basic commodity, like salt, that no one could do without. Elisha told the widow to collect as many empty vessels as possible and then behind closed doors pour her little bit of oil into the jars. She followed the prophet's orders and soon all the jars she and her children could lay their hands on were filled. Unsure what to do next, the widow returned to Elisha, who advised her to sell the oil to her neighbors, use some of the money to pay off her debt, and use the leftover oil for personal use. Soon the miracle the widow experienced started flowing into her neighborhood. Many people in an unnamed town benefited from the oil, no one knowing its source. With the income she received from selling the oil, the widow saved the lives of her children and secured a future for her family. Previously hamstrung by the locust of loss and debt and pushed into uncertain resentment, the widow experienced boundless grace.

Such is the nature of the water that flows from God's house. People's lives are enriched, communities and cities are transformed, yet the source of the transformation often remains hidden. We hear echoes of Jesus's life and ministry, of a few loaves and fish that fed five thousand people, of water that assures one will never thirst again and of bread that keeps one from being hungry.[40] Joel's ending, as we stated, is open-ended. The flow of blessing and acts of restoration never end. The Christian myth tells us that we find ourselves living downstream from Eden, a garden home forever lost. There we find locusts, droughts, and rivers turning into blood. Thank God that we also live downstream from the water that flows from God's house. Going outside, we see water flowing to devastated lives and desolated lands, for the locusts of life can linger. Many persons and communities have no experience of God's restorative work. Yet God's promises are true for all. God's spirit is alive in all, also the ones living with the locusts of life today. Joel's vision invites all people to the water to drink deeply and to splash and play together. Go outside, join God in making a difference, and get your feet wet!

Conclusion

The book of Joel is the millennial narrative. It is for all young people who know loss and trauma, crisis and mourning, the only experiences the locusts of life bring. It is for those who gather and build community. The narrative is for all longing to meet God, merciful and compassionate, very patient, full of faithful love, and ready to forgive—the God who restores. It beckons those who seek to deepen their spirituality, who want to dream dreams and see visions in hope. Joel's narrative is for millennials who believe accountability is important, for we will face the consequences of our decisions and actions. And it is the narrative for all who are already making a positive difference in this world or who seek to do so. The narrative invites one into a larger narrative, a story that resonates deeply with one's lived experience. That the narrative remains inspiring after twenty-five hundred years speaks to its enduring wisdom.

The book of Joel, thankfully, is not *only* for millennials. Rather, it is a book for every generation seeking to live a life of faith in an archetypal, age-old, and personal way. All people, regardless of age, need to be intentional in how they live life, which includes a life of faith. Joel offers us a compelling narrative to live into:

> There was a person who knew the locusts of life. The locusts caused devastation, loss, and trauma. He/she/they mourned the losses and sought healing for the traumas by building life-giving communities and nurturing his/her/their spirituality. He/she/they discovered the compassionate God who promises restoration and pours the Spirit over all. The person(s) embraced accountability, knowing that decisions made and actions taken have consequences. He/she/they participated in God's restorative work toward a just society and a sustainable earth. The person(s) lived the good life.

Throughout the book we have drawn on the power of scripture to invite transformation by disclosing a validated or new reality. Scripture shares this power with all narratives, but the ones in scripture are different, for people have found divine inspiration in them for three thousand years. Hebrew Bible scholar Christopher Seitz is correct when he writes that "the Book of Joel is a solemn, dramatic presentation of [the Day of the Lord] in which the generation depicted and all generations to come are to find a template for repentance, a turning to the Lord and in consequence the promise of forgiveness and deliverance."[1] If the challenge of pastoral leadership is "making God real," then inviting millennials into a larger narrative where they can discover that God is a wise choice.[2]

Using a prophetic text to guide restoration of lives and renewal of faith communities has validity. Old Testament scholar Walter Brueggemann reminds us that prophets bring an alternative consciousness , creating "the sense that new realities can be trusted and relied upon just when the old realities had left us hopeless. It is the task of the prophet to bring to expression the new realities against the more visible ones of the old order. Energizing is closely linked with hope."[3]

The prophet Joel brings hope for a time such as ours

The Millennial Narrative joins authors who recognize our narrative existence. Pastor Tim Keel argues in his *Intuitive Leadership* that we live "a storied life." "People want to see and hear stories and experience their own stories in the context of larger, maybe more dramatic, more explicit, or more intense ones....Stories connect our little lives with the world around us and help us discover who we are. The Bible is a storybook."[4] Keel sees us moving from a "storied life" to a "storied faith," for "we are story-generating people. We are not passive observers of others and their goings-on."[5] Our storied existence helps shape and create our identities. Evocative and compelling narratives such as Joel's become a mirror in which we can see ourselves. Intuitive leaders—we used the language of significant leaders—recognize the importance of narrative and invite persons into larger narratives where they can discover themselves anew. They recognize that people generally do not connect their own story with larger ones, for the illusion that we create our own narratives is alluring. Narrative, Keel reminds us, is the saving grace in a "post-" world of postmodernity, post-Enlightenment, and post-Christendom, as it allows for embodiment, authenticity, and integration (when fragmentation would be the norm).[6] Keel writes that intuitive leaders carry certain postures. "Postures refer to a person's bearing or attitude" and "a way to engage the world."[7] Keel recommends avoiding a defensive posture, for that leads others to experience you as suspicious and passive-aggressive. He identifies nine postures supporting effective leadership: listening, vulnerability, availability, stillness, surrender (to chaos), cultivation (of a hospitable environment), trust, joy, and a posture of dependence. Since postures live in the background, Keel inspects his postures, for postures "reveal what we believe about God, the Bible, the world, and ourselves."[8]

Leaders who can embrace our storied existence will find in Joel a narrative that opens a new way forward.

For individuals, a community and a congregation

One can argue that *a person* does not exist. There is only a person *with* her body; a person *with* family, friends, and neighbors; a person *with* a society; a person *with* the creator; a person *with* locusts. It is an illusion, fueled by a principle such as Descartes's "I think, therefore I am," that we are independent. We are tied to many layers of different relationships. Being utterly alone is nearly impossible, for we also internalize our relationships and carry people with us, even when no one is in sight. Still, loneliness in our culture is pandemic and a heavy burden to carry. To question whether this book is for individuals or communities is thus easy to answer.

The Millennial Narrative is for every person, every community, and every congregation. I have yet to meet a person or a people untouched by the locusts of life. Joel says: "Gather!" He knows that there is only a person *with* a community as the narrative oscillates between the individual and the communal. When God pours out the Spirit over young and old, men and women, and those free and those tied to masters, God does so, not for individual enrichment, but in order to restore persons and the world. The narrative speaks most powerfully if read by individuals *in* community: groups of friends, recovery or Bible study groups, or congregations (see the study guide and listen to the music album, *We Will Remember*, supporting this book). We all can gain much from Joel.

As you've noticed, every chapter of *The Millennial Narrative* ends with certain practices given to facilitate meeting, partnering with, and learning from the millennial generation. In all, thirty practices are identified, all of which a congregation can embrace. Philosopher Alasdair MacIntyre defines a practice as "any coherent and complex form of socially established cooperative human activity through which goods internal to that form of activity are realized in the course of trying to achieve those standards of excellence which are appropriate to and partially definitive of, that form of activity."[9] For MacIntyre, practices teach and inform. They are inherently political as they shape our reality and carry with them moral values. The internal goods of a practice mean that we gain certain things by engaging the practice. In practicing mourning we lament, discover a new identity, and hope is awakened. For MacIntyre, practices enrich both the individual and the community, the external goods of a practice. Through practices we seek, individually and communally, to change our world. For persons of faith, we seek to change the world according to God's values and norms. We know that practices are *historical*—people do things over time; *social*—people do things together; *universal*—they are fundamental to humankind and are in all societies; *local*—people in different cultures and contexts engage practices differently; and practices are *transformational*—they are done in response to and in the light of God's active presence. In addition, they have a *witnessing* aspect—they imply certain beliefs about God, ourselves, our neighbors.[10]

The practices identified in these pages seek to empower transformation—of leaders, their communities, and the people the leaders and the communities will meet and welcome. There might be no revitalization for the church without living into a wide range of customs and habits. Traditional practices such as baptism, communion, prayer, worship, and marriage are important, but not sufficient. In the chapters, we identified thirty leadership practices that serve especially, but certainly not exclusively, the millennial generation:

•Awareness
•Empathy
•Mourning
•Empowerment
•Hope

RECOGNIZE

•Joining
•Witnessing
•Warmth
•Rites and Rituals
•Participatory Leadership

GATHER

•Mirroring
•Memory
•Invitation
•Appreciation
•Advocacy

DISCOVER

Leadership Practices Serving Millennials

RECEIVE

•Openheartedness
•Spirituality
•Bracketing & Holding
•Vision Catching
•Clarity

•Accountability
•Transparency
•Non-defensiveness
•Responsiveness
•Paradox

BE ACCOUNTABLE

RESTORE

•Participation
•Volunteerism
•Generativity
•Collaboration
•Self-care

RECOGNIZE

For the church to be revitalized, pastoral leaders have to empower their communities to meet, learn from, and work with millennials. Where a leader would resist this work, the community is likely to resist the work too. Leaders, after all, wield much power in establishing the customs and habits a congregation extends to itself and offers the world.

Is The Millennial Narrative a "half-story"?

In *The Next Christians: Seven Ways You Can Live the Gospel and Restore the World*, author Gabe Lyons raises an important point. "God's story," he writes, "is made up of four key parts: creation, fall, redemption, restoration.... The truncated Gospel that is often recounted is faithful to the fall and redemption pieces of the story, but largely ignores the creation and restoration components."[11] "Half-story versions," Lyons continues, "begin abruptly in Genesis 3, where the separation of humanity from God is the opening scene."[12] The (millennial) generation, Lyons contends, sees itself and creation as good and wants to restore the world, when the church focuses on sin and redemption. The disconnect is obvious.

Between "relearning restoration," being "Creators" and "In Community," but also being "Civil" and "Countercultural," which are various ways Lyons offers to live the gospel and restore the world, there is much overlap between his project and *The Millennial Narrative*. Both projects seek to inform meaningful living, reach the millennial generation, and empower renewed faith communities. However, the two books also differ significantly, and this difference, no doubt, was felt by readers throughout. Whereas Lyons has a christological reading of a life of faith, we accept the historical and narrative integrity of the book of Joel. To argue that the book of Joel, without Jesus, is a half-narrative would be poor biblical interpretation and rash. Jesus is not the hermeneutical lens one needs to read Joel, even if the first believers in "the Upper Room" made a connection between their experience and the Spirit poured out in Joel (Acts 2) and references to Jesus's life and ministry can be found throughout *The Millennial Narrative*. A christological lens, with its focus on Jesus's ministry and teachings as well as his role in salvation, would be appropriate for interpreting all of the New Testament, but may not be so to understand the rest of scripture. We can agree or disagree on the importance of a christological focus, but very few Hebrew Bible scholars studying Joel would embrace a christological reading. Rather, we can place Jesus's life in the framework Joel provides, from knowing the locusts of life, to being compassionate and participating in the restoration of lives.

This book is written for pastoral leaders rooted in the Christian tradition. I imagine them making associations to the life and ministry of Jesus throughout. Such a reading would be supported by reception theory's understanding that readers of texts make the texts their own, always reading through multiple personal and cultural lenses. *The Millennial Narrative* envisions inviting a generation of persons who are not Christian—the nones and the somes—into a larger narrative, one that can lead to discover the person of Jesus. If we accept Lyons's argument that "God's story" has four components—creation, fall, redemption, restoration—then Joel is a full story, offering a complete narrative for a life of faith. It needs no additions or lenses to read through, even if such choices by the reader are valid.

So, is *The Millennial Narrative* a "half-story"? No, the book of Joel is a complete narrative, unfolding in various acts. The question may hide security found in doctrine and tradition, but does not reckon with how narrative functions in our lives. The question avoids the centrality of lived experience in finding purpose and meaning in one's life. It also has a weak understanding of the millennial generation and the cultural dynamics that shape them. Their deep distrust in institutions and what institutions offer is a hindrance all pastoral leaders have to overcome. Joel can help.

Still, we have not discussed aspects of worship, the use of small groups, or even using social media, to name but three ministry components pastoral leaders often focus on. The reasons for not doing so have been stated, though not directly tied to these components. If the call of Joel is to meet millennials where they already are making a difference in the world, worship, at least initially, should not be a primary focus. Millennials are not so much interested in what kind of worship they receive as in seeking to be part of worship leadership.[13] When church leadership invites young adults to shape worship, practicing openheartedness (see chapter 4), the congregation's worship will change. Likewise, a program such as a small group for millennials will never be stronger than the quality of relationships the church leadership has with young adults and that group's activity in their neighborhood and city. Most if not all congregations have a website, a Facebook page, maybe even a Twitter or Instagram account. These platforms are part of the public face of a congregation. Social media, however, is mostly ineffective without existing relationships being the link between persons and groups. If the main purpose of social media is to bring persons to a congregation, it's likely to fail. The nature and effectiveness of a congregation's social media will change radically once leadership and members of the congregation have joined millennials around the various issues and causes they are passionate about.

One can imagine a life of faith and a ministry built around the book of Joel in terms of directional difference. Whereas traditional approaches would do anything to get millennials *into* the church and "save" them, *The Millennial Narrative* has argued for the building of relationships *outside* and *beyond* the church's walls and recognizes the spiritual gifts millennials received. Join millennials in what they are already doing and learn from them about bringing God's justice and restoration to all of humanity and creation. We envision doing ministry *with* millennials.

So what can a leader do next?

We argued that Joel's narrative does not end, that the water that flows from God's house never runs dry. Though this is a hopeful image and a significant theological truth, what should one do next? *The Millennial Narrative* is one of four complementary components that supports this project. In addition to this book, there are online sermon outlines to help leaders preach through the book of Joel (find it at www.themillennialnarrative.com), a study guide to work through Joel in adult education settings or small groups, and a music album featuring core texts set to music (find *We Will Remember: Songs inspired by the Book of Joel* on iTunes and anywhere music can be downloaded). If we need a narrative to live into, the most basic argument this book makes, then finding that narrative through music offers another possibility. Music flows to us, and through song, we can flow to others. Millennials, we know, love music.

As you continue to travel with Joel, here are ten recommendations that can assist you in discerning your next steps:

1. As a leader, revisit the book of Joel now that you have been shown its significance. Take the time to live into the narrative until it shapes you. Resist the rush to find a sermon series for next week.

2. Choose *one* practice from each chapter highlighted in *The Millennial Narrative* and start living into those practices. No

doubt you are already practicing many of the suggested habits, customs, and ways of living, but be intentional about it.

3. Invite eight to ten core leaders in your congregation, possibly persons already flowing with God's love beyond your church's walls, to read *The Millennial Narrative* with you. Together choose *one* highlighted practice from each chapter and live into those practices as a group.

4. Preach through the book of Joel. Find assistance at www.the millennialnarrative.com.

5. Ask your church musician(s) to teach the congregation the music from the companion album specially created to support *The Millennial Narrative*. The music can support your worship. Find the music on iTunes and other download sites, or at www.the millennialnarrative.com.

6. Begin an adult education series on the book of Joel and use *The Millennial Narrative Participant Guide* to assist you. The series can complement your preaching through the book of Joel.

7. Invite the millennial members of your congregation to read through *The Millennial Narrative* with you.

8. Join millennials as they make a difference in your neighborhood, town, or city. Discover what they do online, look out for flyers posted in coffee shops, or contact a local campus ministry to hear what services the students are involved in.

9. Invite members of your congregation, beginning with the group you identified in #3, to join you in working at a Habitat for Humanity build with millennials, cleaning up a river stream, writing the city council, volunteering, and participating in other forms of service and advocacy.

10. Prayerfully wait for God's restorative work to unfold in your congregation and immediate neighborhood. Because the church is relevant outside its walls, persons will gather with you when you do.

The book of Joel certainly does not offer a miracle fix for a congregation in desperate need of new members or finances. Rather, Joel's promise is that it gives meaning and purpose to all who make the narrative their own. It will restore lives and renew communities as God's blessings first flow to you and then on to others. Millennials are willing to take risks and act for something they believe in. Joel affirms their commitments. Accept the invitation to walk with others in God's ways. You and your community will be restored and grow.

Notes

Introduction

1. Neil Howe and William Strauss, *Millennials Rising: The Next Great Generation* (New York: Vintage Books, 2000).

2. See Ronald Alsop, *The Trophy Kids Grow Up: How the Millennial Generation Is Shaking Up the Workplace*, 1st ed. (San Francisco: Jossey-Bass, 2008); Tim Elmore, *Generation iY: Our Last Chance to Save Their Future* (Atlanta: Poet Gardener Publishing, 2010); Jon Perrin, *The Coming Post-Christian Tsunami: Connecting with an Increasingly Unchurched Culture* (Lexington: Jon Perrin, 2016); Jean M. Twenge, *Generation Me: Why Today's Young Americans Are More Confident, Assertive, Entitled—and More Miserable Than Ever Before* (New York: Free Press, 2006); Christian Smith et al., *Lost in Transition: The Dark Side of Emerging Adulthood* (Oxford: Oxford University Press, 2011); Jennifer M. Silva, *Coming Up Short: Working-Class Adulthood in an Age of Uncertainty* (New York: Oxford University Press, 2013); Lynne C. Lancaster and David Stillman, *When Generations Collide: Who They Are, Why They Clash, How to Solve the Generational Puzzle at Work* (New York: HarperCollins, 2002).

3. The Pew Research Center, "U.S. Public Becoming Less Religious," http://www.pewforum.org/2015/11/03/u-s-public-becoming-less-religious/, accessed October 11, 2016.

4. Elizabeth Drescher, *Choosing Our Religion: The Spiritual Lives of America's Nones* (Oxford: Oxford University Press, 2016), 20.

5. *The Concise Oxford Dictionary of English Etymology*, ed. T. F. Hoad (Oxford: Oxford University Press, 2003), www.oxfordreference.com, accessed October 21, 2016.

6. Alan Cooperman, Gregory Smith, and Katherine Ritchey, "America's Changing Religious Landscape: Christians Decline Sharply as Share of Population; Unaffiliated and Other Faiths Continue to Grow," http://www.pewforum.org/2015/05/12/americas-changing-religious-landscape/, accessed June 9, 2015.

7. Drescher, *Choosing Our Religion*, 16.

8. Ibid., xi, 31.

9. Ibid., 5.

10. For moralistic therapeutic deism, see Christian Smith and Melinda Lundquist Denton, *Soul Searching: The Religious and Spiritual Lives of American Teenagers* (New York: Oxford University Press, 2005), 118.

11. Dietrich Bonhoeffer, *Letters and Papers from Prison* (New York: Macmillan, 1972), 279.

12. Ibid., 360.

13. Anthony C. Thiselton, "Reception Theory, H. R. Jauss and the Formative Power of Scripture," *Scottish Journal of Theology* 65, no. 3 (2012): 289.

14. The essay "Culture and Personality: A Conceptual Scheme" first appeared in 1944. Pastoral theologians will find interest in Kluckhohn and Murray's essay, for they find the source of personal uniqueness—like no other person—in trauma and group membership. Fellow Harvard psychologist Gordon Allport warns against "one pitfall" in Kluckhohn and Murray's formula: the individual can be seen as "only a handful of residual and perhaps negligible, idiosyncrasies, a leftover when we have accounted for most of his behavior in terms of universal or group norms. The facts are otherwise. . . . [A person] weaves them all into a unique idiomatic system." See Gordon W. Allport, *Pattern and Growth in Personality* (New York: Holt, 1961), 14-15. For the use of this dictum in pastoral theology, see Emmanuel Yartekwei Lartey,

In Living Color: An Intercultural Approach to Pastoral Care and Counseling, 2nd ed. (New York: Jessica Kingsley, 2003).

15. Generational observations about baby boomers and their children (who are now young adults) over the past thirty years are not as predictable as they seemed to be in the early 1990s. The generalizations can now be nuanced by massive amounts of digital data from government census taking, consumer preferences about purchases (including reading, food, entertainment, and much more), and behaviors or group affinities analyzed among billions of individuals around the world on social media. These data have been organized regionally into more than seventy lifestyle demographics by database brokers such as Experion. For further information on how lifestyle demographics affect churches trying to reach young adults in a community, see Thomas G. Bandy, *Sideline Church: Bridging the Chasm Between Churches and Cultures* (Nashville: Abingdon Press, 2018).

16. Joy D'Souza, "Xennials, the Microgeneration between Gen X and Millennials," *The Huffington Post,* http://www.huffingtonpost.ca/2017/06/28 /xennials_a_23006562, accessed July 11, 2017.

17. Pew Research Center, "Millennials Overtake Baby Boomers as America's Largest Generation" (2016), http://www.pewresearch.org/fact -tank/2016/04/25/millennials-overtake-baby-boomers, accessed October 12, 2016.

18. Pew Research Center, "Millennials in Adulthood: Detached from Institutions, Networked with Friends" (2014), http://www.pewsocialtrends. org/2014/03/07/millennials-in-adulthood, accessed October 12, 2016.

19. Ad Age Insights and Univision, "The Cultural Connection: How Hispanic Identity Influences Millennials," http://gaia.adage.com/images/bin /pdf/Hispanic%20Millennials.pdf, accessed August 14, 2017.

20. For select texts, see Twenge, *Generation Me* (New York: Atria Books, 2014); Don Tapscott, *Grown Up Digital: How the Net Generation Is Changing Your World* (New York: McGraw-Hill, 2009); Howard Gardner and Katie Davis, *The App Generation: How Today's Youth Navigate Identity, Intimacy, and Imagination in a Digital World* (New Haven: Yale University Press, 2013); Paul Verhaeghe and Jane Hedley-Präole, *What About Me?: The Struggle for*

Identity in a Market-Based Society (London: Scribe, 2014); Gabe Lyons, *The Next Christians: Seven Ways You Can Live the Gospel and Restore the World* (Colorado Springs, CO: Multnomah Books, 2010); Drescher, *Choosing Our Religion* (New York: Oxford, 2016); Perrin, *The Coming Post-Christian Tsunami: Connecting with an Increasingly Unchurched Culture* (Boerne, TX: Perrin Ministries, 2016); Derryck McLuhan, *From Religion to Relationship* (self published, 2015); Victor Shane, *The Authentic Life: A Guidebook for Millennials* (Bloomington, IN: Westbow, 2017); Silva, *Coming Up Short*: Working-Class Adulthood in an Age of Uncertainty (New York: Oxford, 2015); Joshua Best, *Y: Christian Millennial Manifesto* (Holland, MI: Unprecedented Press, 2017); Kara Powell, Jake Mulder, and Brad Griffin, *Growing Young: Six Essential Strategies to Help Young People Discover and Love Your Church* (Grand Rapids, MI: Baker Books, 2016); Bob Whitesel and Kent R. Hunter, *A House Divided: Bridging the Generation Gaps in Your Church* (Nashville: Abingdon Press, 2000); Chuck Underwood, *The Generational Imperative: Understanding Generational Differences in the Workplace, Marketplace, and Living Room* (North Charleston, SC: BookSurge, 2007); William Strauss and Neil Howe, *Generations: The History of America's Future, 1584 to 2069* (New York: Quill, 1991); Thom S. Rainer and Jess W. Rainer, *The Millennials: Connecting to America's Largest Generation* (Nashville: B & H, 2011); John G. Palfrey and Urs Gasser, *Born Digital: Understanding the First Generation of Digital Natives* (New York: Basic Books, 2008); Terry Nance, *Awaken: Letters from a Spiritual Father to This Generation* (New Kensington, PA: Whitaker House, 2016); Jeff Myers, *Cultivate: Forming the Emerging Generation through Life-on-Life Mentoring* (Deluth, GA: Legacy Worldwide 2010); Carolyn A. Martin and Bruce Tulgan, *Managing the Generation Mix: From Urgency to Opportunity*, 2nd ed. (Amherst: HRD, 2006); Lancaster and Stillman, *When Generations Collide*; New York: HarperBusiness, 2003); David Kinnaman, *Unchristian: What the New Generation Really Thinks About Christianity... and Why It Matters* (Grand Rapids, MI: Baker Books, 2007); N. J. A. Humphrey, *Gathering the NeXt Generation: Essays on the Formation and Ministry of GenX Priests* (New York: Morehouse Publishing, 2000); Linda Gravett and Robin Throckmorton, *Bridging the Generation Gap: How to Get Radio Babies, Boomers, Gen Xers, and Gen Yers to Work Together and Achieve More* (Franklin Lakes, NJ: Career Press, 2007); Richard Flory and Donald Miller, *Finding Faith: The Spiritual Quest of the Post-Boomer Generation* (New Brunswick, NJ: Rutgers University Press, 2008); Elmore, *Generation iY* (Los Angeles: Elevate Entertainment, 2015); Pew Research Center, "Millennials Projected to Overtake Baby Boomers as America's Largest Generation" (www.pewresearch.org, March 1, 2018); Misti Burmeister, *From Boomers to Bloggers: Success Strategies across Generations* (Fairfax, VA: Synergy, 2008); Alsop, *The Trophy Kids Grow Up* (San Francisco: Jossey-Bass, 2008); Monte Sahlin and David Roozen, *How Religious Congregations Are Engaging Young Adults in America* (Hartford, CT: Hartford Institute for Religion Research, 2015).

21. Strauss and Howe, *Generations.*

22. Arthur Levine and Diane R. Dean, *Generation on a Tightrope: A Portrait of Today's College Student*, The Jossey-Bass Higher and Adult Education Series (San Francisco: Jossey-Bass, 2012), x–xi.

23. Robin Wilson, "An Epidemic of Anguish," Special Issue: Today's Anguished Students—and How to Help Them, *Chronicle of Higher Education*, (2015): 4.

24. Mordecai Schreiber, "I Will Pour out My Spirit on All Flesh (Joel 3:1)," *Jewish Bible Quarterly* 41, no. 2 (2013): 123.

25. Elie Assis, *The Book of Joel: A Prophet between Calamity and Hope*, Library of Hebrew Bible/Old Testament Studies (New York and London: Bloomsbury/T&T Clark, 2013), 3.

26. Ibid., 216.

27. Aaron Schart, "The First Section of the Book of the Twelve Prophets: Hosea-Joel-Amos," *Interpretation* (2007): 148.

28. James L. Crenshaw, "Joel," *The Anchor Bible* (New York: Doubleday, 1995), 35.

29. Ronald L. Troxel, *Joel: Scope, Genres, and Meaning*, Critical Studies in the Hebrew Bible (Winona Lake, IN: Eisenbrauns, 2015), 38; John Barton, *Joel and Obadiah: A Commentary*, The Old Testament Library (Louisville: Westminster John Knox, 2001), 1.

30. Crenshaw, *Joel*, 45.

31. Troxel, *Joel*, ix, 97. See Troxel for a discussion on the functioning of genre in the prophetic tradition and how the book of Joel has been received.

32. Barton, *Joel and Obadiah*, 19.

33. Here Joel follows Ezekiel, who has a similar message for the exiles living in Babylon. See Ezekiel 37. Deutero-Isaiah had a similar word of comfort. Assis, *The Book of Joel*, 23.

34. Troxel, *Joel*, 97.

35. Crenshaw, *Joel*, 11. Seven biblical books are shorter: Obadiah (twenty-one verses), Haggai (thirty-eight verses), Nahum (forty-seven verses), Jonah (forty-eight verses), Zephaniah (fifty-three verses), Malachi (fifty-five verses), and Habakkuk (fifty-six verses).

36. See Assis, *The Book of Joel* (23–39) for a discussion of these theories.

37. Ronald T. Hyman, "The Prophecy of Joel: The Prophet's Message, Beliefs, and Prophetic Style," *Jewish Bible Quarterly* 39, no. 4 (2011): 225.

38. Assis, *The Book of Joel*, 11.

39. Troxel, *Joel*, 11.

40. Ibid.

41. Ibid., 69.

42. Theodore R. "Ted" Sarbin (1911–2005) is recognized as a pioneer of narrative psychology, a topic he researched from 1985 until the time of his death. See Joseph De Rivera and Theodore R. Sarbin, *Believed-in Imaginings: The Narrative Construction of Reality*, 1st ed. (Washington, DC: American Psychological Association, 1998); Theodore R. Sarbin, *Narrative Psychology: The Storied Nature of Human Conduct* (New York: Praeger, 1986).

43. Bradford J. Hall, *Among Cultures: The Challenge of Communication*, 2nd ed. (Belmont, CA: Thomson Wadsworth, 2005), 73.

44. Ibid.

45. Ibid., 74–81.

46. John Barton, "Reflections on Biblical Criticism," in *Method Matters: Essays on the Interpretation of the Hebrew Bible in Honor of David L. Petersen*, ed. David L. Petersen, Joel M. LeMon, and Kent Harold Richards (Atlanta: Society of Biblical Literature, 2009), 533.

47. Hans Robert Jauss (1921–97), a colleague of Wolfgang Iser, remains the effective founder of reception theory or reception history. Following Hans-Georg Gadamer's *Wirkungsgeschichte* (history of effect or history of influence), Jauss insisted that texts carry unfinished meaning, vulnerable to historical interpretation. Readers, when interpreting texts, complete the meaning of the text as the text satisfies, surpasses, disappoints, or refutes the reader's expectations. *Wirkungsgeschichte* leads to *Rezeptionsgeschichte* (or reception theory). See Hans Robert Jauss, *Toward an Aesthetic of Reception* (Minneapolis: University of Minnesota Press, 1982); Choon Leong Seow, "Reflections on Reception History," in *Method Matters: Essays on the Interpretation of the Hebrew Bible in Honor of David L. Petersen*, ed. David L. Petersen, Joel M. LeMon, and Kent Harold Richards (Atlanta: Society of Biblical Literature, 2009).

48. Thiselton, Anthony C. Thiselton, "Reception Theory, H. R. Jauss and the Formative Power of Scripture," 295.

49. Denise Ackermann, *After the Locusts: Letters from a Landscape of Faith* (Grand Rapids, MI: Eerdmans, 2003).

50. Douglas Rushkoff, *Present Shock: When Everything Happens Now* (New York: Current, 2013), 39.

51. Ibid., 77.

52. For a discussion of the paradoxical nature of narratives, see Kenneth J. Gergen and Mary M. Gergen, "Narrative Tensions: Perilous and Productive," *Narrative Inquiry* 21, no. 2 (2011): 380.

Chapter 1: Recognize

1. See "A Family Crisis or Families in Crisis," in Craig Kennet Miller and MaryJane Pierce Norton, *Making God Real for a New Generation: Ministry*

with Millennials Born from 1982 to 1999 (Nashville: Discipleship Resources, 2003), 45–52.

2. Jacques Derrida, Pascale-Anne Brault, and Michael Naas, *The Work of Mourning* (Chicago: University of Chicago Press, 2001), 171.

3. Kathleen M. O'Connor, *Lamentations and the Tears of the World* (Maryknoll, NY: Orbis Books, 2002), 89.

4. Emily Kaiser, "How Millennials Mourn," *The Washingtonian*, January 11, 2015, https://www.washingtonian.com/2015/01/11/how-millennials -mourn/, accessed July 26, 2017.

5. Christopher R. Seitz, *Joel*, The International Theological Commentary (New York: Bloomsbury, 2016), 116.

6. Victor Avigdor Hurowitz, "Joel's Locust Plague in Light of Sargon II's Hymn to Nanaya," *Journal of Biblical Literature* 112, no. 4 (1993): 597.

7. Douglas Watson, "Divine Attributes in the Book of Joel," *Journal for the Study of the Old Testament* 37 (2012): 113.

8. Augustine, *The City of God* (Buffalo, NY: Christian Literature, 1887), http://www.newadvent.org/fathers/1201.htm. Book 3 ends with this narrative.

9. Ackermann, *After the Locusts*; Pablo Andiñach, "The Locusts in the Book of Joel," *Vetus Testamentum* 42, no. 3 (1992); Assis, *The Book of Joel*, 44.

10. Elie Assis, "The Structure and Meaning of the Locust Plague Oracles in Joel 1,2–2,17," *Zeitschrift für die alttestamentliche Wissenschaft* 122 (2010): 401; Josef Lossl, "When Is a Locust Just a Locust? Patristic Exegesis of Joel 1:4 in Light of Ancient Literary Theory," *Journal of Theological Studies* 55, no. 2 (2004): 579–80. Assis identifies *four* distinct oracles referring to similar destructive events. Each oracle describes the devastation and the human response to destruction in greater detail. See also Leslie C. Allen, *The Books of Joel, Obadiah, Jonah, and Micah*, The New International Commentary on the Old Testament (Grand Rapids, MI: Eerdmans, 1976), 29. Allen suggests the four types of locusts can refer to "peoples, languages, rulers and kingdoms."

11. Assis, *The Book of Joel*, 41.

12. Ibid., 47.

13. Ibid., 58.

14. Troxel, *Joel*, 43.

15. Ibid., 49. Troxel references John Strazicich's study of Joel as being "double-voiced"; Joel, as a *schriftgelehrte Prophetie*, engages in "hermeneutics of resignification."

16. Andiñach, "The Locusts in the Book of Joel," 435.

17. Crenshaw, *Joel*, 88; John Wesley, *Joel: Explanatory Notes and Commentary* (Lexington, KY: Hargraves, 2015), 11; Assis, *The Book of Joel*, 76. Exodus 10 tells of *arbeh*. Psalm 78:46 describes the *gasil* and the *yelek*. Amos 4:10 links *gazam* to God's judgment.

18. Lossl, "When Is a Locust Just a Locust?" 585.

19. Seitz, *Joel*, 122.

20. Hyman, "The Prophecy of Joel," 223.

21. Assis, *The Book of Joel*, 11.

22. Seitz, *Joel*, 122.

23. Assis, *The Book of Joel*, 78.

24. John Swinton, *Raging with Compassion: Pastoral Responses to the Problem of Evil* (Grand Rapids, MI: Eerdmans, 2007). Swinton, a British pastoral theologian, defines theodicy as "[concerning the] intellectual defense of the love, goodness and power of God in the face of evil and suffering in the world" (p. 12). He argues for a pastoral theodicy (versus a theological theodicy) that resists evil by embracing lament, friendship, hospitality, compassion, forgiveness, faithfulness, and thoughtfulness.

25. Assis, "The Structure and Meaning of the Locust Plague Oracles in Joel 1,2–2,17," 407.

26. For a discussion of the three ways metaphor can be understood, see Wallace Martin, "Metaphor," in *The New Princeton Handbook of Poetic Terms*, ed. Terry V. F. Brogan (Princeton: Princeton University Press, 1994), 184.

27. Assis, *The Book of Joel*, 97.

28. Kenneth R. Mitchell and Herbert Anderson, *All Our Losses, All Our Griefs: Resources for Pastoral Care* (Philadelphia: Westminster Press, 1983), 35.

29. Ibid., 36.

30. Mauricio Soto, "Pension Shock," *Finance and Development*, June 2017, 14. https://www.imf.org/external/pubs/ft/fandd/2017/06/pdf/soto.pdf, accessed August 31, 2017.

31. Mitchell and Anderson, *All Our Losses, All Our Griefs*, 38.

32. Ibid., 40.

33. Ibid., 41.

34. Ibid., 42.

35. Lancaster and Stillman, *When Generations Collide*, 66; Elmore, *Generation iY*, 126.

36. Mitchell and Anderson, *All Our Losses, All Our Griefs*, 44.

37. J. William Worden, *Grief Counseling and Grief Therapy: A Handbook for the Mental Health Practitioner*, 3rd ed. (New York: Springer, 2009), 18–23.

38. Ibid., 24.

39. Ibid., 25.

40. Ibid., 25–31.

41. Ibid., 50.

42. Ibid., 57–73.

43. Silvano Arieti and Jules Bemporad, *Psychotherapy of Severe and Mild Depression* (Northvale, NJ: J. Aronson, 1993), 109.

44. For a link between devastation and drought and shame, see Jer 12:13, "They have sown wheat and reaped weeds; they have worn themselves out for nothing. They will be ashamed of their harvest on account of the Lord's fierce anger"; also, Jer 14:3, "The rich send their servants for water, but the wells run dry. They return with empty jars, ashamed, bewildered, and in despair."

45. Matthew J. Lynch, "Neglected Physical Dimensions of 'Shame' Terminology in the Hebrew Bible," *Biblica* 91 (2010): 506. The Hebrew term *bosheth* speaks to the experience of shame.

46. Kyle Cummins is a millennial in youth ministry serving in an urban community.

47. See Donald Capps, *Biblical Approaches to Pastoral Counseling* (Philadelphia: Westminster Press, 1981), 74.

48. The lament used with permission from Kyle Cummins.

49. James F. Dittes, "Ministry as Grief Work," in *Re-calling Ministry,* ed. Donald Capps (St. Louis, MO: Chalice Press, 1999), 15; Jaco J. Hamman, *When Steeples Cry: Leading Congregations through Loss and Change* (Cleveland: Pilgrim Press, 2005), 24.

50. Powell, Mulder, and Griffin, *Growing Young*, 88.

51. Ibid., 91–92.

52. Ibid., 97–99.

53. Ibid., 95.

54. Bob Yoder, *Helping Youth Grieve: The Good News of Biblical Lament* (Eugene, OR: Wipf and Stock, 2015).

55. Ibid., 4.

56. Ibid., 117–18.

57. Ariel Meirav, "The Nature of Hope," *Ratio* 22, no. 2 (2009): 228.

58. Ibid., 229.

59. Matthew W. Gallagher and Shane J. Lopez, *The Oxford Handbook of Hope*, Oxford Library of Psychology (New York: Oxford University Press, 2018), 4.

60. Ibid., xviii.

61. Jonathan Lear, *Radical Hope: Ethics in the Face of Cultural Devastation* (Cambridge, MA: Harvard University Press, 2006), 106.

62. Miguel A. De La Torre, *Embracing Hopelessness* (Minneapolis: Fortress, 2017), ix.

63. Ibid., 117.

64. Gallagher and Lopez, *The Oxford Handbook of Hope*, 20.

65. For a positive assessment of nostalgia, see Svetlana Boym, *The Future of Nostalgia* (New York: Basic Books, 2001).

66. Crenshaw, *Joel*, 91.

Chapter 2: Gather

1. Angie Thurston and Casper ter Kuile, "How We Gather: A New Report on Non-Religious Community," (2015), https://caspertk.files.word press.com/2015/04/how-we-gather.pdf, accessed September 1, 2017.

2. Ibid., 2.

3. Ibid., 6.

4. See http://thedinnerparty.org/about/, accessed September 1, 2017.

5. The other communities discussed in *How We Gather* include CTZN-WELL, a group mobilizing the well-being industry to change the world and increase practices of personal transformation; The US Department of Arts and Culture, an action network of artists and cultural workers whose creativity serves social justice; The Millennial Trains Project, that leads crowd-funded train journeys across America for diverse groups of young innovators; Live in the Grey, a group that seeks to inspire purpose and meaning in

employment; Juniper Path, a group bringing meditation to modern life; and Camp Grounded, a summer camp for adults.

6. Thurston and ter Kuile, *How We Gather*, 9.

7. See https://www.soul-cycle.com/our-story/, accessed September 1, 2017.

8. See http://thesanctuaries.org/about/, accessed September 1, 2017.

9. Thurston and ter Kuile, *How We Gather*, 5.

10. Nancy T. Ammerman, *Sacred Stories, Spiritual Tribes: Finding Religion in Everyday Life* (Oxford: Oxford University Press, 2014).

11. Ibid., 24.

12. Ibid., 259.

13. Ibid., 298.

14. Ibid., 2.

15. Ibid., 45.

16. Crenshaw, *Joel*, 47. Similarities between Joel and the cult of Baal include references to spears, honey flowing in streams, locusts, mourning like virgins, rain-making rituals, mourning rites, oracles of salvation in a vegetative cult, and more.

17. Troxel, *Joel*, 44.

18. Assis, *The Book of Joel*, 19.

19. Ibid.

20. Seitz, *Joel*, 135.

21. For information on spending the night in sackcloth, see 1 Kings 21:27; 2 Samuel 12:16.

22. Hans Walter Wolff and S. Dean McBride, *Joel and Amos: A Commentary on the Books of the Prophets Joel and Amos* (Philadelphia: Fortress Press, 1977), 32.

23. Seitz, *Joel*, 139.

24. Assis, *The Book of Joel: A Prophet between Calamity and Hope*, 104. See also Wolff and McBride, *Joel and Amos*, 33.

25. Other than the book of Joel, the Day of the Lord is named eleven times in the Old Testament: Amos 5:18a, 18b, 20; Zechariah 1:7, 14a, 14b; Malachi 3:23; Ezekiel 13:5; Isaiah 13:6, 9; and Obadiah 15. Joel mentions the Day of the Lord five times: 1:15; 2:1, 11; 3:4; and 4:14 (in the Hebrew text).

26. Assis, *The Book of Joel*, 108.

27. Sebastian Junger, *Tribe: On Homecoming and Belonging* (New York: Twelve, 2016), xvii.

28. Ibid., 17.

29. Levine and Dean, *Generation on a Tightrope*, 53.

30. Ibid., 69.

31. Drescher, *Choosing Our Religion*, 122. Drescher draws on the work of sociologist Abby Day in her discussion of "believing in belonging."

32. Ibid., 123.

33. Ibid.

34. Ammerman, *Sacred Stories, Spiritual Tribes*, 10.

35. Ibid., 21.

36. Ibid., 82.

37. Ibid., 40–44.

38. Ibid., 304.

39. This section was cowritten with Julian Galette. He holds a masters in theological studies degree from Vanderbilt Divinity School. Some of Galette's work can be found on the web at http://www.philome.la/rapbattlegenius.

40. Assis, *The Book of Joel: A Prophet between Calamity and Hope*, 19.

41. Seitz, *Joel*, 135.

42. Walter Brueggemann, *Theology of the Old Testament: Testimony, Dispute, Advocacy* (Minneapolis: Fortress Press, 1997), 664.

43. Ibid., 665.

44. Hall, *Among Cultures*, 95.

45. Ibid., 85–92.

46. Ibid., 94.

47. Michael B. Hundley, "Sacred Spaces, Objects, Offerings, and People in the Priestly Texts: A Reappraisal," *Journal of Biblical Literature* 132, no. 4 (2013).

48. See Leviticus 21:18-21 and Ezekiel 4–5 for the setting up and disruption of holiness codes.

49. Powell, Mulder, and Griffin, *Growing Young*, 166.

50. Ibid.

51. Ibid., 169.

52. Best, *Y: Christian Millennial Manifesto*, 109.

53. Ibid.

54. Ibid., 110.

55. Watson, "Divine Attributes in the Book of Joel," 115.

56. Drescher, *Choosing Our Religion*, 118.

57. Ibid., 117. Drescher cites professor of journalism Michael Pollan.

58. Ibid., 120.

59. Elmore, *Generation iY*, 19, 36–47.

60. Dietrich Bonhoeffer, *Life Together*, 1st ed. (New York: Harper & Row, 1954), 83.

61. Perrin, *The Coming Post-Christian Tsunami*, 40.

62. Ibid., 123.

63. Ibid., 124.

64. Margaret Mead, *Culture and Commitment: A Study of the Generation Gap* (Garden City, NY: Natural History Press, 1970), 2.

Chapter 3: Discover

1. Smith and Denton, *Soul Searching*. In 2002–3, the authors conducted the National Survey of Youth and Religion with 3,370 teenagers ranging from thirteen to seventeen years of age throughout the United States. In included 267 personal interviews of these teens representing forty-five of the fifty states, to "develop a better scholarly and public understanding of the religious and spiritual lives of American adolescents" (p. 4).

2. Ibid., 166.

3. Ibid., 120.

4. Ibid., 130.

5. Ibid., 162–63.

6. Ibid., 166.

7. Ibid., 171.

8. Ibid., 166.

9. Ibid.

10. Kara Powell, Jake Mulder, and Brad Griffin, *Growing Young: Six Essential Strategies to Help Young People Discover and Love Your Church* (Grand Rapids, MI: Baker Books, 2016), 166.

11. Smith and Denton, *Soul Searching*, 149.

12. Abraham Joshua Heschel, *The Prophets* (New York: HarperPerennial, 2001), 242.

13. Ibid., 291.

14. Ibid., 618.

15. Ibid., 297.

16. Ibid., 299.

17. Ibid., 412.

18. Ibid., 299.

19. Ibid., 305.

20. Ibid., 306.

21. Ibid., 307.

22. Seitz, *Joel*, 171; Troxel, *Joel*, 55.

23. Heschel, *The Prophets*, 620.

24. Assis, *The Book of Joel*, 122. See also John Barton, *Joel and Obadiah: A Commentary*, The Old Testament Library (Louisville: Westminster John Knox Press, 2001), 69.

25. Assis, *The Book of Joel*, 139.

26. Ronald T. Hyman, "The Prophecy of Joel: The Prophet's Message, Beliefs, and Prophetic Style," *Jewish Bible Quarterly* 39, no. 4 (2011): 228.

27. Barton, *Joel and Obadiah*, 77.

28. Wolff and McBride, *Joel and Amos*, 52.

29. Barton, *Joel and Obadiah*, 79.

30. Assis, *The Book of Joel*, 143.

31. Crenshaw, *Joel*, 134.

32. Seitz, *Joel*, 163.

33. Nathan C. Lane, *The Compassionate, but Punishing God: A Canonical Analysis of Exodus 34:6-7* (Eugene, OR: Pickwick Publications, 2010), 1.

34. Phyllis Trible, *God and the Rhetoric of Sexuality,* Overtures to Biblical Theology (Philadelphia: Fortress Press, 1978), 35.

35. Ibid., 38.

36. Ibid., 39.

37. Lane, *The Compassionate, but Punishing God*, 28.

38. Ibid.

39. See Numbers 14:18 (Moses reminds Israel of who God is as they lament having left Egypt); 2 Samuel 12:22 (David laments the death of his son); Psalm 86:15 (a *tephillah*—prayer—of David, who is in some distress); Psalm 103:8 (a psalm of praise); Psalm 145:8 (a psalm of gratitude and praise; the Psalter); Nahum 1:3 (Nahum's vision of God; Joel, Jonah, and Nahum from the Twelve); Jonah 4:2 (Jonah, angry that Nineveh was spared, prays to God, merciful and compassionate); and Nehemiah 9:17 (remembering the exodus, the prophet reminds Israel of God's character). In the Torah: Exodus 20; Numbers 14; and Deuteronomy 5. See also Micah 7:18-20.

40. Joseph Ryan Kelly, "Joel, Jonah, and the YHWH Creed: Determining the Trajectory of the Literary Influence," *Journal of Biblical Literature* 132, no. 5 (2013): 806.

41. Lane, *The Compassionate, but Punishing God*, 6.

42. Hosea 14:1 and Amos 4:6-11 also call on Israel to "return to God."

43. Barton, *Joel and Obadiah*, 76.

44. Seitz, *Joel*, 166.

45. Ibid.

46. Crenshaw, *Joel*, 134.

47. Hyman, 221. The terms of the covenant were stated in Leviticus 26:1-13; Deuteronomy 7:12-26; 8:1-20; 10:12-22; 28:1-69.

48. Assis, *The Book of Joel*, 15.

49. Ibid., 178.

50. Ibid., 182.

51. Ibid., 184.

52. Crenshaw, *Joel*, 159.

53. This form of repetition is called *dittography*, used for poetic effect. Emmanuel Tov defines dittography as "erroneously doubling of a letter, letters, word, or words." Emanuel Tov, *Textual Criticism of the Hebrew Bible* (Minneapolis: Fortress Press, 1992), 240.

54. Assis, *The Book of Joel*, 14.

55. Crenshaw, *Joel*, 17.

56. Douglas Watson, "Divine Attributes in the Book of Joel," *Journal for the Study of the Old Testament* 37 (2012): 112ff.

57. Ana-Maria Rizzuto, *The Birth of the Living God: A Psychoanalytic Study* (Chicago: University of Chicago Press, 1979), 177–78.

58. Ibid., 90.

59. Ibid., 179.

60. Ibid., 149–51.

61. Ibid., 171.

62. Ibid., 173.

63. This section was cowritten with Kelsey Davis. She holds a master of divinity degree from Vanderbilt Divinity School. She has served as a chaplain for young adults at St. Augustine's Episcopal Chapel in Nashville, TN. She currently serves as the Curator for Emerging Communities in the Episcopal Diocese of El Camino Real. Heather, her wife and partner, worked on staff at Thistle Farms (https://thistlefarms.org/), where Kelsey volunteered. It is the mission of Thistle Farms to heal, empower, and employ women survivors of trafficking, prostitution, and addiction.

64. For information about Thistle Farms in Nashville, Tennessee, see https://thistlefarms.org/.

65. David L. Cooperrider and Diana Whitney, "Appreciative Inquiry: A Positive Revolution in Change," in *The Change Handbook: The Definitive Source on Today's Best Methods for Engaging Whole Systems*, ed. Peggy Holman, Tom Devane, and Steven Cady (San Francisco: Berrett-Koehler Publishers, 2006). Available in a different version at http://www.tapin.in/Documents/2 /Appreciative%20Inquiry%20-%20Positive%20Revolution%20in%20 Change.pdf, accessed November 12, 2017.

66. Marcus J. Borg, *Jesus, a New Vision: Spirit, Culture, and the Life of Discipleship*, 1st ed. (San Francisco: Harper & Row, 1987), 129.

67. Lane, *The Compassionate, but Punishing God*, 11.

68. Walter Brueggemann refers to the mercy formula as "a credo of adjectives." See Brueggemann, *Theology of the Old Testament*, 215.

69. Lane, *The Compassionate, but Punishing God*, 27.

70. Rob Lee, *Stained-Glass Millennials: Coincidental Reformers* (Macon, GA: Smyth & Helwys, 2016), xvi.

71. Ibid., 3.

72. Ibid., 19.

73. Ibid., 21.

74. The supremacist meeting took place on August 12, 2017. The MTV Video Music Awards event was held on August 27, 2017.

75. See https://www.npr.org/sections/thetwo-way/2017/09/05/54870 8431/lee-relative-who-denounced-white-supremacy-resigns-as-pastor-of-n -c-church, accessed November 13, 2017.

76. See http://auburnseminary.org/rev-robert-wright-lee-iv-statement -leaving-church-speaking-white-supremacy-mtv-video-music-awards/, accessed November 13, 2017.

77. Lee, *Stained-Glass Millennials*, 19.

Chapter 4: Receive

1. William James, *The Varieties of Religious Experience* (New York: Vintage Books, 1990), 34.

2. Drescher, *Choosing Our Religion*, 152.

3. Ibid., 154.

4. Ibid., 8.

5. Ibid., 154.

6. Rudolf Otto, *The Idea of the Holy: An Inquiry into the Non-Rational Factor in the Idea of the Divine and Its Relation to the Rational*, 2nd ed. (London: Oxford University Press, 1958).

7. Ibid., 7.

8. Ibid., 12–13.

9. Ibid., 12.

10. Seitz, *Joel*, 199.

11. Ibid., 185. For a discussion on how Joel 2:28-32 (or Joel 3:1-4 in the Hebrew text) relates to the second half of the book, see Troxel, *Joel*, 73.

12. Barton, *Joel and Obadiah: A Commentary*, 94.

13. Crenshaw, *Joel*, 163.

14. Steven E. Runge, "Joel 2:28-32a in Acts 2:17-21: The Discourse and Text-Critical Implications of Variation from the Lxx," in *The Library of New Testament Studies: Early Christian Literature and Intertextuality*, ed. Chris Keith (New York: Bloomsbury, 2009).

15. Elmore, *Generation iY*, 19, 36-37.

16. Allen, *The Books of Joel, Obadiah, Jonah, and Micah*, 98.

17. Barton, *Joel and Obadiah*, 95.

18. Wolff and McBride, *Joel and Amos*, 65.

19. Barton, *Joel and Obadiah*, 92.

20. Schreiber, "I Will Pour out My Spirit on All Flesh (Joel 3:1)," 127; Larry McQueen, *Joel and the Spirit: A Cry for a Prophetic Hermeneutic* (Cleveland, TN: CPT Press, 2009), 33; Crenshaw, *Joel*, 43.

21. Troxel, *Joel*, 79; Seitz, *Joel*, 194; Assis, *The Book of Joel*, 202.

22. Troxel, *Joel*, 80. Troxel quoting commentator Julius A. Bewer.

23. Assis, *The Book of Joel*, 202.

24. Schreiber, "I Will Pour out My Spirit on All Flesh (Joel 3:1)," 128.

25. Barton, *Joel and Obadiah*, 96.

26. Troxel, *Joel*, 82.

27. Norbert Saracco, "I Will Pour out My Spirit on All People: A Pastoral Reading of Joel 2:28-30 from Latin America," *Calvin Theological Journal* 46 (2011): 270.

28. Rhys H. Williams, Courtney Ann Irby, and R. Stephen Warner, "Church in Black and White: The Organizational Lives of Young Adults," *Religions* 7, no. 90 (2016).

29. Ibid., 3. The authors are quoting Jason Shelton and Michael O. Emerson's *Blacks and Whites in Christian America: How Racial Discrimination Shapes Religious Convictions* (New York: New York University Press, 2012).

30. Ibid., 11.

31. Allen, *The Books of Joel, Obadiah, Jonah, and Micah*, 96.

32. Ibid., 97.

33. Eugene H. Peterson, *The Message: The Bible in Contemporary Language* (Chicago: ACTA Publications, 2013). Style changed for easy reading.

34. McQueen, *Joel and the Spirit*, 45.

35. See http://gothamist.com/2014/08/25/millennials_mcdonalds_lol .php, accessed December 11, 2017.

36. See http://www.businessinsider.com/millennials-are-killing-list-2017-8#, accessed December 11, 2017.

37. See http://mashable.com/2017/07/31/things-millennials-have-killed/; also https://www.buzzfeed.com/ahmedaliakbar/millennial-murder-spree; and https://www.boredpanda.com/business-insider-titles-millenials-against-industries/.

38. See https://www.brethrenchurch.org/articles-stories/10-ways-mil lennials-are-shaping-churches-today; http://www.outreachmagazine.com/fea tures/23830-reach-millennials-church.html; also, http://www.outreachmag azine.com/features/21195-churches-dont-reach-millennials.html; https://www.foxnews.com/opinion/ten-reasons-millennials-are-backing -away-from-god-and-christianity, accessed December 11, 2017.

39. Jürgen Moltmann, *The Spirit of Life: A Universal Affirmation* (Minneapolis: Fortress Press, 2001), 50–51.

40. See https://iona.org.uk/.

41. Jaco J. Hamman, *Becoming a Pastor: Forming Self and Soul for Ministry*, 2nd ed. (Cleveland: Pilgrim Press, 2014), 104.

42. See https://heartfulness.org/cme/#faq, accessed December 11, 2017.

43. Elizabeth A. Livingstone, *The Concise Oxford Dictionary of the Christian Church* (Oxford: Oxford University Press, 2006), http://www.

oxfordreference.com/view/10.1093/acref/9780198614425.001.0001
/acref-9780198614425, accessed December 11, 2017.

44. Arndt Büssing, Federico Baiocco, and Klaus Baumann, "Spiritual Dryness in Catholic Laypersons Working as Volunteers Is Related to Reduced Life Satisfaction Rather Than to Indicators of Spirituality," *Pastoral Psychology*, Online First (2017).

45. George Graen and Miriam Grace, "Positive Industrial and Organizational Psychology: Designing for Tech-Savvy, Optimistic, and Purposeful Millennial Professionals' Company Cultures," *Industrial and Organizational Psychology* 8, no. 3 (2015): 397.

46. Ibid., 399.

47. Robert Wuthnow, *After Heaven: Spirituality in America since the 1950s* (Berkeley: University of California Press, 1998), 3–4.

48. Ibid., 8.

49. Ibid., 6.

50. Ibid., 16.

51. Ibid., 179–98.

52. Ibid., 173.

53. Ibid., 175.

54. Ibid., 196.

Chapter 5: Be Accountable

1. Read more about YIMBYs in San Francisco's Mission District, https://missionlocal.org/2017/11/sf-mission-yimby-movement-wants-to-speed-up-affordable-housing/, accessed December 19, 2017.

2. See https://en.wikipedia.org/wiki/NIMBY, accessed December 19, 2017.

3. The article first appeared August 23, 2017. See https://www.sierraclub
.org/sierra/2017-5-september-october/grapple/pro-housing-urban
-millennials-say-yes-my-backyard, accessed December 19, 2017.

4. Ibid.

5. Ibid.

6. The meeting was reported in *The Guardian*, https://www.theguardian
.com/cities/2017/oct/02/rise-of-the-yimbys-angry-millennials-radical
-housing-solution, accessed December 19, 2017.

7. Marcus J. Borg, *Jesus, a New Vision: Spirit, Culture, and the Life of Discipleship*, 1st ed. (San Francisco: Harper & Row, 1987), 129.

8. Levine and Dean, *Generation on a Tightrope* 137.

9. The Oxford English Dictionary (Online) (London: Oxford University Press, 2017).

10. Danielle Y. Hairston-Green and LaRachelle S. Smith, "Accountability, Growth, and Excellence: Mentorship through the Ages," *Proceedings of the New Mexico Mentoring Institute* 9 (2016): 1276.

11. Drescher, *Choosing Our Religion*, 45.

12. Schart, "The First Section of the Book of the Twelve Prophets," 150.

13. Ibid.

14. Drescher, *Choosing Our Religion*, 45.

15. The theme of the Day of the Lord, a day that can mean either blessing or curse, can also be found in Isaiah 13:6; Ezekiel 13:5; Amos 5:18; Obadiah 15-17; Zephaniah 1:7, 14-16. See Crenshaw, *Joel*, 48.

16. Troxel, *Joel*, 87.

17. The New Testament passages are Acts 2:20; 1 Thessalonians 5:2; 2 Thessalonians 2:2; and 2 Peter 3:10. See also indirect references to "The Day of the Lord" in 2 Peter 3:10; 1 Thessalonians 1:10; 1 Corinthians 1:8,

5:5; 2 Corinthians 1:14; 2 Thessalonians 1:10; 2 Timothy 1:12; Matthew 25:13.

18. Assis, *The Book of Joel*, 197.

19. Troxel, *Joel*, 18, 22.

20. Schreiber, "I Will Pour out My Spirit on All Flesh (Joel 3:1)," 128.

21. Barton, *Joel and Obadiah*, 92.

22. Assis, *The Book of Joel*, 226.

23. For the concept of Jerusalem's eternal nature, see Psalms 46, 48, and 76. Also Jeremiah 7:1-15, 26 and 8:19. Jeremiah was against the eternal sanctity of Jerusalem, stating that the actions of the people will determine that. With the destruction of the temple, Jeremiah was proven right.

24. Allen, *The Books of Joel, Obadiah, Jonah, and Micah*, 109; Assis, *The Book of Joel*, 216.

25. Crenshaw, *Joel*, 175.

26. Allen, *The Books of Joel, Obadiah, Jonah, and Micah*, 109.

27. Watson, "Divine Attributes in the Book of Joel," 125.

28. Paul R. Raabe, "The Particularizing of Universal Judgment in Prophetic Discourse," *The Catholic Biblical Quaterly* 64 (2002): 665.

29. Assis, *The Book of Joel*, 207.

30. See, for example, Genesis 4:6; 12:8; 13:4; 21:33; 26:25; Exodus 34:5; Deuteronomy 28:10; 1 Kings 18; Isaiah 64:6; 65:1.

31. Assis, *The Book of Joel*, 208.

32. Ibid., 228.

33. Ibid.

34. Will Kynes, "Beat Your Parodies into Swords, and Your Parodied Books into Spears: A New Paradigm for Parody in the Hebrew Bible," *Biblical Interpretation* 19 (2011): 307.

35. Barton, *Joel and Obadiah*, 104.

36. Crenshaw, *Joel*, 179. See also Assis, *The Book of Joel*, 220–21.

37. See Amos 5:18-20 for the Day of the Lord as a day of dread.

38. Assis, *The Book of Joel*, 199.

39. Ibid.

40. Seitz, *Joel*, 184.

41. Ibid., 185. For his argument, Seitz draws on James Marr's concept of interpretation being guided by a "resultant system," a priori in the mind of the interpreter that determines understanding of the text.

42. Allen, *The Books of Joel, Obadiah, Jonah, and Micah*, 39.

43. Isaiah 7:10-14, "Again the LORD spoke to Ahaz: 'Ask a sign from the LORD your God. Make it as deep as the grave or as high as heaven.' But Ahaz said, 'I won't ask; I won't test the LORD.' Then Isaiah said, 'Listen, house of David! Isn't it enough for you to be tiresome for people that you are also tiresome before my God? Therefore, the LORD will give you a sign. The young woman is pregnant and is about to give birth to a son, and she will name him Immanuel.' "

44. For judgment that flows from the particular to the universal, see Isaiah 10:22-23; 28:14-22; Jeremiah 12:7-13; Obadiah 8-15.

45. For a complete list of transgender persons killed in the United States and elsewhere, see https://en.wikipedia.org/wiki/List_of_unlawfully_killed _transgender_people#United_States_2, accessed February 12, 2018.

46. See https://www.hrc.org/resources/violence-against-the-transgender -community-in-2017, accessed December 12, 2018.

47. See Amos 5:24: "But let justice roll down like waters, and righteousness like an ever-flowing stream."

48. See: http://southernersonnewground.org/, accessed February 12, 2018.

49. Danita Bye, *Millennials Matter: Proven Strategies for Building Your Next-Gen Leader* (Racine, WI: Broad Street Publishing 2017). The seven traits she discusses are courage, determination, awareness, knowledge, optimism, trustworthiness, and accountability.

50. *The Oxford English Dictionary* (Online), accessed December 20, 2017.

51. Bye, *Millennials Matter*, 61.

52. Ibid., 63.

53. See https://www.ccl.org/articles/white-papers/learning-about-learning-agility/, accessed December 22, 2017.

54. Ibid., 4.

55. Ibid., 6.

56. Bye, *Millennials Matter*, 65.

57. Ibid.

58. Robert J. Anderson and W. A. Adams, *Mastering Leadership: An Integrated Framework for Breakthrough Performance and Extraordinary Business Results* (Hoboken, NJ: Wiley, 2016), 66.

59. Ibid., 67.

60. Ibid., 68.

61. Ibid., 80.

62. *The Oxford English Dictionary* (Online), accessed December 22, 2017.

63. For a discussion of paradox in ministry, see H. Newton Malony, *Living with Paradox: Religious Leadership and the Genius of Double Vision* (San Francisco: Jossey-Bass, 1998).

64. Ibid., 17–117.

65. Hamman, *Becoming a Pastor: Forming Self and Soul for Ministry*, 47.

66. "Blue Boat Home" is a song written by Peter Mayer set to the hymn "Hyfrydol" by the Welsh musician Rowland Prichard (1811–87). Prichard wrote the hymn in 1830. The song appears on the album *Earth Town Square*. See http://www.petermayer.net/music/. For the hymn, see https://hymnary.org/tune/hyfrydol_prichard.

Chapter 6: Restore

1. Rushkoff, *Present Shock*, 39.

2. The 2017 Millennial Impact Report is sponsored by the Case Foundation, a nonprofit supporting and researching changemakers (https://casefoundation.org/), and conducted by Achieve, a research firm (http://www.achieveagency.com/). The report, released in three phases, can be downloaded from its own website, http://www.themillennialimpact.com/, accessed December 24, 2017.

3. The Millennial Impact Project, The Millennial Impact Report—Phase 1, December 24, 2017, http://www.themillennialimpact.com, ii.

4. Ibid., 4.

5. The Millennial Impact Project, The Millennial Impact Report—Phase 2: The Power of Voice: A New Era of Cause Activation and Social Issue Adoption (2017), accessed December 24, 2017, http://www.themillennialimpact.com/, 13.

6. The Millennial Impact Project, The Millennial Impact Report—Phase 1, 6.

7. The Millennial Impact Project, The Millennial Impact Report—Phase 2, 23.

8. The Millennial Impact Project, The Millennial Impact Report—Phase 1, 8.

9. The Millennial Impact Project, The Millennial Impact Report—Phase 2, 2, 10–11.

10. Ibid., 12.

11. Ibid., 14.

12. Barton, *Joel and Obadiah*, 108.

13. For arguments for and against the inclusion of the last verses of Joel, see Assis, *The Book of Joel*, 246–47.

14. Barton, *Joel and Obadiah*, 108–9.

15. Seitz, *Joel*, 219.

16. For references to "milk and honey," see Exodus 3:8; Leviticus 20:24; Numbers 13:27; Deuteronomy 6:3; and Joshua 5:6.

17. Assis, *The Book of Joel*, 248.

18. Allen, *The Books of Joel, Obadiah, Jonah, and Micah*, 124.

19. Assis, *The Book of Joel*, 254.

20. Crenshaw, *Joel*, 200.

21. Wolff and McBride, *Joel and Amos*, 84.

22. Assis, *The Book of Joel* 257.

23. This section was cowritten with Rev. Lindsey Krinks. Lindsey holds a masters degree in theological studies from Vanderbilt Divinity School.

24. Discover more about Open Table Nashville at http://opentablenash ville.org/.

25. See http://opentablenashville.org/story.

26. James M. Gustafson, "Participation: A Religious Worldview," *Journal of Religious Ethics* 44, no. 1 (2016): 148.

27. Ibid.

28. Ibid., 149.

29. For a discussion on participation in evil, see Benjamin Splichal Larson, "Participation in Evil: The Problem of Doing Evil When Attempting to Fight Evil," *Currents in Theology and Mission* 33, no. 9 (2012).

30. Gustafson, "Participation," 160.

31. The Millennial Impact Project, The Millennial Impact Report—Phase 1, 6.

32. Erik H. Erikson, *Identity and the Life Cycle* (New York: Norton, 1980), 129. See also Donald Capps and Don S. Browning, *Life Cycle Theory and Pastoral Care*, Theology and Pastoral Care Series (Philadelphia: Fortress Press, 1983), 18.

33. Christopher J. Adams et al., "Clergy Burnout: A Comparison Study with Other Helping Professions," *Pastoral Psychology* 66 (2017).

34. Christina Maslach and Michael P. Leiter, "Understanding the Burnout Experience: Recent Research and Its Implications for Psychiatry," *World Psychiatry* 15, no. 2 (2016): 103.

35. Adams, et al., "Clergy Burnout," 150.

36. See https://missamazing.org/, accessed December 25, 2017.

37. See http://lucentevententertainment.com/cuddle-the-world/, accessed December 25, 2017.

38. See https://www.facebook.com/strongerthanstigma, accessed December 25, 2017.

39. This is a paraphrase of "the poor widow" (2 Kgs 4).

40. For "Feeding the Five Thousand," see Matthew 14:13-21; Mark 6:31-44; Luke 9:12-17; John 6:1-14. For never being thirsty, see John 4:14-15. For never going hungry, see John 6:35.

Conclusion

1. Seitz, *Joel*, 222–23.

2. Miller and Norton, *Making God Real for a New Generation*, 9.

3. Walter Brueggemann, *The Prophetic Imagination* (Minneapolis: Fortress Press, 2001), 14.

4. Tim Keel, *Intuitive Leadership: Embracing a Paradigm of Narrative, Metaphor, and Chaos* (Grand Rapids, MI: Baker Books, 2007), 29.

5. Ibid., 32.

6. Ibid., 103–5.

7. Ibid., 225.

8. Ibid., 226.

9. Alasdair C. MacIntyre, *After Virtue: A Study in Moral Theory*, 3rd ed. (Notre Dame, IN: University of Notre Dame Press, 2007), 218.

10. Benjamin T. Conner, *Practicing Witness: A Missional Vision of Christian Practices* (Grand Rapids, MI: Eerdmans, 2011), 56–59.

11. Lyons, *The Next Christians*, 51.

12. Ibid., 52.

13. Miller and Norton, *Making God Real for a New Generation*, 134.

Bibliography

Ackermann, Denise. *After the Locusts: Letters from a Landscape of Faith*. Grand Rapids, MI: Eerdmans, 2003.

Ad Age and Univision Insights. "The Cultural Connection: How Hispanic Identity Influences Millennials." Last modified 2012. http://gaia.adage.com/images /bin/pdf/Hispanic Millennials.pdf.

Adams, Christopher J., Holly Hough, Rae Jean Proeschold-Bell, Jia Yao, and Melanie Kolkin. "Clergy Burnout: A Comparison Study with Other Helping Professions." *Pastoral Psychology* 66 (2017): 147–75.

Allen, Leslie C. *The Books of Joel, Obadiah, Jonah, and Micah*. The New International Commentary on the Old Testament. Grand Rapids, MI: Eerdmans, 1976.

Allport, Gordon W. *Pattern and Growth in Personality*. New York: Holt, 1961.

Alsop, Ronald. *The Trophy Kids Grow Up: How the Millennial Generation Is Shaking Up the Workplace*. 1st ed. San Francisco: Jossey-Bass, 2008.

Ammerman, Nancy T. *Sacred Stories, Spiritual Tribes: Finding Religion in Everyday Life*. Oxford: Oxford University Press, 2014.

Anderson, Robert J., and W. A. Adams. *Mastering Leadership: An Integrated Framework for Breakthrough Performance and Extraordinary Business Results*. Hoboken, NJ: Wiley, 2016.

Andiñach, Pablo. "The Locusts in the Book of Joel." *Vetus Testamentum* 42, no. 3 (1992): 433–42.

Arieti, Silvano, and Jules Bemporad. *Psychotherapy of Severe and Mild Depression.* Northvale, NJ: J. Aronson, 1993.

Assis, Elie. *The Book of Joel: A Prophet between Calamity and Hope.* Library of Hebrew Bible/Old Testament Studies. New York and London: Bloomsbury/ T&T Clark, 2013.

———. "The Structure and Meaning of the Locust Plague Oracles in Joel 1, 2–2, 17." *Zeitschrift für die alttestamentliche Wissenschaft* 122 (2010): 401–16.

Augustine. *The City of God.* Buffalo, NY: Christian Literature Publishing Company, 1887. http://www.newadvent.org/fathers/1201.htm.

Barton, John. *Joel and Obadiah: A Commentary.* The Old Testament Library. Louisville: Westminster John Knox Press, 2001.

———. "Reflections on Biblical Criticism." *Method Matters: Essays on the Interpretation of the Hebrew Bible in Honor of David L. Petersen*, edited by David L. Petersen, Joel M. LeMon, and Kent Harold Richards, 523–40. Atlanta: Society of Biblical Literature, 2009.

Best, Joshua. *Y: Christian Millennial Manifesto.* Holland, MI: Unprecedented Press, 2017.

Bonhoeffer, Dietrich. *Letters and Papers from Prison.* New York: Macmillan, 1972.

———. *Life Together.* 1st ed. New York: Harper & Row, 1954.

Borg, Marcus J. *Jesus, a New Vision: Spirit, Culture, and the Life of Discipleship.* 1st ed. San Francisco: Harper & Row, 1987.

Boym, Svetlana. *The Future of Nostalgia.* New York: Basic Books, 2001.

Brueggemann, Walter. *The Prophetic Imagination.* Minneapolis: Fortress Press, 2001.

———. *Theology of the Old Testament: Testimony, Dispute, Advocacy.* Minneapolis: Fortress Press, 1997.

Burmeister, Misti. *From Boomers to Bloggers: Success Strategies across Generations.* Fairfax, VA: Synergy Press, 2008.

Büssing, Arndt, Federico Baiocco, and Klaus Baumann. "Spiritual Dryness in Catholic Laypersons Working as Volunteers Is Related to Reduced Life Satisfaction Rather Than to Indicators of Spirituality." *Pastoral Psychology,* Online First (2017): 1–15.

Bye, Danita. *Millennials Matter: Proven Strategies for Building Your Next-Gen Leader.* Racine, WI: Broad Street Publishing, 2017.

Capps, Donald. *Biblical Approaches to Pastoral Counseling.* Philadelphia: Westminster Press, 1981.

Capps, Donald, and Don S. Browning. *Life Cycle Theory and Pastoral Care.* Theology and Pastoral Care Series. Philadelphia: Fortress Press, 1983.

The Concise Oxford Dictionary of English Etymology. Edited by T. F. Hoad. Oxford: Oxford University Press, 2003. http://www.oxfordreference.com/.

Conner, Benjamin T. *Practicing Witness: A Missional Vision of Christian Practices.* Grand Rapids, MI: Eerdmans, 2011.

Cooperman, Alan, Gregory Smith, and Katherine Ritchey. "America's Changing Religious Landscape: Christians Decline Sharply as Share of Population; Unaffiliated and Other Faiths Continue to Grow." Last modified 2015. Accessed June 9, 2015. http://www.pewforum.org/2015/05/12/americas -changing-religious-landscape/.

Cooperrider, David L., and Diana Whitney. "Appreciative Inquiry: A Positive Revolution in Change." *The Change Handbook: The Definitive Source on Today's Best Methods for Engaging Whole Systems.* Edited by Peggy Holman, Tom Devane, and Steven Cady, 73–88. San Francisco: Berrett-Koehler, 2006.

Crenshaw, James L. Joel. *The Anchor Bible.* New York: Doubleday, 1995.

De La Torre, Miguel A. *Embracing Hopelessness.* Minneapolis: Fortress Press, 2017.

De Rivera, Joseph, and Theodore R. Sarbin. *Believed-in Imaginings: The Narrative Construction of Reality.* 1st ed. Washington, DC: American Psychological Association, 1998.

Derrida, Jacques, Pascale-Anne Brault, and Michael Naas. *The Work of Mourning.* Chicago: University of Chicago Press, 2001.

Dittes, James E. "Ministry as Grief Work." *Re-Calling Ministry.* Edited by Donald Capps, 15–29. St. Louis: Chalice Press, 1999.

Drescher, Elizabeth. *Choosing Our Religion: The Spiritual Lives of America's Nones.* Oxford: Oxford University Press, 2016.

D'Souza, Joy. "Xennials, the Microgeneration between Gen X and Millennials." *The Huffington Post.* Last modified 2017. Accessed July 11, 2017. http://www.huffingtonpost.ca/2017/06/28/xennials_a_23006562/.

Elmore, Tim. *Generation iY: Our Last Chance to Save Their Future.* Atlanta: Poet Gardener Publishing, 2010.

Erikson, Erik H. *Identity and the Life Cycle.* New York: Norton, 1980.

Flory, Richard, and Donald Miller. *Finding Faith: The Spiritual Quest of the Post-Boomer Generation.* New Brunswick: Rutgers University Press, 2008.

Gallagher, Matthew W., and Shane J. Lopez. *The Oxford Handbook of Hope.* Oxford Library of Psychology. New York: Oxford University Press, 2018.

Gardner, Howard, and Katie Davis. *The App Generation: How Today's Youth Navigate Identity, Intimacy, and Imagination in a Digital World.* New Haven: Yale University Press, 2013.

Gergen, Kenneth J., and Mary M. Gergen. "Narrative Tensions: Perilous and Productive." *Narrative Inquiry* 21, no. 2 (2011): 374–81.

Graen, George, and Miriam Grace. "Positive Industrial and Organizational Psychology: Designing for Tech-Savvy, Optimistic, and Purposeful Millennial

Professionals' Company Cultures." *Industrial and Organizational Psychology* 8, no. 3 (2015): 395–410.

Gravett, Linda, and Robin Throckmorton. *Bridging the Generation Gap: How to Get Radio Babies, Boomers, Gen Xers, and Gen Yers to Work Together and Achieve More.* Franklin Lakes, NJ: Career Press, 2007.

Gustafson, James M. "Participation: A Religious Worldview." *Journal of Religious Ethics* 44, no. 1 (2016): 148–75.

Hairston-Green, Danielle Y., and LaRachelle S. Smith. "Accountability, Growth, and Excellence: Mentorship through the Ages." *Proceedings of the New Mexico Mentoring Institute* 9 (2016): 1275–78.

Hall, Bradford J. *Among Cultures: The Challenge of Communication.* 2nd ed. Belmont, CA: Thomson Wadsworth, 2005.

Hamman, Jaco J. *Becoming a Pastor: Forming Self and Soul for Ministry.* 2nd ed. Cleveland: Pilgrim Press, 2014.

———. *When Steeples Cry: Leading Congregations through Loss and Change.* Cleveland: Pilgrim Press, 2005.

Heschel, Abraham Joshua. *The Prophets.* New York: HarperPerennial, 2001.

Howe, Neil, and William Strauss. *Millennials Rising: The Next Great Generation.* New York: Vintage Books, 2000.

Humphrey, N. J. A. *Gathering the Next Generation: Essays on the Formation and Ministry of GenX Priests.* Harrisburg: Morehouse, 2000.

Hundley, Michael B. "Sacred Spaces, Objects, Offerings, and People in the Priestly Texts: A Reappraisal." *Journal of Biblical Literature* 132, no. 4 (2013): 749–66.

Hurowitz, Victor Avigdor. "Joel's Locust Plague in Light of Sargon II's Hymn to Nanaya." *Journal of Biblical Literature* 112, no. 4 (1993): 597–603.

Hyman, Ronald T. "The Prophecy of Joel: The Prophet's Message, Beliefs, and Prophetic Style." *Jewish Bible Quarterly* 39, no. 4 (2011): 221–31.

James, William. *The Varieties of Religious Experience*. New York: Vintage Books, 1990.

Jauss, Hans Robert. *Toward an Aesthetic of Reception*. Minneapolis: University of Minnesota Press, 1982.

Junger, Sebastian. *Tribe: On Homecoming and Belonging*. New York: Twelve, 2016.

Kaiser, Emily. "How Millennials Mourn." *The Washingtonian*. January 11, 2015. https://www.washingtonian.com/2015/01/11/how-millennials-mourn/, accessed July 26, 2017.

Keel, Tim. *Intuitive Leadership: Embracing a Paradigm of Narrative, Metaphor, and Chaos*. Grand Rapids, MI: Baker Books, 2007.

Kelly, Joseph Ryan. "Joel, Jonah, and the Yhwh Creed: Determining the Trajectory of the Literary Influence." *Journal of Biblical Literature* 132, no. 5 (2013): 805–27.

Kinnaman, David. *Unchristian: What the New Generation Really Thinks About Christianity . . . and Why It Matters*. Grand Rapids, MI: Baker Books, 2007.

Kluckhohn, Clyde, and Henry A. Murray. *Personality in Nature, Society, and Culture*. New York: Knopf, 1959.

Kynes, Will. "Beat Your Parodies into Swords, and Your Parodied Books into Spears: A New Paradigm for Parody in the Hebrew Bible." *Biblical Interpretation* 19 (2011): 276–310.

Lancaster, Lynne C., and David Stillman. *When Generations Collide: Who They Are, Why They Clash, How to Solve the Generational Puzzle at Work*. New York: HarperCollins, 2002.

Lane, Nathan C. *The Compassionate, but Punishing God: A Canonical Analysis of Exodus 34:6-7*. Eugene, OR: Pickwick Publications, 2010.

Larson, Benjamin Splichal. "Participation in Evil: The Problem of Doing Evil When Attempting to Fight Evil." *Currents in Theology and Mission* 33, no. 9 (2012): 249–58.

Lartey, Emmanuel Yartekwei. *In Living Color: An Intercultural Approach to Pastoral Care and Counseling.* 2nd ed. New York: Jessica Kingsley, 2003.

Lear, Jonathan. *Radical Hope: Ethics in the Face of Cultural Devastation.* Cambridge, MA: Harvard University Press, 2006.

Lee, Rob. *Stained-Glass Millennials: Coincidental Reformers.* Macon, GA: Smyth & Helwys Publishing, 2016.

Levine, Arthur, and Diane R. Dean. *Generation on a Tightrope: A Portrait of Today's College Student.* The Jossey-Bass Higher and Adult Education Series. San Francisco: Jossey-Bass, 2012.

Livingstone, Elizabeth A. *The Concise Oxford Dictionary of the Christian Church.* Oxford: Oxford University Press, 2006. http://www.oxfordreference.com /view/10.1093/acref/9780198614425.001.0001/acref-9780198614425.

Lossl, Josef. "When Is a Locust Just a Locus? Patristic Exegesis of Joel 1:4 in Light of Ancient Literary Theory." *Journal of Theological Studies* 55, no. 2 (2004): 575–94.

Lynch, Matthew J. "Neglected Physical Dimensions of 'Shame' Terminology in the Hebrew Bible." *Biblica* 91 (2010): 499–517.

Lyons, Gabe. *The Next Christians: Seven Ways You Can Live the Gospel and Restore the World.* Colorado Springs: Multnomah Books, 2010.

MacIntyre, Alasdair C. *After Virtue: A Study in Moral Theory.* 3rd ed. Notre Dame, IN: University of Notre Dame Press, 2007.

Malony, H. Newton. *Living with Paradox: Religious Leadership and the Genius of Double Vision.* San Francisco: Jossey-Bass, 1998.

Martin, Carolyn A., and Bruce Tulgan. *Managing the Generation Mix: From Urgency to Opportunity.* 2nd ed. Amherst: HRD Press, 2006.

Martin, Wallace. "Metaphor." *The New Princeton Handbook of Poetic Terms.* Edited by Terry V. F. Brogan, 184–90. Princeton: Princeton University Press, 1994.

Maslach, Christina, and Michael P. Leiter. "Understanding the Burnout Experience: Recent Research and Its Implications for Psychiatry." *World Psychiatry* 15, no. 2 (2016): 103–12.

McLuhan, Derryck. *From Religion to Relationship.* Self-published, 2015.

McQueen, Larry. *Joel and the Spirit: A Cry for a Prophetic Hermeneutic.* Cleveland, TN: CPT Press, 2009.

Mead, Margaret. *Culture and Commitment: A Study of the Generation Gap.* Garden City, NY: Natural History Press, 1970.

Meirav, Ariel. "The Nature of Hope." *Ratio* 22, no. 2 (2009): 216–33.

The Millennial Impact Project. The Millennial Impact Report—Phase 1: Millennial Dialogue on the Landscape of Cause Engagement and Social Issues. 2017.

———The Millennial Impact Report—Phase 2: The Power of Voice: A New Era of Cause Activation and Social Issue Adoption. 2017.

Miller, Craig Kennet, and MaryJane Pierce Norton. *Making God Real for a New Generation: Ministry with Millennials Born from 1982 to 1999.* Nashville: Discipleship Resources, 2003.

Mitchell, Kenneth R., and Herbert Anderson. *All Our Losses, All Our Griefs: Resources for Pastoral Care.* Philadelphia: Westminster Press, 1983.

Moltmann, Jürgen. *The Spirit of Life: A Universal Affirmation.* Minneapolis: Fortress Press, 2001.

Myers, Jeff. *Cultivate: Forming the Emerging Generation through Life-on-Life Mentoring*. Dayton: Passing the Baton International, Inc., 2010.

Nance, Terry. *Awaken: Letters from a Spiritual Father to This Generation*. New Kensington: Whitaker House, 2016.

O'Connor, Kathleen M. *Lamentations and the Tears of the World*. Maryknoll, NY: Orbis Books, 2002.

Otto, Rudolf. *The Idea of the Holy: An Inquiry into the Non-Rational Factor in the Idea of the Divine and Its Relation to the Rational*. 2nd ed. London: Oxford University Press, 1958.

The Oxford English Dictionary (Online). London: Oxford University Press, 2017.

Palfrey, John G., and Urs Gasser. *Born Digital: Understanding the First Generation of Digital Natives*. New York: Basic Books, 2008.

Perrin, Jon. *The Coming Post-Christian Tsunami: Connecting with an Increasingly Unchurched Culture*. Lexington: Jon Perrin, 2016.

Peterson, Eugene H. *The Message: The Bible in Contemporary Language*. Chicago: ACTA Publications, 2013.

Pew Research Center. *Millennials in Adulthood: Detached from Institutions, Networked with Friends*. 2014.

———*Millennials Overtake Baby Boomers as America's Largest Generation*. 2016.

———"U.S. Public Becoming Less Religious." Last modified 2015. http://www.pewforum.org/2015/11/03/u-s-public-becoming-less-religious/, accessed October 11, 2016.

Powell, Kara, Jake Mulder, and Brad Griffin. *Growing Young: Six Essential Strategies to Help Young People Discover and Love Your Church*. Grand Rapids, MI: Baker Books, 2016.

Raabe, Paul R. "The Particularizing of Universal Judgment in Prophetic Discourse." *The Catholic Biblical Quaterly* 64 (2002): 652–85.

Rainer, Thom S., and Jess W. Rainer. *The Millennials: Connecting to America's Largest Generation.* Nashville: B & H, 2011.

Runge, Steven E. "Joel 2:28-32a in Acts 2:17-21: The Discourse and Text-Critical Implications of Variation from the Lxx." *The Library of New Testament Studies: Early Christian Literature and Intertextuality.* Edited by Chris Keith, 103–13: New York: Bloomsbury, 2009.

Rushkoff, Douglas. *Present Shock: When Everything Happens Now.* New York: Current, 2013.

Sahlin, Monte, and David Roozen. *How Religious Congregations Are Engaging Young Adults in America.* Hartford, CT: Hartford Institute for Religion Research, 2015.

Saracco, Norbert. "I Will Pour out My Spirit on All People: A Pastoral Reading of Joel 2:28-30 from Latin America." *Calvin Theological Journal* 46 (2011): 268-77.

Sarbin, Theodore R. *Narrative Psychology: The Storied Nature of Human Conduct.* New York: Praeger, 1986.

Schart, Aaron. "The First Section of the Book of the Twelve Prophets: Hosea-Joel-Amos." *Interpretation* (2007): 138-53.

Schreiber, Mordecai. "I Will Pour out My Spirit on All Flesh (Joel 3:1)." *Jewish Bible Quaterly* 41, no. 2 (2013): 123–31.

Seitz, Christopher R. *Joel.* The International Theological Commentary. New York: Bloomsbury, 2016.

Seow, Choon Leong. "Reflections on Reception History." *Method Matters: Essays on the Interpretation of the Hebrew Bible in Honor of David L. Petersen.* Edited by David L. Petersen, Joel M. LeMon, and Kent Harold Richards, 561–86. Atlanta: Society of Biblical Literature, 2009.

Shane, Victor. *The Authentic Life: A Guidebook for Millennials.* Bloomington, IN: Westbow Press, 2017.

Silva, Jennifer M. *Coming Up Short: Working-Class Adulthood in an Age of Uncertainty.* New York: Oxford University Press, 2013.

Smith, Christian, Kari Christofferson, Hillary Davidson, and Patricia Snell Herzog. *Lost in Transition: The Dark Side of Emerging Adulthood.* Oxford: Oxford University Press, 2011.

Smith, Christian, and Melinda Lundquist Denton. *Soul Searching: The Religious and Spiritual Lives of American Teenagers.* New York: Oxford University Press, 2005.

Smith, Christian, and Patricia Snell. *Souls in Transition: The Religious and Spiritual Lives of Emerging Adults.* Oxford: Oxford University Press, 2009.

Soto, Mauricio. "Pension Shock." *Finance and Development,* June, 2017.

Strauss, William, and Neil Howe. *Generations: The History of America's Future, 1584 to 2069.* New York: Quill, 1991.

Swinton, John. *Raging with Compassion: Pastoral Responses to the Problem of Evil.* Grand Rapids, MI: Eerdmans, 2007.

Tapscott, Don. *Grown Up Digital: How the Next Generation Is Changing Your World.* New York: McGraw-Hill, 2009.

Thiselton, Anthony C. "Reception Theory, H. R. Jauss and the Formative Power of Scripture." *Scottish Journal of Theology* 65, no. 3 (2012): 289–308.

Thurston, Angie, and Casper ter Kuile. *How We Gather.* Cambridge, MA, 2015. Download at https://caspertk.files.wordpress.com/2015/04/how-we-gather.pdf.

Tov, Emanuel. *Textual Criticism of the Hebrew Bible.* Minneapolis: Fortress Press, 1992.

Trible, Phyllis. *God and the Rhetoric of Sexuality.* Overtures to Biblical Theology. Philadelphia: Fortress Press, 1978.

Troxel, Ronald L. *Joel: Scope, Genres, and Meaning.* Critical Studies in the Hebrew Bible. Winona Lake, IN: Eisenbrauns, 2015.

Twenge, Jean M. *Generation Me: Why Today's Young Americans Are More Confident, Assertive, Entitled—and More Miserable Than Ever Before.* New York: Free Press, 2006.

Underwood, Chuck. *The Generational Imperative: Understanding Generational Differences in the Workplace, Marketplace, and Living Room.* North Charleston, SC: BookSurge, 2007.

Verhaeghe, Paul, and Jane Hedley-Präole. *What About Me? The Struggle for Identity in a Market-Based Society.* London: Scribe, 2014.

Watson, Douglas. "Divine Attributes in the Book of Joel." *Journal for the Study of the Old Testament* 37 (2012): 109–29.

Wesley, John. *Joel: Explanatory Notes and Commentary.* Lexington, KY: Hargraves, 2015.

Whitesel, Bob, and Kent R. Hunter. *A House Divided: Bridging the Generation Gaps in Your Church.* Nashville: Abingdon Press, 2000.

Williams, Rhys H., Courtney Ann Irby, and R. Stephen Warner. "Church in Black and White: The Organizational Lives of Young Adults." *Religion* 7, 90 (2016): 1–20.

Wilson, Robin. "An Epidemic of Anguish." *Chronicle of Higher Education*, Special Issue: Today's Anguished Students—and How to Help Them (2015): 1–28.

Wolff, Hans Walter, and S. Dean McBride. *Joel and Amos: A Commentary on the Books of the Prophets Joel and Amos.* Philadelphia: Fortress Press, 1977.

Worden, J. William. *Grief Counseling and Grief Therapy: A Handbook for the Mental Health Practitioner.* 3rd ed. New York: Springer, 2009.

Wuthnow, Robert. *After Heaven: Spirituality in America since the 1950s.* Berkeley: University of California Press, 1998.

Yoder, Bob. *Helping Youth Grieve: The Good News of Biblical Lament.* Eugene, OR: Wipf and Stock, 2015.

CPSIA information can be obtained
at www.ICGtesting.com
Printed in the USA
LVHW041220131218
600251LV00003B/6/P